Anti-Semitism in Hungary

Anti-Semitism in Hungary
Appearance and Reality

EXECUTIVE EDITOR
Jeffrey Kaplan

ASSOCIATE EDITORS
Zsófia Tóth-Bíró · Sáron Sugár · Lídia Papp · Tamás Orbán · Dávid Nagy

Helena History Press

Copyright © Jeffrey Kaplan et al. 2022
All rights reserved

KKL Publications LLC, Helena History Press
Reno, Nevada USA

Publishing scholarship about and from Central and East Europe

www.helenahistorypress.com

Distributed by IngramSpark and available through all major e-retail sites

info@helenahistorypress.com

The essays in this volume are transcriptions of the presentations made at the June 28–29, 2021 conference in Budapest sponsored by the Danube Institute (established by the Batthyány Lajos Foundation in 2013) titled *Anti-Semitism in Hungary: Appearance and Reality*.

ISBN 978-1943596-27-0
ISBN 978-1-943596-28-7 (ebook)

Contents

Part 1 Introductory Material
Jeffrey Kaplan, *Introduction* 3
Tamás Orbán, *Preface* 21
Zsófia Tóth-Bíró, *Preface* 25
Sáron Sugár, *Preface* 29
Jeffrey Kaplan, *Foreword* 33

Part 2 Welcoming Speeches
Ambassador Yacov Hadas-Handelsman 39
Rabbi Báruch Oberlander 43
Rabbi Róbert Frölich 45
András Heisler 47
Rabbi Slomó Köves 53
György Szabó 57
Rabbi Andrew Baker 59
Tristan Azbej 63

Part 3 Historical Issues
Béla Bodó, *Responses to Terror* 69
Rabbi Róbert Frölich, *The History of Military Chaplaincy* 81
Tibor Pécsi, *"Nothing New Under the Sun…"* 85
Menachem Keren-Kratz, *Does Anti-Zionism Equal Anti-Semitism?*
 —The Satmar Rebbe's Extreme Orthodox Hungarian Ideology 89
Jehuda Hartman, *Modernity and Jewish Perceptions of Anti-Semitism* 93

Part 4 Current Research & Contemporary Issues
Dr. Tamás Kovács, *Educational and Scientific Projects in a Changing World* 103
Tamir Wertzberger, *Old and New Anti-Semitism* 107
Kálmán Szalai, *The Work of the Action and Protection League* 111

Part 5 Media and Popular Culture
Ruth Isaac, *Personal Experiences with Anti-Semitism* 117
László Kürti, *The Culture of Hungarian Anti-Semitism* 121
Virág Gulyás, *The War of Public Opinion—Social Media & Influencer Marketing* 129

Part 6 International Perspectives

Shaul Magid, *Is Anti-Semitism a "Problem" in America Today?* 145
Marek Kucia, *Anti-Semitism in Poland* 159
Sebastian Rejak, *Anti-Semitism in Central Europe* 167

Part 7 Concluding Remarks

Jeffrey Kaplan, *Anti-Semitism in Hungary: Appearance and Reality
    Concluding Remarks* 177

Part 8 Articles

Menachem Keren-Kratz, *Can Jews Be Anti-Semitic?: The Case of Neturei
    Karta's Extreme Orthodox Anti-Zionist and Anti-Israel Ideology* 185
László Bernát Veszprémy, *The Jewish Press in Hungary* 213
Jeffrey Kaplan, *When the Cultic Milieu Goes Mainstream: Anti-Semitism
    and Violence in the Digital Age* 227

Contributors 251
Articles Glossary 259
Index 263

Part

1

Introductory Material

Introduction[1]

Jeffrey Kaplan

Introduction

On 28–29 June 2021, the Danube Institute sponsored a conference titled "Anti-Semitism in Hungary: Appearance and Reality." The conference brought together leading figures from the Hungarian Jewish community, Hungarian and foreign scholars, and a representative of the Hungarian government. A broad range of views was presented, but there was unanimous agreement that the problem of Hungarian anti-Semitism has declined significantly in the last decade and that the Hungarian government has played an active role in this decline. This is the reality that was reflected not only in conference proceedings, but in reports issued by the EU, the United States government, and NGOs concerned with anti-Semitism.

By contrast, the portrayal of Hungary in the Western media presents a much more dire picture. Indeed, when I came to Hungary in the summer of 2020, a close reading of the *New York Times* assured me that the Hungarian Parliament had been closed to allow the Prime Minister to assume near dictatorial power and that the ruling party's appeal was in part powered by a wave of anti-Semitism that threatened the Hungarian Jewish community. To my surprise, the Parliament was very much open for business and there had been only one violent anti-Semitic incident reported in the country in the last two years.

The contrast between appearance and reality could not be more stark, and it was this dissonance that was the real genesis of the conference, and of the studies to follow.

---

1 An earlier version of this article appeared in "The Hungarian Jewish Community and the Question of Anti-Semitism Today," *Hungarian Conservative*, 1:3, (2021), 60–9.

The Hungarian Jewish Community

The most reliable estimate of the Jewish population in Hungary is 47,000, although a more politicized estimate from MAZSIHISZ (Federation of the Hungarian Jewish Communities) ranges as high as 100,000.[2] But the real question is who is doing the counting and who is being counted. Prof. András Kovács sheds a good deal of light on the problem. In the aftermath of the Holocaust, with Orthodoxy nearly destroyed and remnants emigrated, no more than 10% of Hungarian Jews aligned with any religious community while long standing assimilationist tendencies reasserted themselves. In terms of measurables, in 2020 only 12,000 Jews paid the voluntary tax to Jewish groups and only perhaps 1% of Jews actually attend synagogue regularly. Thus while the Jewish population of Hungary is the third largest in the EU, the number of active Jews is really quite small.[3]

Visits to Jewish synagogues in Budapest and interviews with Hungarian Jews well illustrate the problem. The Dohány Street Synagogue in Budapest's Jewish Quarter, the second largest Jewish synagogue in the world, is an architectural wonder. For a first time visitor, it evokes the echoes of the beautiful, Moorish influenced architecture in Morocco from the outside while evoking a strange synthesis of Jewish, Catholic and Anglican designs on the inside. It even boasts a pipe organ once played by Franz Liszt, which must have scandalized the Orthodox of the time. Yet within its cavernous interior, still boasting tiered balconies that were once reserved for the women of the congregation, an average Sabbath service is composed of no more than perhaps 30 souls, with many of these being tourists. Smaller congregations of Orthodox Jews have much the same problem. How dire the issue has become is well illustrated by an anecdote regarding an Orthodox rabbi in Budapest. Having suffered a family tragedy, he was unable to gather a *minyan*—the *halakhically* (*Halakha* translates to Jewish law) mandated 10 adult males needed to constitute a religious service—in order to offer prayers for the family member without having to find foreign Jewish visitors on the street to join in.

---

2   Berman Jewish DataBank, "World Jewish Population, 2018," (2019), https://www.jewishdatabank.org/content/upload/bjdb/2019_World_Jewish_Population_(AJYB,_DellaPergola)_DataBank_Final.pdf. For the MAZSIHISZ estimate, https://www.worldjewishcongress.org/en/about/communities/HU.

3   András Kovács and Barna Ildiko, "Zsidók és zsidóság Magyarországon 2017: Egy szociológiai kutatás eredményei," (2018). Interview with Prof. András Kovács, June 3, 2021.

In conducting interviews with the Hungarian Jewish community, the immemorial issue of 'who is a Jew' was frequently raised. According to *Halakha,* a Jew is defined solely as the child of a Jewish mother or a convert who has undergone an Orthodox conversion ceremony. The issue in Israel is starkly political. The Israeli Law of Return, fashioned in 1950 and revised in 1970 with Holocaust history in mind, defines a Jew qualifying for citizenship under the Law of Return as anyone with a Jewish family member, however distant, and an Orthodox convert to Judaism. In March 2021, the Israeli Supreme Court widened the gates further to include converts from any stream of Judaism.[4]

The US approach is typically American. For all but the Orthodox streams, a Jew is anyone who feels he or she is Jewish, giving cultural and *Halakhic* Jews equal recognition. How all-encompassing this embrace can become is wonderfully illustrated by the 18-minute video "The Tribe," which contrasts the history of the ubiquitous Barbie doll with the many flavors of cultural Judaism. Who would have thought the blond and seemingly Aryan Barbie was actually Jewish, or that there was such a thing as a "Bujew" for Jews who also practice Buddhism?[5]

The question in Hungary is equally complex. Orthodox rabbis interviewed for this research are in rare agreement with Neolog rabbis associated with MAZSIHISZ that the definition of a Jew must be according to *Halakha,* while secular Jewish leaders, particularly the current leadership of MAZSIHISZ, assert that cultural identity is more important. The crux of the argument however is not simply about what is needed to form a *minyan* or fill a synagogue. Rather, the real issue is about access to resources, specifically, subsidies from the Hungarian government to the Hungarian Jewish community. And therein lies a story.

The Great Divide

There is a joke among Hungarian Jews that should serve as a cautionary tale for all that follows in this section. Once there was a Hungarian Jew who was

---

4   Noah Feldman, "Who Is a Jew? Israel's Supreme Court Expands the Answer," *Bloomberg Opinion*, March 2, 2021, https://www.bloomberg.com/opinion/articles/2021-03-02/israel-expands-its-right-of-return-and-sparks-a-debate.
5   For a link to the video and a long in-depth discussion of the film, see "The Tribe," *The Moxie Institute*, http://www.moxieinstitute.org/films/the-tribe/.

washed up on the proverbial desert island after a shipwreck. Years later he is found, and his rescuers are astonished to find that he has built not one but two synagogues. They ask him why he needs two synagogues. He replies, "This is the one where I go to pray and that is the one that I will NEVER pray in!"

The great divide of Hungarian Judaism is much like the apocryphal desert island. The great majority of Hungarian Jews are Neologs, which has been long represented by MAZSIHISZ. MAZSIHISZ, which emerged as the successor organization to the communist era MIOK (Magyar Izraelitak Országos Képriselete—National Representation of Hungarian Israelites), was formed in 1992.[6] It has become the umbrella organization for not only the Neolog community but also for the small groups of American influenced Conservative and Reform Jews. MAZSIHISZ estimates that they represent as many as 90% of Hungarian Jews, and on paper, this is probably close to the truth.

In 1989, Rabbi Baruch Oberlander arrived in Budapest and would assume the title Chief Representative of Chabad Hungary. A brilliant scholar, he quickly won respect and some admiration throughout the Hungarian Jewish community.[7] There is a story that is current among women in EMIH, the Chabad branch in Hungary, which goes something like this. When the Lubavitcher Rebbe, Rabbi Schneerson, sent Rabbi Oberlander to Budapest, his instruction was that you can stay in Hungary only if you find a *mikva*, a ritual bath for women. Amazingly, one mikva survived, in a small alley near the Dohány Street Synagogue. It is still active today and can be found adjacent to a small, only very recently renovated Orthodox synagogue a few hundred meters from Dohány Street. So with this sign, Rabbi Oberlander set down roots in Budapest.

He soon attracted an acolyte, also brilliant and charismatic but more abrasive by far, in Rabbi Slomó Köves. Köves, born Máté Köves in Budapest, went to yeshiva in Pittsburgh and brought back with him a very American assertiveness and boundless energy, which did not play as well with much of the staid Jewish community of Hungary.

---

6 Raphael Patai, *The Jews of Hungary: history, culture, psychology* (Detroit, MI: Wayne State University Press, 2015), 614–5, 48–50.
7 Interview with Rabbi Róbert Frölich, May 12, 2021.

Rabbi Köves' background was utterly typical of Hungarian Jews of his generation. His upbringing was secular, and although his Jewish roots were not hidden from him as they were from many of his generation, they were not stressed either. In 1991 he met Rabbi Oberlander and embarked on a very different path—one that is the *leitmotif* of the Chabad mission. To understand the nature of the conflict which followed, a few words about Chabad are in order.

Chabad, known in the English language media as the Lubavitcher movement, developed into the only Jewish missionary group with their target audience being secular Jews, whom they seek to bring to Orthodox practice. The movement is global in scope and boundless in ambition. Its origins can be found in the emerging Hassidic world of the 1780s, when Rabbi Shneur Zalman of Liady founded the group in present day Belarus. But it was not until the 1950 ascension of Rabbi Menachem Mendel Schneerson, the seventh Lubavitcher Rebbe, that the group turned decisively toward messianism. An intense cult grew around the Rebbe that saw him as the long awaited Meshaiach (Messiah) for whom Jews have waited for millennia. Even his 1994 death did not quell the messianic excitement around Rebbe Schneerson.[8] Even after his death, Chabad members throughout the world continue to consult him through the multi-volume collection of his letters on such personal issues as education, marriage and even real estate.[9]

Rabbis Oberlander and Köves attracted a small but growing following, marked for their energy and zeal, which stood in stark contrast to MAZSIHISZ, which under the leadership of András Heisler had become more a civic than a religious organization. Rabbi Köves in particular appears to be as tireless as he is combative. In 2004, he was a founder of EMIH (Unified Hungarian Jewish Congregation), which is the religious base from which all Hungarian Chabad activities spring.

A list of his initiatives would take more word space than can be allotted here, but on the religious side he leads Torah and other religious teachings,

---

8 On early Chabad history, see Immanuel Etkes, *Rabbi Shneur Zalman of Liady: The Origins of Chabad Hasidism* (Waltham, MA: Brandeis University Press, 2014). Biographies of Rebbe Schneerson come in two flavors, academic and hagiographic. For one of each, Joseph Telushkin, *Rebbe: The life and teachings of Menachem M. Schneerson, the most influential Rabbi in modern history* (New York: Harper Collins, 2016). Chaim Miller, *Turning Judaism Outward: A Biography of Rabbi Menachem Mendel Schneerson the Seventh Lubavitcher Rebbe* (Brooklyn, NY: Kol Menachem, 2014).

9 Interview with György Szabó, April 22, 2021.

serves as a congregational rabbi, has formed media groups such as the conservative and often satirical *Neokohn* (itself a pun combining the American term Neocon and the Jewish *Kohen* or priest), a university (Milton Friedman after the American economist), a new Holocaust Museum (House of Fates) and an NGO that tracks anti-Semitic incidents in Hungary (Tett és Védelem Alapítvány / Action and Protection), to name a few.[10]

But it is the Chabad alliance championed by Rabbi Köves with the Hungarian government that makes him the particular Golem in the world of András Heisler. Which brings us to the question of resources. At the "Anti-Semitism in Hungary: Appearance and Reality" conference, Mr. Heisler quoted an article that had appeared "recently" in the *Times of Israel* newspaper that said that "it is unacceptable" that "in our countries" Jewish organizations are not treated in the same way and those that "sympathize" with the government are given preferential treatment. He then also quoted the statement of 10 international Jewish organizations that turned to the European Commission asking that Jewish "representative organizations" with an "historical embeddedness" in a given country be treated equally to others, whether "in terms of support in the public arena or financing." The statement said that "several European governments do not ensure that and provide preferential treatment to non-representative Jewish denominations." Heisler said that in her response, President of the European Commission, Ursula Von der Leyen, said the Commission calls on governments to "make sure there is a diverse Jewish public life."[11]

The statement was clear enough, though its meaning is multi-layered. On the one hand, MAZSIHISZ receives as much as 80% of the normal government distribution of resources to the Jewish community. On the other, Rabbi Köves has nurtured and often served as go between in the special relationship between prime ministers Viktor Orbán and Benjamin Netanyahu, which has flowered into close relations with Israel. This has opened the gates to considerable governmental largesse, which has allowed EMIH to flourish and undertake such high profile but extremely expensive undertakings as the House of Fates, Tett és Védelem Alapítvány and Milton Friedman University, which seeks to import world class Jewish scholars to join its faculty.

---

10   Interview with Rabbi Slomó Köves, June 1, 2021.
11   András Heisler conference address, June 28, 2021. Translated by Zsófia Tóth-Bíró.

András Heisler, an implacable foe of the Orbán government and all things EMIH, was suitably outraged. This led to the bizarre spectacle of two Orthodox communities, EMIH and MAOIH (Autonomous Orthodox Jewish Community of Hungary) suing MAZSIHISZ for US$33 million in the Bet Din, or rabbinical court in Jerusalem. The Bet Din obviously has no enforcement power in Hungary, but it is a moral force that would be hard for a Jewish group to simply ignore.

The EMIH goal is to renegotiate the 2012 agreement for the restitution of funds for property seized in WWII under the term of a 1991 law. The agreement gave MAZSIHISZ 80% of the funds, or about US$5 million annually. EMIH and MAOIH each got US$600,000 per year.[12] In this, MAOIH is very much the junior partner, with a total membership of perhaps 50. But it is better established than EMIH with a stronger historical claim to be the successor of the thriving Orthodox community that once comprised hundreds of thousands but who were decimated by the Holocaust. MAOIH's current leader, Robert Deutsch notes that he was advised to front the law suit by his own rabbis, whom he does not name but who are probably named Oberlander and Köves.

Which brings us full circle to the 'who's a Jew' argument. András Heisler notes that while all three groups use the money for the Jewish community, MAZSIHISZ is much bigger and so the 2012 agreement should be upheld. In reply, Rabbi Köves alludes to the 12,000 Jews who earmark 1% of their taxes for the Jewish group of their choice. It's a small number, however:

> The fact that people give their 1% to a Jewish community doesn't mean they're Jewish, and it doesn't mean they're a constituent. It just means that they prefer this money go to the Jewish community rather than the government.[13]

In other words, many of those 12,000 are not *halakhically* Jewish, and if the figure of only about 1,000 Jews as active participants in the Jewish community is sound, the MAZSIHISZ claim to represent most of the roughly

---

12 Yaakov Schwartz, "Israeli rabbis order Hungary government to freeze payouts to sparring local Jews," *Times of Israel*, April 23, 2021, https://www.timesofisrael.com/israeli-rabbis-order-hungary-government-to-freeze-payouts-to-sparring-local-jews/.

13 Ibid.

47,000 member of the Hungarian Jewish community rings hollow indeed. Again, it depends on who is doing the counting and who is being counted. This is the $33 million question.

For his part, Mr. Heisler is already all but conceding defeat in the Bet Din, given that it is an Orthodox institution judging a case brought by two Orthodox communities. In his view surely, the Slomó Köves golem looms large. Not only is Rabbi Köves connected to the Israeli government but he has been the host of key figures in the Jewish world when they visit Hungary.

"Ashkenazi Chief Rabbi David Lau visited Hungary three times, and not once did he inform my organization that he was coming," said Heisler. "He came to Budapest, visited the prime minister together with EMIH, and afterward we saw it in the newspaper."

"I wrote him a letter saying that this isn't proper, that if you're the Ashkenazi chief rabbi and you come to Budapest, please inform us. At least let us invite you to sit down for a coffee—we are the biggest Jewish community in East-Central Europe. And the second time he came, nothing. The third time, nothing. So while this is not a religious court ruling per se, it's a very strong sign for us," he said.[14]

With such high drama in the Jewish community itself, the problem of anti-Semitism in Hungary seems prosaic indeed. But it was not always so.

Anti-Semitism in Hungary Today

The Strange Saga of Jobbik

In 2011, Hungary had an anti-Semitism problem and it was serious. Its parliamentary face was the Jobbik Party, which formed in 2003. It initially met with little success, garnering a mere 2.2% of the vote in the 2006 parliamentary elections. Shortly thereafter, Jobbik formed the Magyar Gárda (Hungarian Guard Movement), which was all too reminiscent of the pre-war Arrow Cross for comfort. In 2007, Jobbik gained 14.77 % of the vote in the

---

14 Ibid.

European Parliamentary elections and topped this with 16.67 % of the vote in the 2010 Hungarian parliamentary elections. It was now the third largest party in the Hungarian Parliament.[15]

The Magyar Gárda was the most high profile of a number of small but active far right paramilitary groups who acted in concert in 2011 and 2012 to conduct violent anti-Roma and anti-Jewish demonstrations throughout the country. Actions of this sort were occurring throughout Europe, most notably in Germany at the time, and so they attracted little notice in the Western media. That changed when Jobbik MP Márton Gyöngyösi introduced a proposal for the creation of a 'Jewish list' of Jews in government who posed a security risk. It was a bridge too far, and although Jobbik immediately claimed that Gyöngyösi's proposal was misunderstood, it was the beginning of the end for Jobbik. There were anti-Jobbik demonstrations across the country, its vote tallies began a precipitous decline, and in 2018 its leader Gábor Vona resigned.

Eventually, Jobbik's story ended in farce when Csanád Szegedi, one of the party's leading anti-Semitic firebrands, was confronted with the fact that he was Jewish. More than that, Szegedi's grandmother survived Auschwitz and his grandfather survived the labor camps that in fact saved the lives of many Jewish men during the Holocaust. This is an old story with a particularly Hungarian twist. In the early 1960s, the charismatic leader of the American Nazi Party, George Lincoln Rockwell, drew an idiosyncratic band of misfits and lunatics to his banner, where they all lived together in a wildly dysfunctional 'barracks' and dressed up in imitation Third Reich brown shirt uniforms. One of the most rabid was Dan Burros, who wrote the group's official *Stormtrooper's Manual* and 'endeared' himself to the group by strangling their only loyal friend; a pet dog affectionately named Gas Chamber. He was confronted by the *New York Times* with evidence that not only was Burros Jewish, but his father was a cantor in the local synagogue and Dan had been duly given a Bar Mitzva and had himself studied in a yeshiva. Unable to

---

15 András Bíró Nagy, Tamás Boros, and Zoltán Vasali, "More Radical than the Radicals: the Jobbik Party in international comparison," in *Right-Wing extremism in Europe: Country Analyses, Counter-Strategies and Labor-Market Oriented Exit Strategies* (2013), 229. On Jobbik, see also András Kovács, "Antisemitic Prejudices and Dynamics of Antisemitism in Post-Communist" (Berlin: Jüdisches Museum Berlin, 2013). Jeffrey Stevenson Murer, "The rise of Jobbik, populism, and the symbolic politics of illiberalism in contemporary Hungary," *The Polish Quarterly of International Affairs* 24, no. 2 (2015): 79–102.

bear the dissonance, Burros committed suicide.[16] The Hollywood film "The Believer" is loosely based on Burros' life.

Szegedi's path was less traumatic but much more Hungarian than that of Dan Burros. As noted, a common trope among Hungarian Jews is that they either were unaware of their Jewishness or were raised in a secular, assimilationist atmosphere and so their Jewish heritage was little more than a family anecdote. Moreover, Hungary has the highest rate of Ashkenazi Jewish blood of any country in the world save Israel[17]—a testament to the success of the Hungarian policy of assimilation of non-Roma minorities. Certainly, Jewish intermarriage rates in Hungary have always been high, again a combination of assimilation and, in an accident of history, the survival of far more Jewish men in labor brigades than of Jewish women, who were deported to death camps in Poland.

Asked to leave the Party and give up his seat in the European Parliament, Szegedi turned to Rabbi Slomó Köves rather than the Grim Reaper. Following profuse apologies to the Jewish community and a visit to the Holocaust Museum, Szegedi has become an advocate for Israel, Zionism and the Jewish community.[18] A very Hungarian cautionary tale.

Jobbik today is, at least rhetorically, a very different animal. In 2020, Péter Jakab, whose heritage is openly Jewish, took over as party chair and expelled some of the party's most extreme members. Jobbik no longer uses anti-Semitic rhetoric, though an anti-Roma barb may slip out now and then. It has moved toward the conservative mainstream by rebranding itself Jobbik Magyarországért Mozgalom (Jobbik—Movement for a Better Hungary). In 2018 it gained 16.7% of the vote and holds 47 seats in Parliament.[19]

---

16 A. M. Rosenthal and Arthur Gelb, *One more victim: The Life and Death of an American-Jewish Nazi* (New York: New American Library, 1967). Jeffrey Kaplan, *Encyclopedia of White Power: a Sourcebook on the Radical Racist Right* (Walnut Creek: AltaMira Press, 2000), 33–35.
17 Cnaan Liphshiz, "Hungarians show highest rate of Ashkenazi genes after Israelis, company says," *Times of Israel*, August 13, 2019, https://www.timesofisrael.com/hungarians-show-highest-rate-of-ashkenazi-genes-after-israelis-company-says/.
18 Eyder Peralta, "Leader Of Anti-Semitic Party In Hungary Discovers He's Jewish," *NPR*, August 14, 2012, https://www.npr.org/sections/thetwo-way/2012/08/14/158773637/leader-of-anti-semitic-party-in-hungary-discovers-hes-jewish.
19 Shaun Walker, "Does electing a leader with Jewish roots prove Jobbik has changed?," *Guardian*, February 12, 2020, https://www.theguardian.com/world/2020/feb/12/electing-leader-jewish-roots-jobbik-changed-hungary-shift. *Norsk Senter for Forskningsdata*, "Hungary—Political parties," https://o.nsd.no/european_election_database/country/hungary/parties.html.

Introduction

Hungarian Anti-Semitism Today

In Hungary today, public expressions of anti-Semitism are proscribed by law. There are no anti-Semitic demonstrations as there were a decade ago, and since 2019 there has been only one violent anti-Semitic incident reported according to both international and Hungarian sources.[20] The Action and Protection Foundation's annual reports illustrate the dearth of anti-Semitic incidents. In 2019, there was one reported assault, 6 cases of damage to property and 27 incidents of hate speech. From January to June 2020, there was only one report of discrimination, 4 cases of damage to property and 11 incidents of hate speech.[21] All sources agree that anti-Semitic violence in Hungary today is statistically negligible and among the lowest in Europe.

Despite these numbers, perception and reality differ considerably. According to the 2018 Eurobarometer anti-Semitism survey:

> The December 2018 Eurobarometer survey asked questions about antisemitism of the general public. Among those surveyed, 45% of Hungarian respondents said antisemitism was a "very" or "fairly" important problem in Hungary, significantly less than the 77% of Hungarian Jews in the FRA survey. Other significant findings include:
>
> • Just 26% believe antisemitism had increased over the past five years, significantly lower than the 38% EU average, and 22% believe antisemitism had decreased, the largest percentage in the EU after Romania.
>
> • 46% believe "expressions of hostility and threats towards Jewish people in the street or other public places" is a problem.

---

20 *Antisemitism in Europe: Implications for U.S. Policy*, United States Commission on International Religious Freedom (Washington, DC), 20–1, https://www.uscirf.gov/sites/default/files/Antisemitism%20in%20Europe.pdf.

21 *Anti-Semitic Hate Crimes in Incidents in Hungary 2019. Annual Short Report*, Action and Protection Foundation (Budapest, 2020), 6, https://tev.hu/wp-content/uploads/2020/09/APL_annual-short_2020JAN-JUN_72dpiKESZ.pdf. *Anti-Semitic Hate Crimes and Hate Incidents in Hungary 2019. Annual Short Report, January-June 2020*, Action and Protection Foundation (Budapest, 2021), 4, https://tev.hu/wp-content/uploads/2020/09/APL_annual-short_2020JAN-JUN_72dpiKESZ.pdf. Interview with Kálmán Szalai, June 2, 2021.

- 46% believe "people denying the genocide of the Jewish people, the Holocaust" is a problem.

- 40% believe "antisemitism in schools and universities" is a problem.[22]

Although there is now a general sense of physical security in the Hungarian Jewish community, the perception that anti-Semitism in Hungary is a significant problem is widespread and a matter of near certainty in the Western media. How to account for this dissonance is a fascinating exercise. It is made more complex by an observation made in an interview by Mr. György Szabó, the president of the Hungarian Jewish Heritage Public Foundation. He is a former Fidesz MP and remains close to the Hungarian government. More to the point however, he is an EMIH member and dresses the part of an Orthodox Jew. In our interview with him, he wondered how Jews who report public anti-Semitic incidents or remarks can be recognized as Jewish. There is nothing to distinguish them from other Hungarians.[23]

It's a fair question, and one that can be in part answered by one of the more liberal members of the Jewish community, Adam Schönberger, President and CEO of MAROM. MAROM is a youth group affiliated with the Conservative stream of Judaism which is centered in the United States but has affiliates in Israel as well. He recalls:

> Yes. In my childhood, definitely in the 80s and early 90s in school, and there was of course, a difference between me and the other kids in the school. It always stopped with verbal attacks, but it could be harsh also. So, it was a bit of anti-Semitism in the beginning. Then I went to Jewish school, so then I just didn't really meet with such things. But when I got involved with the Hungarian university system, it became very real for me. I went to university not in Budapest but in Pécs. I was in the liberal arts, and I had a lot of encounters with students of history. And at that time, at least of those people I met, 70 to 80 percent had a sort of anti-Semitic sensability. It was a lot of years ago, like 15 years ago or so,

---

22 European Commission, "Perceptions of Antisemitism," January 2019, https://ec.europa.eu/commfrontoffice/publicopinion/index.cfm/ResultDoc/download/DocumentKy/85035.
23 Interview with György Szabó, April 22, 2021.

but those were my, my tensions. And if I went to a party, after a couple of beers they started to chant far-right wing or sort of Nazi slogans and these kinds of things. In Pécs there were also German faculty members, and a lot of Germans and Hungarians went there to study. I met with a lot of them, and there were a lot of anti-Semitic feelings in that community as well.

Among the young people, yeah, definitely. And it's interesting, because when I started to work in this organization, and at that time this whole social media bubble was created, and therefore I found my place in this bubble and I just had fewer and fewer encounters with those people than when I went to University and before that to school. That type of encounter with that other bubble almost cease to exist in my life. And then where I meet with anti-Semitism was actually on the internet, in comments and the other things one can easily find on different pages. So my physical encounters with anti-Semitic people have been significantly reduced, and therefore I didn't really meet with this in my personal life. I didn't really work in those type of environments where people are actually verbally anti-Semitic, so after university, I never met with this type of atrocity and this type of people and groups. [24]

Internet born Anti-Semitism is both ubiquitous and global. It knows no state boundaries and shares information, speculation and vitriol freely across borders. It is beyond our scope, so we return to Hungary and a more academic take.

An Academic Interlude

Prof. András Kovács[25] notes that the overall rates of anti-Semitism are as follows:

---

24 Interview with Adam Schönberger, April 16, 2021. In 2019, the MAROM community center was attacked and vandalized by neo-Nazis. However, Mr. Schönberger notes that this was not an anti-Semitic attack. Rather, it was anti-LGBT and stemmed from his work with LGBT groups.

25 All data and tables in this section are from Ildikó Barna and András Kovács, "Religiosity, Religious Practice, and Antisemitism in Present-Day Hungary," *Religions* 10, no. 9 (2019), https://www.mdpi.com/2077-1444/10/9/527/pdf.

Table 1. The percentage of antisemites among the Hungarian adult population, 2006–2017.

	Extreme Antisemites	Moderate Antisemites	Non-Antisemites/Unclassifed
2006	18	16	66
2017	26	10	64

Overall, the numbers indicate that while those who are not anti-Semitic remain over the decade steady at 66% of the Hungarian population, there have been some changes in extreme anti-Semitism, which has grown, and moderate anti-Semitism, which has declined. This can in part be accounted for by the rise of left-wing anti-Semitism stemming from anti-Zionism and opposition to Israeli policies in Palestine.

He further identifies three strands of anti-Semitism in Hungary. Religious anti-Judaism encompasses a range of beliefs such as the existence of a global Jewish conspiracy, charges of deicide in the killing of Christ and the like. Secular anti-Semitism ranges from opposition to Israeli policies to the belief that Jews have too much power in Hungary and the like. Emotional anti-Semitism is the hardest to quantify. The issue is a simple scale of sympathy for Jews and antipathy towards Jews.

Table 8. Different types of antisemitism in 2011 and 2017 (percentage).

	2011	2017
Religious anti-Judaism		
Non-antisemites	55	45
Moderate antisemites	19	20
Extreme antisemites	10	14
Unclassifiable	10	21
Secular antisemitism		
Non-antisemites	27	25
Moderate antisemites	27	26
Extreme antisemites	16	19
Unclassifiable	30	30

Emotional antisemitism		
Non-antisemites	59	63
Moderate antisemites	13	8
Extreme antisemites	20	22
Unclassifiable	8	7

In sum, anti-Semitism exists in Hungary as it does in every nation of the world. The increase in left-wing anti-Semitism is notable, while the other forms of anti-Semitism have remained stable or declined over the last decade.

The View from Abroad

The case against Hungary which can be found in the Western press and in elite discourse follows two primary tributaries. In Israel, the collective memory of Hungarian Holocaust survivors remains strong and continues to shape popular perceptions of Hungary.[26] The close diplomatic relationship between Israel and Hungary, and the even closer relationship between prime ministers Orbán and Netanyahu play exceedingly well on the Israeli right, but in the slightly more than 50% of Israelis who detest the former Israeli prime minister, the imagery is less sanguine. The Israeli view will of course change and evolve over time, but archetypal beliefs change more slowly than ongoing political trends.

In the US, the case is much more complex. There is little or no popular awareness of Hungarian Holocaust history. Rather, the view of Hungary is shaped by the memory of the Cold War. 1956 is the dominant theme and it is reinforced by the many Hungarian refugees who came to the West in the wake of the Soviet invasion. Hungarians are seen as the brave freedom fighters who stood against Soviet oppression.

The evidence presented against Hungary in the Western media is therefore much more contemporary in nature. The *causus belli* in this indictment centers on the György Soros campaign. The short lived poster campaign and some of the more extreme rhetoric did seem to have an element of classical anti-Semitism. With headlines like "Viktor Orbán's anti-Semitism problem" and "A Friend to Israel, and to Bigots: Viktor Orbán's 'Double Game'

---

[26] Interview with Prof. Jehuda Hartman, January 4, 2021.

on Anti-Semitism," Hungary and the Orbán regime are commonly depicted as both anti-Semitic and anti-democratic, with each trope intertwined and mutually supporting.[27]

In reading more deeply into the charges, we find a familiar cast of characters. A very cautious witness for the prosecution is none other than András Heisler, whose grievance is less with the anti-Soros poster campaign, which depicted the financier in a way that was strikingly reminiscent of the 1930s vintage 'Smiling Jew' German propaganda poster, than with the cover of *Figyelő*, a Hungarian magazine that depicted a cover shot of his face as a gentle rain of forint notes falls all about him. He took this as an anti-Semitic attack, and there may have been an element of truth in that, but he is no favorite of the prime minister—an antipathy that may date to his invitation to a gathering with Israeli Prime Minister Benjamin Netanyahu. Before Netanyahu's arrival, the Soros posters were removed, but Heisler—who is no one's idea of a diplomat—raised the topic in front of the Israeli prime minister. That embarrassment was an element in the EMIH-Fidesz embrace that is seldom remarked but very much there.[28]

> "There is this double game," Mr. Heisler said in an interview. He described the Orbán administration's relationship with Hungary's 100,000-strong Jewish population as "incredibly positive," but added that officials often make gestures that "ruin the values that they purport to espouse."[29]

And if András Heisler is the witness for the prosecution, who else but Rabbi Slomó Köves would take the stand for the defense?

> "When the prime minister of the country openly praises the Jewish state and the leader of the Jewish state, I don't think there's any other tool which is more effective at decreasing the anti-Semitism of the local population," Köves told *The Times of Israel*.[30]

---

27 William Echikson, "Viktor Orbán's anti-Semitism problem," *Politico*, May 13, 2019, https://www.politico.eu/article/viktor-Orbán-anti-semitism-problem-hungary-jews/. Patrick Kingsley, "A Friend to Israel, and to Bigots: Viktor Orbán's 'Double Game' on Anti-Semitism," *New York Times*, May 14, 2019, https://www.nytimes.com/2019/05/14/world/europe/Orbán-hungary-antisemitism.html.
28 Interview with Rabbi Slomó Köves, June 1, 2021.
29 Patrick Kingsley, "A Friend to Israel, and to Bigots: Viktor Orbán's 'Double Game' on Anti-Semitism."
30 Yaakov Schwartz, "Fans of Orbán or not, Hungarian Jews are optimistic ahead of PM's Israel visit,"

Conclusion

What has come out of this research is that, in contrast to the Western press, very few Jews we have interviewed believe that the Soros campaign was in fact anti-Semitic either in intent or execution. With only a few exceptions, the Soros campaign is seen by those we have interviewed as entirely political, and that moreover, neither he nor the rhetoric surrounding his activities is seen as having any connection to the Jewish community in Hungary whatsoever. A significant exception to this consensus is the Chief Rabbi of Hungary, Róbert Fröhlich, who sees a more ominous reading of the anti-Soros campaign, although he does not state that the intent was explicitly anti-Semitic.[31]

This view though was lost on the Western media, or simply ignored. Rather, the charge of Hungarian anti-Semitism became an element of a wider critique of what has come to be called *illiberal democracy* and could thus be rolled into an indictment of conservative parties in Europe, which could then be equated with fears that the Trump administration constituted a threat to American democracy as well. This media driven view of Hungary as anti-Semitic and anti-democratic however has not taken deep root in the US, and after the events in Washington on 6 January has drawn increasingly little public interest.

In sum, the Hungarian government has taken significant steps to combat anti-Semitism, and this has led to the dramatic decrease in the anti-Semitic violence that was common in Hungary a decade ago. The government's embrace of Rabbi Slomó Köves does not draw rave reviews in the wider Hungarian Jewish community, and the MAZSIHISZ/EMIH divide grows ever more heated and colors much of the perception of the steps taken by the Orbán government to support the Jewish community. The complaint that the government favors EMIH is obvious and has a good deal of truth to it. That however is a political question for the Hungarian Jewish community. What all agree is that under the Orbán government, Jews in Hungary are more secure than a decade ago and significant steps to combat anti-Semitism have been undertaken with some considerable degree of success.

Times of Israel, https://www.timesofisrael.com/fans-of-Orbán-or-not-hungarian-jews-are-optimistic-ahead-of-pms-israel-visit/.
31　Interview with Rabbi Róbert Frölich, May 12, 2021.

Preface

Tamás Orbán

Knowledge can only be built upon understanding deeper connections, for which the humility to actually look without prejudice and preconceived conclusions is a prerequisite. To understand is to see with one's own eyes. For me, the desire for such understanding was what made me feel intrigued about this project in the first place. To try to understand anti-Semitism in Hungarian society not only by looking at ambiguous statistics but by looking at the phenomenon through the eyes of those it concerns the most, the Hungarian Jews themselves.

At first, it was just that. It was a new, direct approach to uncover the depths of a system of deeply rooted and fascinating societal prejudices, hatreds and misconceptions. But as time went by, it became much more than that. Through the personalized accounts of many of these testimonies we could not only glimpse into the nature of anti-Semitism but into the surprisingly complex world of Jewish society, which at certain points felt like a parallel world to what I was used to live in every day.

Let us take a step back first, to where this project started. I remember that not long after Professor Kaplan's arrival to the Danube Institute we had a long talk about the evolution of different ancient cultures and religions and naturally we touched on Judaism. Until that point, I never felt any kind of connection towards the religion—its doctrines, beliefs and ideology—apart from the fact that it served as much of the basis of Christianity in the form of the Old Testament (the Torah). Of course, as a history major back in my undergraduate studies, I always felt fascinated by the incredible endurance Jewish culture proved to possess throughout the millennia of its existence—outliving all of its early civilizational counterparts, despite the frequent hardships it had to go through in ancient times—and later, during my studies in international relations and especially the geopolitics of the 20th century, I marvelled at the ability of Israel, this tiny speck of Western civilization in the middle of a sea of Arab and Muslim nations, to defy all odds for its survival through countless wars and regional upheavals. Yet, my eyes were never truly open to the deeply embedded mysticism in the Judaic world view nor the religious symbols and historical necessities behind them which made Judaism what it is today. And Professor Kaplan told us just enough, casually at our lunch table, to get our imagination working. I and the other research fellows became immediately hooked and just wanted to know more.

During those days more lunchtime cultural anthropology classes followed that memorable first one, until we inevitably touched the subject of anti-Semitism. It turned out that the Professor arrived with quite a skewed view on Hungary in this regard, unsurprisingly I might add. Western media has developed a real knack for portraying the current Hungarian government as extreme right, a narrative which would be incomplete without a good amount of anti-Semitism. As an American academic, he arrived in Hungary believing that Jews here were persecuted daily, or at least were close to being, by either the government's own actions or the societal atmosphere it created. Nevertheless, his experiences, as he pointed out to us, have led him to reconsider everything he previously thought about this country, while also opening up an opportunity to look further into the strangeness and uniqueness of the Hungarian Jewish community. One thing led to another, and we ended up at the beginning of a months-long journey to map out the reality of Hungarian anti-Semitism, primarily through the eyes of its real and supposed victims.

What followed was three months of intensive research which started with identifying our primary interview subjects. The task, which initially seemed simple, quickly proved to be anything but. As a young researcher from Transylvania for whom Budapest is still relatively new after living here only for a couple of years, I haven't had any connections or ties with the Hungarian Jewish community before, so I never imagined it being this complex and divided in its structure. The synergies of different denominations, factions and organizations—belonging to the Neolog, Orthodox, Hasidic and Progressive streams—simply amazed me. No matter how small the Jewish community is (from a few thousand to more than 150 thousand depending on definition), it felt overwhelming to single out enough leaders and representatives to get all sides of the story. Nonetheless, it happened, and we could move on to the next phase.

Once the interviews started, it quickly became apparent that asking only about anti-Semitism is barely scratching the surface. Everyone had a different—sometimes contradicting—story to tell, often based on their affiliation to the different organizations. Scholars talked about the roots of anti-Semitism, identifying it in Hungarian history and sometimes in our political traditions. Jewish journalists focused on street violence, while attributing either its relatively recent disappearance *or* growth to the political elite. Those with closer ties to the state of Israel usually praised the government's foreign policy commitment to it, while some NGO leaders talked about domestic intersectional oppression. But without any doubt, the most fascinating interviews we had were with leaders—religious and civil—of the Jewish denominations, where the lines that divide them became clearer than ever. It was apparent from the start that members of some denominations experienced significantly less anti-Semitism than others. Those who did have to deal with everyday incidents usually took up an opposing stance to the government and the governing party, while those who didn't were generally supportive of it. Or at least that is what it seemed at first, but it dawned on us that the causation here could be reversed. The deeper we dug, the more connections we seemed to have uncovered that linked perceived anti-Semitism to one's own political affiliations and their connections to other Jewish groups. The task at hand finally became apparent: if we were to come up with definitive answers on Hungarian anti-Semitism, we needed to look past its politization first, as the truth is buried under multiple levels of complex political synergies—of ideological differences, historical enmities and endless competition for resources—which often use the subject of anti-Semitism but rarely have anything to do with it in reality.

As for the reality, it turned out that the Hungarian case is not so different than the state of anti-Semitism in other East Central European countries, but not free of unique characteristics either. There is a sizable population who harbours at least somewhat anti-Semitic thoughts and beliefs, but this mainly stems from general ignorance and lack of connections to the Jewish community. Misconceptions and prejudice are the luxury of those who haven't met a single Jewish person in their life and are usually present in the form of decades old baseless tropes. What is unique—and not only in Central Europe, continent-wide—is the almost complete lack of anti-Semitic violence. Hungary has seen a dramatic decrease in anti-Semitic attacks in the last decade, which directly correlates to the current government's zero tolerance initiatives against it. The governing party, despite all the accusations from the West, not only plays a part in punishing anti-Semitism more harshly while significantly funding 'watchdog' organizations, but is also contributing towards every aspect of Hungarian Jewish life and helps to maintain a surprisingly large network of synagogues, NGOs, charity and cultural organizations as well. Those among the Hungarian Jews (mainly on the political left) who still accuse the government of anti-Semitism seem to have a considerably harder case to defend than those who are generally satisfied with its policies regarding this matter.

The conclusions of this field research are in this book—in the form of the introduction written by Professor Kaplan—while the interviews themselves will make up the second volume. This first one is an anthology of the speeches and presentations given by leading scholars and public figures of the Hungarian Jewish community (many of whom shared their more personalized views during the interviewing phase as well) at our international conference, titled 'Anti-Semitism in Hungary—Appearance and Reality'. The speakers were selected to represent the diversity of opinions we experienced during the research and also to add valuable foreign perspectives to the whole. We did our best to present all sides and narratives of Hungarian anti-Semitism, even though it is more like a *dreidel* in this respect than the proverbial coin.

Hungary presents an undoubtedly curious case both in terms of its Jewish community and its presence of anti-Semitism. Hungarian Jews—in international comparison—are unique in many different ways, which opens the way for a fascinating political atmosphere around them. Diving into this unknown world presented us with more questions than answers, but I am fairly confident that through these books we are able to give all those who are interested a near complete view on our true subject, anti-Semitism in Hungary, while also offering a trip into the mesmerizingly complex world of a Central European Jewish community.

Preface

Zsófia Tóth-Bíró

It was with some hesitation that I embarked on the journey that led our team to this final product of a complex project—the present anthology.

A fourth-year law student and junior researcher with the Danube Institute, with little if no background in Jewish studies, I felt I was ill-equipped for the task. Of course I am not entirely unaware of what Judaism is and what being Jewish in Hungary means. I happen to have Jewish relatives and friends, and thanks to my alma mater, the Pázmány Péter Catholic University's mandatory course on the Holocaust that I took as a freshman, I have a fair knowledge of the horrors of the persecution of Jews during WWII. Yet, I am definitely no expert on the topic of anti-Semitism, and I was worried about making missteps during the research.

But as a member of a great team made up of seasoned researchers I enjoyed the months-long process every step of the way, and have realized from the beginning how important was the project of mapping the situation of Hungarian Jewry and anti-Semitism in somewhat novel ways and through fresh eyes.

And that is why the project was launched in the first place—to attempt to present an objective and comprehensive analysis of the state of anti-Semitism in Hungary. By no means is the title of the present monograph, a collection of the contributions to the June 28–29, 2021 homonymous conference, *Anti-Semitism in Hungary: Appearance and Reality*, accidental. We have unfortunately seen distorted facts and at times deliberate misinformation, as well as disingenuous insinuations in public discussions of the topic in recent years at home and abroad. What our team strived to do was to provide a snapshot, as realistic as possible, of the situation, without the biases and misconstructions that unfortunately characterize many international analyses.

In order to have a grasp on the issue, we first conducted interviews with credible representatives of the Jewish community, making sure to include stakeholders from a variety of backgrounds and from across the political spectrum. On the basis of the valuable inputs we received, we selected the topics and invited the contributors to the conference, most of whom graciously accepted our request.

We are extremely grateful to all the distinguished presenters who offered us their precious time and expertise. Let me highlight here that we appreciate their confidence in our team's good will and professionalism, and we are thankful for them trusting that we would produce something unbiased and informative.

From among the presentations included in the monograph, I would like to highlight only a few. Let me begin with that of Dr. Róbert Frölich, Chief Rabbi of Hungary/MAZSIHISZ, leading rabbi of the Dohány Street synagogue. The humor and humanism of his remarks as well as his sharing of first-hand experiences as Hungary's first post-WWII Jewish military rabbi greatly helped us all understand the dynamics of the current situation of anti-Semitism in Hungary.

We also highly appreciated it that András Heisler, President of the Federation of Hungarian Jewish Communities (MAZSIHISZ), accepted our invitation and delivered remarks in a frank and open manner, not shying away from highlighting the still existing fears of discrimination among Budapest's Jewry. Mr. Heisler pointed out the concern among actors taking a more critical stance towards the Hungarian government that there are still controversial authors included in the national school curriculum of Hungary, authors whose apparent track record of anti-Semitism offends our Jewish-Hungarian compatriots.

Chief Rabbi of the Unified Hungarian Jewish Congregation (EMIH) Slomó Köves delivered eye-opening remarks about the trends over the past decade regarding anti-Semitic incidents in Hungary, stressing on the one hand that the number of incidents is on a steady decline and is significantly lower than in Western European countries, noting on the other hand that there is still much effort required to change the hearts and minds of those still infected by the plague of anti-Semitism. Similarly, Kálmán Szalai, Executive Director of the Action and Protection Foundation (Tett és Védelem Alapítvány), stressed that the changing of attitudes towards Jews must begin in early childhood. Therefore education plays a crucial role.

The conference provided a chance to also gain important insights into anti-Semitism abroad, with different presenters speaking about both right-wing and left-wing anti-Semitism, as well as about anti-Semitism rooted in radical Islam. This allowed the situation in Hungary to be viewed through the prism of the international context of anti-Semitism.

Tamir Wertzberger, Foreign Affairs Director of the Action and Protection League, highlighted in his seminal speech the anti-Israel bias that is predominant in international organizations, while Virág Gulyás, a Hungarian-born international activist fighting anti-Semitism underscored the enormous anti-Semitic and anti-Israel slant that characterizes most social media and a large part of the mainstream media, in particular liberal and left-leaning outlets.

I must highlight that the *spiritus rector* behind the conference and the present anthology is U.S. scholar, historian Jeffrey Kaplan. He is currently living and working in Hungary as a visiting fellow of the Danube Institute, whose generous and unconditioned moral and material support made the project possible.

I believe there are plenty of lessons one could learn from the conference, whether as a participant, an organizer, or a member of the audience. What hopefully everyone took away from the two productive days of the conference is that in Hungary there is now kind of a moment of grace, when the relationship between Hungary's Jewish and non-Jewish citizens is poised to be better than ever before, and where a pro-Israel government strongly opposed to all forms of anti-Semitism is in power. The other lesson is that the situation is far from perfect, with a lot still to be done, including a more honest reckoning with the past, and taking into account its repercussions for the present. This reckoning includes new approaches to controversial historical and literary figures. Finally, the conference also demonstrated that anti-Semitism is not a Jewish issue, but a national one. It is a problem that affects all Hungarians, and fighting it and attempting to eradicate it is in the interest of our entire nation.

I hope that the anthology will reach many, including some of those who have not been concerned with the topic before. I trust that it will provide food for thought and valuable insights, as well as dispel some misconceptions regarding the state of anti-Semitism in Hungary today.

Preface

Sáron Sugár

As someone who has always been interested in Jewish history, culture and religion and has quite a few Jewish relatives and friends, I was really excited to take part in this research and get to know the life stories and the backgrounds of the major figures of the Hungarian Jewish Community through it.

In 2009 Elie Wiesel, the Nobel-prize-winning author, professor, and Holocaust survivor, visited Hungary, and in one of his speeches, he said the following: "Hungary is going through a moral crisis. Do not let those ghosts of the past bring back the ugliness of the past. Don't let anti-Semitism gain ground. Remember Auschwitz would never happen without anti-Semitism. Remember that minorities have rights—and I include here the Romas as well. I especially want all of you to know that you can make a difference. Remember: shout with all your strength and it will not be for nothing." A little more than a decade later, after our research, we can say that even though anti-Semitism hasn't disappeared, Jews in Hungary do feel safe, as the level of anti-Jewishness has declined greatly in the country.

Since my teenage years, I've always felt a moral responsibility to stand up for Israel and the Jewish community in the case of any anti-Semitic threats or attacks against them. One of my earliest memories of fighting back against anti-Semitism in Hungary was in 2012, when Márton Gyöngyösi, a leading politician of the Jobbik party, urged that the Hungarian Parliament should draw up a list of Jews who pose a "national security risk". Even though at that time I was only 14 years old, it upset me that a Hungarian politician can make an anti-Semitic statement like that. As a reaction, Faith Church (Hit Gyülekezete), a Hungarian nondenominational megachurch, allied with the Jewish community to organize a protest where more than ten-thousand people stood up against Márton Gyöngyösi's anti-Semitic statement. I vividly remember this powerful occasion when we did what Elie Wiesel asked from us in 2009; shouted no to anti-Semitism. Eventually, this resistance and fight achieved its goal as the anti-Semitic part of Jobbik weakened throughout the years—even though it hasn't disappeared fully. This protest was also politically unique as it was the only demonstration in which the right-wing government and the left-wing opposition protested together, which was a huge accomplishment, as we can see how even the topic of anti-Semitism can be overly politicized.

Despite all of this, in many Western countries it's become common to portray Hungary as a country where anti-Semitism is still as strong as during the Second World War. Usually, the reporters making those claims don't ask the Jewish community what are their day-to-day experiences in Hungary. In this research, our aim was to show what representatives of the Jewish community think about the Hungarian situation, as they are the ones who can genuinely tell whether anti-Semitism is still a huge problem in their everyday life or not.

In the conference we held in June many speakers detected anti-Zionism and anti-Israelism as new forms of anti-Semitism. These forms of new anti-Semitism particularly strengthened during the Israeli-Palestine crisis in May 2021, when misinformation spread so fast and effectively in social media that it led to many anti-Semite-filled "free-Palestine rallies" in the very countries usually accusing Hungary of its alleged failure to tackle racism and anti-Semitism. For instance, in many states of the USA, in Vienna, London, and Berlin rallies led to many anti-Semitic attacks: protesters were stabbing and beating up Jews in the streets, burning Israeli flags, and shouting anti-Semitic slogans, saying that the Holocaust never happened. It was a shocking experience to hear that people could believe these lies and turn against their neighbors. Fortunately, these anti-Zionist rallies didn't lead to anti-Semitic attacks in Hungary. Though we must know what is happening around us in the world, as a Holocaust survivor close to me phrased it, "It must always be borne in mind that the genocide of the Jewish people can no longer occur, for these horrors can come so unexpectedly. Now that we know this can happen, we need to pay attention much sooner to everything that is hate and racism. We must be aware of what is happening in the world and we should not hope that things will go well on their own."

When we talk about anti-Semitism in Hungary, we can't forget about the severe historical responsibility of Hungary in the Shoah. As some people mentioned in the interviews, Hungary still hasn't fully faced its historical responsibility that under the often-disputed leadership of Miklós Horthy many Hungarians collaborated with the Germans and took an active part in deportations.

Even though we took some steps to face and process this tragedy as a nation, there is still a lot to be done. Also, it's so heartbreaking to see how deeply this tragedy impacted the Hungarian Jewish community. While before the Holocaust there were approximately 850,000 Jewish people from which 750,000 practiced Judaism, now there are approximately 100,000 Jewish people in Hungary from which only 1000–2000 people practice Judaism religiously. In 2018 I decided to go to the annual March of the Living at Auschwitz with my school, which was an experience that I will never forget in my life. Before we went to Poland, we visited the Dohány Street Synagogue (the largest Jewish synagogue in Europe) where Chief Rabbi Róbert Frölich gave us a short speech in which he mentioned the painful fact that before the Holocaust every week the synagogue was packed at sermons, while now usually there is no need to use the big hall as there are only a few people who come to worship on a weekly basis.

Our two-day journey to Auschwitz was an experience; as Reuven Rivlin the tenth President of Israel put it in his memorial speech: "We marched from death to life. From the Holocaust to the rebirth. From Auschwitz to Jerusalem." I strongly remember that after we visited Auschwitz for the first time and saw the places where one of the darkest, bloodiest and most cruel genocides of history happened, we got sick at even the thought of having to go back there the next day. However, the next day when we arrived at the March of the Living event at Auschwitz the whole camp had a different atmosphere. Auschwitz was filled with life and hope: 12,000 young and old people remembered the dead and celebrated that life triumphed over death, as the final plan of the Nazis didn't succeed. One of the most cathartic moments for me at the March happened when the anthem of Israel, the Jewish people's home, "Hatikvah" (which in Hebrew means "The Hope") intoned as we left the death camp. As we sang Hatikvah, the death camp was filled with that hope and truth that no one will ever be able to eliminate God's chosen people from the Earth.

Even though the Shoah deeply affected the Hungarian Jewish Community, some of the representatives who we interviewed told us that they would like to go beyond their Holocaust identity, which doesn't mean that they'll forget the loss that the Shoah caused to them; they in fact do everything to insure that the new generations will remember as well. Overcoming the Holocaust identity means that they would like to make Judaism attractive again to more and more Jewish people so they can rebuild their communities and fill up the empty synagogues with life. I hope that through the amazing life stories and heart-felt, captivating thoughts of the Hungarian Jewish people, the reader will get closer to them. Many of these stories show us that the Hungarian Jewish community does everything to raise its community from death to life, and by the end of our research, we can gratefully draw the conclusion that in the last decade their work hasn't been obstructed by serious anti-Semitic threats and attacks.

Foreword

Jeffrey Kaplan

Perhaps the most surprising thing about the Anti-Semitism in Hungary: Appearance and Reality conference that took place in Budapest on 28–29 June 2021 was that it took place at all. It was planned in the darkest days of the COVID lockdown in Hungary. There had been no live conferences of any kind for quite some time as all tried to learn to live from Zoom meeting to Zoom meeting. From the earliest planning stages, no thought was given to creating a virtual conference. Participants would either join us in person or no conference would be held. Virtual meetings, like every other form of life on the internet or in the murky netherworld of social media, are at best transitory and are quickly and easily forgotten. A topic as important as anti-Semitism in Hungary deserved a better fate.

That decided, the next hurdle was to bring participants together in a single conference setting. The Hungarian Academy of Sciences (*Magyar Tudományos Akadémia/* MTA) certainly provided an opulent venue, but the location was not the primary issue. Nor it turned out were COVID fears, which by June 2021 was getting better as Budapest was slowly coming back to life, albeit life lived in masks (which for a post-communist country had a certain historical irony). Rather, as many observers of the Hungarian Jewish community as well as community members themselves warned, bringing together the factions of Hungarian Judaism under one roof, much less at the same panel table, was a feat that had not been accomplished in quite some time. Indeed, as one foreign rabbi with much experience with Hungarian Jewry noted, if it could be done, it would be a great *mitzva* (good deed) for all involved.

In the end, all of the leaders of the Hungarian Jewish community came together and, in the spirit of Isaiah 11:6–9, MAZIHISZ and EMIH, a group of global academics and local and foreign activists, representatives of international Jewish organizations and the Hungarian government sat together and held productive, if sometimes sharply worded, sessions. Presentations were offered from widely differing perspectives in both English and Hungarian, the latter of which was translated live with great facility by Ms. Ildikó Biró. The video record of these sessions can be found at https://danubeinstitute.hu/en/videos. Many of the PowerPoint presentations can be found on the Helena History Press website http://helenahistorypress.com/.

The presentations and discussions which followed covered virtually every aspect of contemporary Jewish life in Hungary, as well as delving into Hungarian politics from widely differing perspectives. Most were supportive of the government's strongly enforced zero-tolerance policy with regards to public or media expressions of anti-Semitism and to the remarkable lack of anti-Semitic violence in recent years in Hungary. There was criticism too, stemming from the perception that the government favored a particular faction of the Jewish community over others, but despite this, all agreed that, in sharp contrast to a decade ago, Hungary was now a place where Jews could walk the streets and practice their religion freely.

It was this observation that Hungary was, in sharp contrast to the foreign perception of the country, a remarkably safe place for Jewish life, that inspired the subtitle of the conference: Appearance and Reality. This was a point that was made repeatedly in the many in-depth interviews with Hungarian Jewish leaders that preceded the conference. From the perspective of the researchers involved, Prof. Jeffrey Kaplan, Tamás Orbán, Zsófia Tóth-Bíró, Sáron Sugár, Dávid Nagy and Lidia Papp, it was these in-depth and often very personal interviews that, more than the conference itself, were at the heart of the project. Conferences, however successful, come and go and in time are forgotten. Published research by contrast, leaves a permanent historical record of not only the Hungarian Jewish community today, but of both the realities of Jewish life in Hungary and the remarkably negative ways in which the Hungarian situation is portrayed in the Western media.

This research is contained in the two-volume *Anti-Semitism in Hungary: Appearance and Reality* set published by Helena History Press. The first volume, which you hold in your hands, is the record of the conference itself, as well as the observations of the young researchers who made it possible, and a set of supporting academic articles which serve as supplement to the topics covered in the conference. Volume 2, which will appear shortly, contains the interviews with community leaders and activists that are at the true heart of this research.

It is our hope that the volumes together will leave for future researchers no less than for the Jewish community itself, as accurate a portrait of the state of anti-Semitism in Hungary as possible and will serve as a record of the people and place for many years to come.

Part

2

Welcoming Speeches

Introductory Remarks

Ambassador Yacov Hadas-Handelsman

Thank you very much. Good morning, ladies and gentlemen, honorable guests. It is an honor to take part in this conference at the Danube Institute.

As we look around the streets of Budapest and also around other cities in Hungary, the presence of Jewish tradition and culture is clearly seen and felt. As we travel to other major European capitals, we can also see the existence of Jewish culture, communities, heritage and religion. But there is a difference. And what is the difference? It is the sense of calm and security. This is what Jews feel when living here or coming to visit Hungary.

Hungary has the largest Jewish community in Central Europe, estimated around 100,000 people, mostly living in the capital, Budapest. It is with peace of mind that even someone recognized as a Jew can stroll the streets of Budapest with a sense of ease and security. Moreover, Hungarian Jews have every facility to express without fear their Jewish heritage and religious life.

That in and of itself tells a lot about a country. It tells a lot about a situation that we have to praise 80 years after the Holocaust in Europe, as already was indicated by Mr. [John] O'Sullivan. Well, elsewhere anti-Semitism can be seen and felt, sometimes also by physical assaults. This is not the case here, thank God. Jews in Hungary live in safety and tranquility.

Ladies and gentlemen, just to give you a few statistics. According to data from the ADL website, Hungary is at the bottom of the list for the number of anti-Semitic attacks or assaults in the European Union. In the 2019 survey administrated by the ADL, Hungary was one of the countries with the least amount of anti-Semitic assaults reported. The Hungarian government has made it clear, time and again that the only possible approach to anti-Semitism is zero tolerance.

It is important to mention that there has been a rise of anti-Semitism in Western Europe, North America and elsewhere. Jews around the world are living under threats in cities where anti-Semitism was not particularly present not very long ago. We are now seeing a wave of anti-Semitism being perpetrated by all kinds of people, religious or secular, educated or illiterate, and so on. As we saw on social media, there were individuals in the streets of New York or Los Angeles looking to attack Jews simply because they happen to be Jews.

Another aspect of the rise of anti-Semitism, which is also connected to the phenomenon I just described, is anti-Israelism. Since it is not exactly politically correct or is down-right illegal in certain countries to be anti-Semitic, people are hiding this tendency under the trend of Israel bashing. In recent years there has been a lot of criticism around the world allegedly regarding Israeli politics and particularly the Palestinian / Israeli conflict.

No one is immune from criticism, but I am sure you will agree with my assumption that there is a clear line which separates legitimate criticism and a criticism which is a cover up for anti-Semitism. An example: there are 193 members of the United Nations, yet Israel is the only country whose right of existence is called into doubt occasionally. We have had the famous slogan chanted by people around the world, "From the river to the sea Palestine will be free". This, ladies and gentlemen, is not criticism of Israel, but anti-Semitism, and I don't think I have to elaborate why specifically, not in this forum, but this is the reality. People knowingly or unknowingly, are expressing anti-Semitic ideas under the cover of legitimate criticism of Israeli policy. It is increasingly becoming difficult to have a proper discussion about Zionism or a normal political debate about Israel. Positions have hardened, emotions run high, and hard statements are being made. And we cannot ignore the fact that anti-Semitism is on the rise. I'm not revealing any secret to you, I'm sure.

The above-described phenomenon is not part of reality in this country, but we should remain vigilant and uncover this phenomenon whenever, wherever it may appear. At the end of the day, it hits all segments of human societies, and there is no religion, nationality, color or ethnicity difference. One might start by being anti-Semitic, but it does not end there. And we see this even in countries where there are no Jews or there have never been Jews, but yet they are considered to be one of the top anti-Semitic societies or countries in the world.

Despite the long, bitter past, the Jewish community in Hungary managed to overcome the atrocities of the Holocaust as well as the communist dictatorship era. And today, as said before, the Jewish community seems to be flourishing socially, culturally and religiously. This is all mainly thanks to the great support of the Hungarian government.

So, thank you for that and thank you for making Hungary feel like a home away from home for the Jewish community, and I'm wishing you all fruitful discussions in the next two days. Let us hope that really this will contribute something to the main task of humanity, which is in my opinion apart from climate changes and fighting all kinds of poverty and injustice in the world. But I think that anti-Semitism stands above them, not because I'm an Israeli Jew, but simply because, as I said before, this is a symptom of something which is wrong, sick, and as I said: you start with the Jews, and when you finish with the Jews, you turn to other groups in society.

Thank you very much.

Introductory Remarks

Rabbi Báruch Oberlander

I'm talking to you from New York. For ages the Jewish people have suffered from hatred and persecution. The Jewish calendar is unfortunately full of many outstanding tragic events. Just yesterday we spent Sunday, which was the 17th day of Tammuz in the Jewish calendar, fasting for a full day remembering the day when the Romans breached the walls of Jerusalem when they came there to destroy the Holy Temple. We have to remember all these tragic events. As the saying goes: 'if we don't remember the past, it can repeat in the future'.

In the beginning hatred of the Jewish people was the hatred of the Jewish religion, and we were persecuted in the hope that we would leave our religion for other religions. Then with the separation of church and state the hatred of Jewish people became a personal hatred, a racial hatred of the people. Unfortunately, this hatred turned out to be much more ruthless and vicious. This racial hatred took us to Auschwitz and other death camps, where we lost 6 million innocent people. More than 75 years later this hatred can still be found in different parts of the world from the USA to Europe. This hatred comes from the extreme right and from the extreme left. It can show up with different faces, but we still have to realize that it is still the same old racial hatred.

Is there anything that can be done to fight this ugly anti-Semitism? My father, let his memory be blessed, was a teenager when he survived the Holocaust in the city of Budapest. He and his family stayed in Budapest for a few years after the Holocaust, after that they went to the United States of America. He used to tell me, and he believed, that education is the only effective tool to fight anti-Semitism. People must be educated and brought up to understand, to tolerate the other person who might be different than yourself.

The differences in people enrich our society. As the Talmud says, just as God created us so that our faces are different from each other in the same way our opinions, thinking and mentality are different from each other. This is not a problem. Rather, the many opinions make society more colorful and more beautiful. But education of the people, my father used to stress, has to start at a very young age, in kindergarten. It is never too early to teach this and bring this message to the masses. It is only then that we can hope that as adults we will act with love and kindness toward each other.

As the Chief Rabbi of the Orthodox Rabbinate, I can tell you that thank God that in Hungary we, the Jewish people enjoy complete freedom to practice our religion. We can also walk on the streets freely, send our children to Jewish schools without fear. But in certain quarters there is still a growing culture of hatred and anti-Semitism. This has to be looked at and studied thoroughly, so we can understand what the sources for this hatred are, where it comes from, so it can be confronted and dealt with in the right way.

This is why this conference is so important. I would like to thank the organizers of this conference for their hard work and let God send blessing to your work to have a very fruitful event.

Thank you very much!

Introductory Remarks

Rabbi Róbert Frölich

Rabbi Slomó Köves quotes the fifth book of Moses and I would like to do the same and also quote Moses—from a bit earlier in the Bible from the third book. Moses says: 'rebuke your neighbor and not suffer sin upon him'. Let me quote another important figure who maybe had not such importance as Moses, but he was indeed important: Winston Churchill: 'I only believe in statistics that I falsify myself'. But what's the connection? We heard a lot of statistics in President Heisler's and Rabbi Köves' presentations. Statistics are indeed important, they have only one problem, they do not always cover reality. Because in fact if we compare the presence of anti-Semitism in Hungary to that in Western Europe then we can say that the situation here is not so bad.

If I remember correctly, Rabbi Köves and President Szabó emphasized the importance of education. They are right, I deeply agree. I normally call attention to the fact that education is a long-term issue, so it is important what we teach. But including the works of Hungarian interwar author Albert Wass—who might be a great author but do not forget that he was decorated two times by Ferenc Szálasi[1]—or including Cécile Tormai[2] in the curriculum is not helpful. She was an Hungarian author who is well known for her anti-Semitic views, and her inclusion is perhaps not a good idea. And that's when Moses comes into the picture. So, when we call attention to the fact that the surface is different from the depths, the bottom, we basically behave as decent Jews according to Moses' requirement. We call

---

1 Ferenc Szálasi (1897–1946) was the leader of the Arrow Cross who was installed as Prime Minister by the Nazis during the German occupation of Hungary in 1944. He was tried and executed by the communist government in 1946.

2 Cécile Tormay (1875–1937) was a writer whose work was nominated for the Nobel Prize. She is a controversial figure in Hungary stemming from her lesbian and transgender lifestyle and anti-Semitic writings.

our fellow man's attention to the mistakes they are making or that they are about to make so that they won't carry a sin just because we let them make those mistakes.

Thank you for listening!

Introductory Remarks

András Heisler

With the generous support of the Hungarian government, the Rumbach Street Synagogue was renewed. And a few days after the opening, we were able to enjoy a wonderful religious event. We held a common Bat Mitzvah for 12 Jewish girls, which is a memorable moment for every Jewish family. I wanted to show pictures of this ceremony however, no pictures were taken because the girls' parents chose not to take pictures. Why? Because they are afraid. They are afraid of what will happen if their co-workers, neighbors, their acquaintances recognize them and ask the question: are you Jews? Ladies and gentlemen, my dear friends, this little story tells a lot about reality. Whether the concerns are true or just believed is hard to say, but in recent years, we have heard more about the transmission of trauma across generations, when different generations can pass on their fears without actually talking to each other about it.

We all need to acknowledge that the Holocaust can cause trauma in second-generation members to this day. Of course, it may also arise that religion, faith, is a personal issue for everyone, but do the parents of a Christian think the same way (as the Jewish parents) about baptism? It should be noted that there are fears, but there is no anti-Semitism in Hungary today from which all this can be deduced directly. In Budapest, you can walk freely on the streets, there are no or rare physical atrocities against either Jewish people or Jewish institutions. The situation in Hungary today is better in this respect than in other European countries, and this can be said responsibly.

The principle of zero tolerance was announced by Prime Minister Viktor Orbán. The renovations of synagogues and abandoned cemeteries, the subsidies received for the development of Jewish infrastructure, and physical security are almost paradisiacal to the superficial observer. Yet sociological surveys indicate that members of the Jewish community feel the phenomenon of existing anti-Semitism is becoming more intense, and their civic comfort is not good. In addition, as a responsible Jewish leader, one cannot go without saying a word. It cannot be denied that despite the government decisions listed, anti-Semitism is present in society as a whole; although among the supporters of all parliamentary parties, albeit to varying degrees, research data show that the rejection of Jews is still unacceptable.

In wider society, speech consisting of bitten-off half-sentences, which suggest a lot and hurt us, is still fashionable. Where every year neo-Nazis laugh at the world and are given permission for parades disguised as traditional performance tours, where they are permitted to do a little Arrow Cross, Nazi romanticism—there's something wrong. Where a democratically elected mayor of the capital can be portrayed as one of the greatest evildoers in Hungarian history—Szalasi—there is something wrong.[3] And where the country's Prime Minister can be featured on the front page with a Hitler mustache,[4] there's something wrong. There is something wrong with parliamentarians being singled out for listing in the 21st century.[5] Not only is it forbidden to relativize the Holocaust, but it is also dangerous to play with the signs associated with it. This is what right- and left-wing politicians do, and then they fail to explain what they do to each other. My dear friends, we Hungarians are proud of our origins, our customs, our diversity, even our debates. We may always have disagreements, but we must react if we got hurt regularly, and that will not be a fight but a legitimate self-defense.

After more than half a million martyrs, it would be important for us to pay more attention to each other. It would be important to prevent our undoubted present traumas from becoming overwhelming, but to do so, we cannot go without a word about the hatred in our society, the remarks and beliefs that attack our communities. We cannot turn our heads if a minority is stigmatized, for we know from history that hatred against any minority can sooner or later be a breeding ground for anti-Semitism.

---

3   The reference is to a Fidesz Party Facebook post that depicted Budapest Mayor Gergely Karácsony as the wartime Arrow Cross Party leader Ferenc Szálasi.
4   The picture appeared in the satirical weekly newspaper *Magyar Narancs* [Hungarian orange].
5   The reference is the call by a Jobbik parliamentarian in 2012 for the creation of a Jewish list which would single out Jewish parliamentarians suspected of dual loyalty. This caused a strongly negative reaction across the Hungarian political spectrum.

As Hungary's largest Jewish organization, it is therefore important for us to be aware of the dangers. Not because we love to be afraid, but because we can protect ourselves, while also helping, protecting, and informing society as a whole about the dangers of hatred. MAZSIHISZ established the Ignác Goldziher Jewish Historical and Cultural Research Institute. One of the Institute's most important goals is to conduct theoretical research on issues affecting and occupying the Jewish community, to publish them in domestic and international forums, and to disseminate the results to decision-makers. It helps to monitor and analyze Hungarian anti-Semitism. According to the latest analysis based on attitude surveys, there is still work to be done in Hungary. The survey distinguishes between physical atrocity, threat, vandalism, anti-Semitic hate speech, conspiracy theory, and so-called public anti-Semitism. In Hungary, the number of cases in the first three types is extremely low, and there is a decreasing trend.

Compared to Western Europe, the situation is much more favorable, we all feel this, of course, comparing multicultural societies and Hungary's relatively homogeneous national community is a more complicated task than comparing individual data. Anti-Semitic manifestations in the online sphere, on the other hand, are on the rise everywhere. Conspiracy theories about the epidemic have emerged, and perhaps the most sensitive and critical area is public anti-Semitism. It is critical because this category does not contain anything that would be a misdemeanor according to the letter of the law. Yet it is one of the insidious forms of anti-Semitism that fundamentally affects the well-being of our community. What can my 96-year-old, Holocaust survivor mother think, who returned home from Auschwitz, when she hears that Horthy was a defender of the Jews? Do we have to believe that the Jews, deprived of everything, their human dignity, could have lived the year 1944 in great condition?

The Hungarian gendarmes crowded them into wagons and the Arrow Cross members shot them into the Danube. The recognition of historians who contributed to the revision of the Horthy era, relativizing the events of the Holocaust, the raising of former anti-Semitic public figures onto a pedestal, or the inauguration of the Horthy statue today frustrates members of the Hungarian Jewish community, creating uncertainty and fear. Let's face it, according to Median's survey, 20% of Hungarian society is strongly anti-Semitic and 16% is moderately anti-Semitic. Compared to previous years, there is no significant shift, which can be said to be good, despite the strong growth of anti-Semitism in Western Europe.

Even with Orbán's zero-tolerance, we cannot be satisfied, as one-third of society is more or less infected with anti-Semitism. The proportion of Holocaust deniers and relativizers is also high, which jumped in 2018: 20% of the population was characterized by Holocaust denial and 10% by relativization. The importance of education on this issue would be obvious, it cannot be stressed enough, but as long as it is the responsibility of those who profess or accept racist views to design curricula, we should not expect real results on this issue.

According to the survey, the rejection of Jews goes hand in hand with the rejection of other minorities, so I ask everyone not to be surprised when we react sensitively to action or incitement to hatred against any other minority group. Anti-Zionism against Israel is a form of anti-Semitism. Domestic public life and public discourse are better in this respect than in many other countries. The clear position of the Hungarian government in favor of Israel is important. Anti-Zionism is not accepted in Hungary and the Hungarian government plays a significant role in this. All this is reassuring and the Jews are grateful.

Ladies and Gentlemen, overall, there is something to do, there is room for improvement. We have to evaluate Prime Minister Viktor Orbán and his government's efforts against anti-Semitism. However, existing mistakes must be addressed. Anti-Semitism destroys public life throughout the country.

I can't avoid mentioning another phenomenon. I've read an article in the *Times of Israel* that is important for the future of all European Jewry in our countries, and I quote, "Do not allow discrimination between Jewish organizations." If governments can choose the Jews they love and those they don't, it leads to inadmissible manipulation. In Hungary, only one group receives the vast majority of funding, in exchange for political support the *Times of Israel* writes.[6] This is unacceptable to the majority of Hungarian Jews, but also the European Union.

---

6   The reference is to EMIH, the Hungarian Chabad movement led by Rabbi Slomó Köves. EMIH for its part disputes this contention. See the Introduction to this volume for details of the controversy.

I would not have highlighted a newspaper article if the ten most important Jewish advocacy organizations had not approached the European Commission to ensure that historically embedded and legitimately represented denominations, both in terms of public recognition and funding, were treated equally. At present, many European governments do not adhere to this principle, and power and funding are concentrated in the hands of a single, unrepresentative denomination, says a statement by ten international Jewish organizations. In response, European Commission President Ursula von der Leyen prioritizes the fight against anti-Semitism, is deeply concerned about the escalation of violence on the streets of Europe, and recommends that Jewish life in Europe be helped.

Ladies and Gentlemen, we are facing a two-day conference, and there is nothing more boring than to be able to model the results of the conference in advance, so I respectfully ask all participants to analyze the situation of Hungarian Jewry in many ways. Let there be pluralism because there is something to rejoice about, there are results that cannot mean circumventing, trivializing, or silencing existing mistakes or shortcomings.

Finally, I would like to send a message to Hungarian Jews, Neologs, Orthodox, Lubavitchers, members of progressive movements, or even secularists: be proud of our values, be independent in our thinking and be courageous in accepting our opinions. Don't let yourself be intimidated or scared. Let us not allow any of us to be harmed by our faith and we can continue to walk freely in Hungary and take photos of the Bat Mitzva that can be posted on social media. This is what I wish for ourselves, this is what I am asking of you, all of us, and thank you for listening.

Introductory Remarks

Rabbi Slomó Köves

Ladies and gentlemen, dear Ambassador, dear State Secretary, distinguished guests, speakers, I would like to start with a quote from the Bible, our common heritage. The fifth book of Moses says: 'God will bless you in all your endeavors in the work of your hand'. The sages in the Talmud say it is not only a blessing but it is also a way to teach us how to get that blessing. A Jew should always know that to get a blessing he has to use the work of his hand in order to create a vessel for the blessing.

What I would like to speak about today is what the actual actions are that we can do to change the current situation and what the tools and the vessels are through which we can combat and abolish—if we cannot totally annihilate—the virus of anti-Semitism in Hungary and in other parts of the world. In the last year and a half, we all have become handmade virologists, and we know that in order to fight a virus, an unseen sickness, we first have to make a map, we have to see what we are dealing with, we have to see who carries the virus and in what way they pass on the virus to someone else.

I would like to bore you with some facts and show you some types of tendencies that we have seen in the last couple of years. I will focus on Hungary, although we could do the same type of mapping in the rest of the EU or any other country where data is available. I will speak about the different perceptions that Hungarian Jews have about their situation, which does not necessarily go in parallel with the actual facts. As we know, perception is not always parallel with facts—there was a study, a pretty famous one, done by the European Union Agency for Fundamental Rights, a.k.a. FRA. In 2012 this study was done in 12 Member States which had a sizeable Jewish community, and the study was done again in 2018. This study involved close to 17,000 individuals who were identified as Jewish. I want to cite some of the questions that were asked, and give you the data from 2012 and then from 2018.

Out of all the states listed, Hungary in 2012 had 91% of Jewish people thinking anti-Semitism had increased in the previous five years. The same question was asked in 2018. The same answer came from only 70%. Next question: perceptions of changes in the level of expression of anti-Semitism on the Internet. In 2012, the answer from Hungary was 88%, while in 2018, 73%. Respondents were very worried or fairly worried about a family member or a person close to them becoming a victim of an anti-Semitic assault in 2012, the figure in Hungary was 66%, which was in third place in the EU. In 2018, it was 29%. Another figure is about concerns that a family member or a person close to the respondent could become the victim of verbal insults or harassment because of anti-Semitism. This figure in 2012 was 28%, as opposed to 18% in 2018. Well, I could go on and on about the different figures, but what we do see throughout the study and the comparison between the 2012 and 2018 studies is that Hungary's place on this list has become considerably better in that six-year period between 2012 and 2018.

We can look at another figure: in 2015, the number of anti-Semitic assaults in Hungary—physical and verbal—was 52, this is 5.3 per million inhabitants. The same figure in most Western countries was higher, in the USA it was 942, which is 2.9. In Great Britain though, it was 960, which is 14.5 per million inhabitants. Compare that to France which had 808 assaults and it's 12 assaults per million. And in comparison, the Hungarian number of 2015 is 52 assaults, which is 5.3 per million.

Now let's look at the latest data available from 2019. In the U.S., there is a considerable increase. In 2018 it was 5.7 per million. In Great Britain it was 25 per million. There were almost 1700 cases of anti-Semitic assaults in Great Britain. In Hungary, the cases dropped in 2018: it was 32 cases, which is 3.3, the figure almost dropped to half from 2015. What is the reason for this decrease? Well, there can definitely be many reasons, but I strongly believe, as follows from the quote from the Bible which I have started with, that our actions can actually change our existence; they can change our environment and there have been some very recognizable actions taken in the last 5–10-year period.

In 2012, seeing that the situation was worsening in Hungary, and seeing that 90% of Hungarian Jews felt that anti-Semitism had increased in the previous five years, we decided to create an organization to combat anti-Semitism. This is how the Action and Protection League came into existence with the cooperation of all Jewish communities and all Jewish streams. We strongly believed that we have to raise the fight against anti-Semitism to a professional level. This included first and foremost the initiative to try to push back on physical assaults. The actions that have been taken together with the government, for example, include a change in the Hungarian constitution, the Fourth Amendment, which made it possible for the Hungarian civil and penal code to include more tools in order to fight anti-Semitism and Holocaust denial, and this has proven to be a very effective tool. From 2014 on, the number of physical assaults as well as Holocaust denial cases has dropped significantly. There is still a long way to go and what we do see is, as was mentioned by Mr. Heisler, that Hungary is still struggling with a high level of anti-Semitism in minds and hearts. There is almost no physical assault, but at the same time we do know that Holocaust denial and anti-Semitic attitudes in society are relatively prevalent. Between 35% and 40% of Hungarian society displays some type of anti-Semitic attitude, and almost 20% of Hungarian society has some belief in Holocaust denial.

What is the way forward? I strongly believe that the same way we have diminished the physical assaults of anti-Semitism and we have changed the perception of Jewish people living in Hungary, we can change the perceptions and the minds and hearts of people, but we also have to understand that this is a long-term job, not something that can be done short term. Education is definitely the most important tool when it comes to changing minds and hearts. This is why I feel it is important that the Hungarian government created very strong cooperation with the Jewish communities when it was working on the national curriculum, in reviewing all the textbooks of history, literature and so forth to try to see what should be included and what should be excluded or presented in a certain way in Hungarian textbooks. I also strongly believe that changing minds and hearts with regard to the remembrance of the Holocaust is the responsibility not only of the Hungarian government but also of the Jewish community. Therefore, the opportunity that the Hungarian Jewish community gained by creating probably the largest holocaust museum in Eastern-Central Europe is a major one; a chance for us to try to present the story of the Holocaust in a way we believe can change the perception of regular Hungarians and especially Hungarian youth in the future.

Dear members and dear speakers, thank you very much for honoring me by inviting me to this conference. I wish you a successful discussion and we should all hope that the next time when we want to hold such a conference there will be nothing to talk about. Thank you very much!

Introductory Remarks

György Szabó

Over the past week on several occasions, I had the chance to meet with commanders of the paratroopers of the Israeli Defense Forces. They asked me what my opinion about anti-Semitism was. When I started listing my opinion about the Holocaust, etc., one of them asked me, "When will we step forward into the future from the past?" I answered him saying that we can never actually move on from the past because there are events that we must always remember, but there are certain concerning developments that we must take into account.

These concerns are actually the more and more radical anti-Jewish and anti-Israeli statements and politics that are appearing in Western Europe and in the United States of America. When with some of my friends who are sitting here now, we said about ten years ago that a new type of anti-Semitism is taking shape in Europe which is based primarily on anti-Israeli sentiments, many laughed at us. By today, unfortunately, we can say that these movements are getting stronger and stronger both in Europe and in America, and currently Hungary is the only secure ally of the state of Israel. Of course, we can interpret Hungarian public speech in this way or another way. When I am asked whether I ever encountered instances of anti-Semitism in the streets, my answer is always that this should be measured by looking, for example, at people like me who are visibly Jewish. When we are asked this question, we usually say that while in France, in Belgium, the Netherlands and in other countries where you can't walk the streets safely with the look that I have, in Hungary you not only can walk freely on the street but you can do so proudly.

The activities of the Hungarian Jewish Heritage Public Foundation [Mazsök] demonstrate that the level of activity of Jewish public life is unprecedented, as one of our main problems is that we don't have sufficient funds to be able to support all 50 Jewish organizations that represent a large variety of

Hungarian Jewish communities. Mazsök supports 150 Jewish themed projects and manages to give assistance to a hundred Jewish families per year. I simply can't say that Jews are afraid in Hungary, as these one hundred families apply for a grant using public applications, and also all those organizations that are Jewish by name and all those projects that are openly and transparently linked to Jewishness in the majority of cases have no experience of anti-Semitism.

Of course, I'm not saying that the situation is perfect or ideal, as there are always things to do and things to improve, and lots of sensitization work is needed. However, I believe that the countries of Europe have a lot to learn from Hungary in the ways to tackle anti-Semitism.

I wish you all very useful, edifying and constructive work during the conference, and I hope that by the end of the conference you'll come to conclusions that will show the way forward not just for Hungary but for Europe as well.

Thank you for your attention.

Introductory Remarks

Rabbi Andrew Baker

Thank you, it's good to be with you if only virtually today. I would like to just offer some rather general reflections on the challenge, the problem of anti-Semitism, as well as the experience essentially of getting governments and international organizations to address the problem as well. And I want to reflect not only on my work for many years with the American Jewish Committee, but also from serving since 2009 as a special envoy of the OSCE, the Organization for Security and Cooperation in Europe.

Many people point to the U.N. conference on racism held 20 years ago in Durban, South Africa, as a kind of turning point. When we look at the resurgence of anti-Semitism, that really marks almost these two decades. That was a conference where Jewish organizations initially had seen to it, I would say simply, to ensure that anti-Semitism was identified as one of the long-standing forms of racism. But instead, the conference itself almost became a place for fomenting anti-Semitism, that saw the renewal of the Zionism is racism canard and was accompanied, as it was, by a breakdown of the peace process in the Middle East. Shortly thereafter, we saw a surge in anti-Semitic incidents, mostly in Western Europe. These were anti-Semitic incidents that initially governments themselves were slow to identify or recognize or perhaps even more troubling, intentionally chose not to recognize. It led eventually to significant international efforts.

The conference organized by the OSCE was the first conference on anti-Semitism by an international organization. It took place in 2003 in Vienna, followed by a high-level conference in Berlin. A year later, a declaration in which all of the OSCE participating states asserted that anti-Semitism had taken on new forms and manifestations. It did state this largely as a way to refute what we had been hearing from some governments, that events in the Middle East, incidents in Israel could never justify anti-Semitism. Of course, we saw how they were at least being pointed to as ways of rationalizing or excusing this increase in incidents.

So where are we now, literally almost two decades later? I think we find ourselves in a challenging situation; in one where there's a genuine, I would say that; puzzle. If we looked at this in a kind of split screen, we would be able to say, and I'll share briefly what are significant positive measures taken by governments, by international bodies and organizations to address the problem of anti-Semitism. And yet that other split-screen shows us what I think the people who are here speaking and listening today know all too well, that the problem has not diminished. If anything, it seems even more acute and more challenging. The fact is, we see anti-Semitism coming from various places and they've been already identified by previous speakers, but just to recount: we see anti-Semitism coming from the far right, and anti-Semitism that we know quite well and that we've been addressing for years. But it remains strong and in some cases even stronger than it was some years back as, disillusioned with the European Union, with anti-immigrant activity in Europe, and in America, there are seething racist white supremacist movements that are inherently anti-Semitic.

We see anti-Semitism coming from the political left, not always and perhaps not frequently taking violent form, but a pernicious form as well. The challenge is often to the Jews own place in the political and social movements on the progressive left. We see that playing out these days in the United States. We saw it reach a kind of high point, if you will a low point, with anti-Zionism as a form of anti-Semitism which was being expressed in the British Labor Party under the chairmanship of Jeremy Corbyn.

We've seen as well over these years, as various people in different Western European countries know all too well, significant incidents of anti-Semitism coming from parts of the Arab and Muslim communities. This kind of anti-Semitism has at times taken even lethal forms, but one that is expressed frequently and on a day-to-day basis in the form of physical or verbal harassment that sees the comfort, the day-to-day sustainability, of Jewish life being challenged. We've seen how anti-Semitism has been folded into efforts to confront the Holocaust era in history. Notable in a country like Hungary, but in Hungary's neighbors as well, a significant development in the 1990s, early 2000s, and in pushing these countries to confront critically, directly their Holocaust-era history. Much of this folded into efforts to secure the restitution of Jewish property, [the restoration of] communal and private property. Anti-Semitism played a role here. We see the honoring of fascist era leaders, perhaps inspiring national identity, but individuals who themselves were complicit, active participants in the Holocaust in various countries. While there was a record really of international historical commissions and other vehicles to address this problem, we've seen now in more recent years that it is almost been pushed aside. One cannot argue this is out of ignorance anymore, but we see a revival of these fascist era figures being honored in various countries in Central and Eastern Europe, countries where Jewish communities themselves are the very victims or the children and grandchildren of the victims of these perpetrators.

We see another form, a real challenge to Jewish life, maybe not anti-Semitic by intent, but in many ways still anti-Semitic in effect. I speak now about efforts to restrict or ban long-standing religious practices essential for Jews and in many cases for Muslims as well. Namely, the practice of *brit milah* circumcision and of *Shechita* or religious slaughter. Often these are movements led by human rights activists, people who are arguing "we're concerned only about the protection of animals or to secure the rights and protection of children". But we've seen in multiple countries success in banning the practice of religious slaughter and movements now to ban circumcision as well. Again, you take all of these together and if they succeed, they really do pose a very real, even existential challenge to the future sustainability of Jewish communities in these countries. These are the multiple problems we face.

At the same time, we've seen over these last two decades remarkable, positive developments in getting governments to take up this problem, to address these issues. Security has been and remains a critical issue for Jewish communities. It is one that is never truly settled and I think we even recognize no one wants to imagine that permanent Jewish life has to exist behind fortified walls and armed guards. Nevertheless, many of the attacks we were witnessing during the first decade of this millennium were taking place because governments were slow or unwilling to really step forward and offer the security necessary. That is today far less the case.

We can still ask for more, we can still understand more may need to be done. But nevertheless, these days governments recognize this is part of recommendations and decisions issued by the OSCE, by the European Union, and by various national governments. We've seen an increase in identifying and appointing individuals with a specific responsibility in their national governments to implement action plans to address anti-Semitism. We've seen the adoption and use now of the working definition of anti-Semitism initially developed with the European Monitoring Center 15 years ago, but since 2016, identified as the IHRA working definition, the definition of the International Holocaust Remembrance Alliance, a tool that can help police, prosecutors, and monitors to understand anti-Semitism and its multiple forms. And hopefully by understanding it, beginning to properly address that definition to some degree remains controversial. But in fact, it has become a formally adopted definition by nearly 30 countries, numerous organizations, sports teams and others, and it is a significant tool to educate the general public as well on the anti-Semitism that we face.

We have much sharper and clearer experience now in identifying and measuring anti-Semitism. Surveys conducted by the EU Agency for Fundamental Rights and other civil society organizations as well, give us a clearer picture of the problem and certainly of how Jews themselves see and experience this. All of this is really quite a remarkable and positive development.

Nevertheless, we're facing many of the same challenges and perhaps in an even more acute form than we did looking back now to 15 to 20 years ago. Perhaps we might conclude that were there not such efforts undertaken by governments, the problem would be even more severe. One cannot really know that, but we surely have our work cut out for us today.

And to add one more point that I think we all have come to recognize: even if there is a great effort and involvement on the part of governments in addressing anti-Semitism, we see all too frequently the challenge that the fight against anti-Semitism itself has become politicized. Those on the left are only willing, maybe too willing, to point to the problem on the right while ignoring what happens in their own camp. There are those who have a real challenge confronting Holocaust-era history, pointing instead to the challenge of Muslims attacking Jews elsewhere in Europe. I think we see here in the United States, where for so very long the fight against anti-Semitism, against racism and intolerance had always been a common bipartisan effort, that now it as well has become a tool of our hyper-partisan political arena.

Thank you very much.

Introductory Remarks

Tristan Azbej

Your Excellency, Honoured Leaders of Jewish Communities, Ladies and Gentlemen. It is a great privilege to be here today. First of all, this is my first international conference in one and a half years. Second, I find this issue very important, and I commend the organisers and the Danube Institute for starting this series of international conferences on such a significant and serious topic. It came to me just before today's event that I'm going to be the only representative of the Hungarian government at this conference, which is a great responsibility. At the same time, though, this has become a personal topic and mission for me having been brought up in Hungary in Central Europe, having served in Israel for four years as a diplomat and leading Hungary's humanitarian program for persecuted religious minorities at present. In these times of rising anti-Semitism globally and also in these times of rising anti-religious sentiments and religious intolerance, I think this should be more than just government policy. I think it should be more than the policy of international organisations. It should be a personal mission for all of us to fight anti-Semitism, anti-religious persecution and violence. So my thoughts will partially be the remarks of a government representative, but they will also serve as a personal greeting to you. I will attempt not to open my prepared speech, which is quite a courageous thing to do when someone is speaking about such a sensitive issue.

As a Christian Democrat politician of the governing Hungarian Christian Democrat parties, I want to emphasize that the cornerstone of our policies is the Judeo-Christian value system, Judeo-Christian social values. These are social values that can be promoted and advocated for by a secular government such as ours, but they all come from the same religious idea shared by Judaism and Christianity. This religious idea is that men and women were created by God in his own image and likeness. Therefore men and women have an inalienable right to human dignity. This human dignity has to be protected by granting basic human rights. Of course, the main task of states and governments is to provide well-being for their citizens. This well-being, however, has no meaning whatsoever if human dignity is not protected. The Hungarian government's policy towards anti-Semitism is led by this approach. This is the policy of zero tolerance, the only possible alternative regarding this issue. It is this approach that has led the Hungarian government to have the ambition of championing and protecting religious freedom in the international arena.

Talking about combatting anti-Semitism in Hungary, I can proudly say that, in the last eleven years, the Hungarian government led by Prime Minister Viktor Orbán implemented a series of measures in this regard which are unprecedented in Hungarian history. And it may be unprecedented in many other countries in Europe also. I was very much honoured and privileged to hear about these measures from leaders of Hungarian Jewish communities as well. I think that perhaps the result and efficiency of these measures can be debated or there can be a discussion about them. However, the Hungarian government's sincere approach to combating anti-Semitism is indisputable. Of course, this conference will be about the success and efficiency of these policies and about their political background. It will be up to you to discuss all this. But I think that the international community should recognise what the Hungarian government has achieved so far in terms of fighting impunity regarding anti-Semitic hate crimes, in terms of raising awareness about anti-Semitism and also in terms of supporting Jewish culture and communities in Hungary.

In terms of fighting impunity, the Hungarian government proposed and the Hungarian legislature adopted and strengthened sanctions against provocations aimed at Jewish and other communities. It also implemented and increased sanctions against any hate crime in the Hungarian Civil and Criminal Code. In addition, Hungarian legislation has introduced a legal term to describe Holocaust denial which imposes sanctions on the hateful act of denying the murder of six million innocent people. As for raising awareness about the issue, the Hungarian government organised the Holocaust Remembrance Year on the 75th anniversary of the Shoah. Also, Hungarian Prime Minister Viktor Orbán was the first head of government to acknowledge and recognise the role and responsibility of the Hungarian state in the Holocaust.

Of course, there has been much debate and discussion in Hungarian public discourse about the historical basis of the Holocaust Remembrance Year. But I would like to remind everyone that this government was the first one in Hungarian history to organise a Holocaust Remembrance Year at all. So therefore, even if the implementation can be subject to criticism, and it should always be subject to criticism as part of politics, the efforts of the Hungarian government should be acknowledged. It was the first occasion to recognise the responsibility of the Hungarian state, to raise awareness about the issue and thus make gestures towards fulfilling this moral obligation. This should be acknowledged when portraying Hungary, the Hungarian government and its efforts to combat anti-Semitism.

Still, our objective is not to stop with these measures. We have two gradual objectives in this respect. The first objective is to create an environment in which all Hungarian Jewish compatriots feel valued and protected in Hungary. The second objective, gradually speaking, is that all of our Jewish compatriots feel valued in Hungary but without a sense of being protected, since the environment is such that they do not need protection anymore, in other words, they are not facing any threat in Hungarian society. Although this conference is about domestic issues, let me give you a brief overview.

When we look to the west of the European Union and to the north, we see an emerging threat of a new wave of anti-Semitism stemming from the appearance of radical Islam. Also, especially in the United Kingdom, there have been reports about a new type of anti-Semitism coming from radical left ideologies. I want to reassure the Hungarian Jewish community and all the international community that Hungary will remain a strong political force in keeping radical Islam out of Hungary and also out of the European Union by stopping illegal migration. In addition, we will be promoting, we will be steady and committed in promoting religious freedom outside of Hungary and on an international scale also. Hungary was the first country that elevated the issue of protecting religious freedom to government level by starting the Hungary Helps Program. It is the first program to provide humanitarian aid to persecuted Christian and other religious minorities all around the world.

Why am I talking about supporting persecuted Christians at a conference about combatting anti-Semitism? By now, the Hungary Helps Program has provided support to persecuted religious communities in more than 40 countries of the world. I would like to speak about one country in particular, and that is Iraq in the Middle East. Iraq was home to a very strong Jewish community for thousands and thousands of years dating back to Biblical times. By now, no Jewish person or community has remained in that country. There is a tragic anecdote which says that, despite the historical fact that at one point about one third of the population of Baghdad was of Jewish cultural background, there is only one elderly Orthodox man who has remained by now. For comparison, when we talk about the fate of Christianity in Iraq, we see that it shows a tragic parallel to Jewish communities. Christianity has a 2,000-year-old presence in that country. Even in 2004, there were 1.5 million Christians living in Iraq. Now, after only 16 years, the number is 275,000. So in the course of one and a half decades, it has decreased to approximately 300,000.

This is why Hungary is championing this cause. In the course of the last four years, we have provided help to about a quarter of a million people persecuted for their faith. And we supported not only Christians; first of all, that wouldn't be Christian-like at all. We also provide support to the Yazidi ethno-religious community in the Middle East. In addition, the Hungarian government, through the Hungary Helps Program, supports the Rohingya community, a persecuted Muslim minority group as well. And it is my great honour to announce to you that, together with the Unified Hungarian Jewish Congregation, the Hungary Helps Program will provide humanitarian aid to the Jewish Sephardic communities in Yemen which have been targeted by discrimination and have suffered a lot during the armed conflicts and violence there.

I would like to close these remarks with a biblical quote. I'm going to turn to the very beginning of the Bible. This is a simple question. Adam, where are you? (Gen 3,9) Adam, in this context, means man. Where is man in the face of inhumanity? Where is man in the face of inhumanity when he fails to act? We will not fail to act. We will not remain silent. We will not abandon those people who are threatened or who are discriminated against, and we will not abandon those people who are persecuted for their faith or ethnic background.

Thank you very much for the invitation and for your attention.

Part

3

Historical Issues

Responses to Terror

Béla Bodó

(This article is a more detailed version of Prof. Bodó's presentation.)

Jewish responses to pogroms and other forms of physical violence took one of five forms: intercessions; anti-defamation (systematic struggle against anti-Semitism in the parliament and the press); armed resistance, private and communal responses, self-defense; geographic mobility and flight from local communities; and emigration from the country.

During the counterrevolution, intercession took place at the local, national and international levels. Intercessions were initiated by the family members of the victims of violence or Jewish organizations on behalf of private individuals or the Jewish community as whole. The goal of private intercessions was to locate family members or free them from captivity. Public intercessions, on the other hand, were meant to change policy. The making of contacts with, and complaining to, the entente representatives and international Jewish organizations also served to put pressure on the Hungarian government to end violence. Both private and public intercessions were based on an unequal relationship (a strong asymmetrical dependency) between the parties. Forced into a historical role, Jews who requested intervention and help were supposed to display humility and even submission. Intercessions often involved offering bribes (disguised as donations) to militia leaders, local officials and politicians.

Private intercessions normally occurred at the local (municipal and country) levels. However, a handful of mainly upper-middle class Jews and their legal representatives were able to gain access to high-ranking civil servants, government officials and even Admiral Horthy to plead the case of their loved ones. Normally the victims' relatives and their legal representatives sought to stir up pity and compassion; they also played on the military leaders' and civil servants' sense of honor and justice to achieve their goals. In many, perhaps the majority of cases, intercession involved the exchange of a large sum of money, or of valuables, such as jewelry. The acceptance of bribes, however, did not necessary lead to the release of prisoners. The paramilitary leaders and county officials were eager to pocket the bribes; yet they were more reluctant to live up to their promises. The same paramilitary leaders could also simply ignore the higher officials, including Horthy's order to release the inmates. Private intercessions often came too late; by the time the order of the political or military official arrived, the victims, in many cases, had already been shot, or tortured to death.

Public intercession involved Jewish delegations visiting military and political leaders, such as Admiral Horthy, the members of the civilian governments, influential aristocrats, such as Archduke Ágost József von Habsburg, counts Albert Apponyi and István Bethlen, as well as Catholic and Protestant dignitaries. They were trying to convince them to rein in the militias and condemn discrimination and anti-Jewish violence. This was not always easy. The relationship with the Catholic elite had been rocky at least since late 19th century (the People's Party, which represented Christian Socialism in Hungary, functioned as one of the main sources of anti-Semitic agitation in the country), and reached its nadir during the two revolutions. The historically correct (cold but fair) relationship also deteriorated rapidly after the war (young aristocrats were overrepresented in the most murderous paramilitary units). The Catholic Church was reluctant to condemn the atrocities against Jews in the first months of the counter-revolution in the fall of 1919.

Change came only in the final months after December 1919. Catholic leaders, such as Prelate János Csernoch and Count János Mikes, the Bishop of Szombathely, often spoke out against the militias and the pogroms; they were also prepared to meet, appear in public and issue joint statements with Jewish religious dignitaries. Still, a small yet influential minority in the Catholic elite, led by Ottokár Prohászka, the Bishop of Székesfehérvár (one of the main figures in the history of modern Hungarian anti-Semitism and a driving force behind the anti-Semitic Numerus Clauses legislation of 1920), continued to reject appeals or to have any meaningful contact with Jewish leaders. Paradoxically, the Catholic Army Bishop, István Zadravecz, a close friend, political ally and admirer of the militia leader Pál Prónay and avowed enemy of "Judeo-Bolshevism," came to the defense of the famous Orientalist and Chief Rabbi of Szeged, Immanuel Löw, accused of *lèse majesté* and treason. Zadravecz even appeared as a character witness at Löw's trial in May 1921. Catholic newpapers such as *Új Nemzedék* continued to spread lies about Jewish participation in the war and remained an important source of anti-Semitic agitation in the 1920s and 1930s.[1]

The aristocratic support for the violent militias declined drastically after December 1920. It is doubtful however, that that the rejection of anti-Semitic violence and its agents had much to do with the intercessions or expressed sympathy for the victims. Influential aristocrats, such as Count Albert Apponyi, who led the peace delegation in 1919, worried that continued attacks on Jews would have a negative impact on the country's reputation and the outcome of peace negotiations. Both church leaders and politically engaged aristocrats were disturbed by the chaos and saw the militias as a seed of disorder. Political and military leaders, such as Admiral Horthy, were even more reluctant to cut the ties with the elite paramilitary groups, which they deemed useful until the end of 1921. Their desire to rein in the militia was informed by concern over law and order and the fear of a possible military coup. Indeed, the greatest opponent of the militias in Horthy's entourage, Count Pál Teleki, harbored strong resentment towards Jews and was a major force behind the Numerus Clausus legislation of 1920 (indeed, he was major force of anti-Semitic agitation until his death in 1941).

Yet the most politically experienced and savvy among them, such as István Bethlen, recognized early on the damage that the pogroms and armed robberies had caused the country's reputation. In early October 1919, a delegation of conservative aristocrats, headed by Count Bethlen, visited Horthy in Siófok to discuss foreign and domestic policy, including the issue of anti-Semitic violence. Bethlen asked Horthy directly if a pogrom would follow the entry of his troops into the capital in November. The visibly irritated Admiral's response was that "there will be no pogrom! But some will have to take a bath!"[2] This was a reference to the paramilitary groups' habits of throwing the remains of their murdered enemies into the river.

---

1   See Jenő Gergely ed., *A püspöki kar tanácskozásai. A magyar katolikus püspökök konferenciáinak jegyzőkönyveiből, 1919–1944* (Budapest: Gondolat, 198), 140–141.
2   Komoróczy, *A ZSIDÓK TÖRTÉNETE MAGYARORSZÁGON*, 380.

In the first half of 1920, legitimist aristocrats, such as Count Albert Apponyi, who led the Hungarian peace delegation to Paris, constantly warned politicians in Budapest, including Horthy, to do something about the armed robberies and the anti-Jewish riots. It was one of their number, Count Pál Teleki, who, as prime minister, proscribed the civic militias in the summer of 1920. Admittedly, the intercessions by Jewish leaders played only a minor role in the growing hostility of the traditional social elite to militias and their rejection of paramilitary violence. Nevertheless, they did help to reinforce the conservative instincts of the political elite.

Regent Horthy, at the intercession of Jews and gentiles such as Zadravecz, pardoned Löw, and after thirteen months in captivity, the chief Rabbi of Szeged was able to leave prison. In 1938, during the debate on the first anti-Jewish law in the Upper House of Parliament, the famous Orientalist thanked Zadravecz for his intervention.

The second form of intercession included asking influential foreigners to intercede with Hungarian officials on behalf of the Jews. The Legal Aid Office of the Pest Community, set up in the fall of 1919 under the direction of Dr. Géza Dombováry, regularly passed on information about the atrocities not only to the Supreme Command of the national army (Horthy) and the prime minister's office, but the entente mission, as well. Western diplomats and military officials listened to Jewish complaints: people like Thomas Hohler, the high commissioner of the British Legation, and the American General Bandholtz met with the leaders of the community and repeatedly raised the issue of anti-Semitic violence with Admiral Horthy and other members of the political elite. At the end of September, at Bandholtz's initiative, the entente sent a fact-finding mission, headed by the American colonel Nathan Horowitz, to Transdanubia. The colonel and his entourage were to gather reliable information about anti-Semitic violence and to speak with local Jewish leaders. Colonel Horowitz, who was of Jewish decent, visited Horthy in Siófok; he also inspected several county prisons and internment camps. Warned about his arrival, prison administrators removed the sickly and the abused to the camp in Zalaegerszeg and other locations. Taking the place of abused inmates and speaking good English, Prónay's young and well-fed officers were able to convince the American colonel that prisoners had been treated decently in the infamous military prison in Siófok. In his final report, published a few weeks after the visit, Colonel Horowitz praised the discipline of Horthy's troops. He stated that "Admiral Horthy's army had done everything within reason to prevent any such "persecutions [of Jews]"; he thought that "no more atrocities had been committed than would ordinarily happen under the stress of such circumstances."[3] Horowitz admitted that the population, due to their experience under Communism, in which Jews played a major role, was strongly anti-Semitic, and that individual atrocities had, indeed, occurred. But the American colonel denied that there was a White Terror in Hungary, or any of these atrocities had to do with Horthy, his national army or the civilian government.

The Horowitz report had a devastating impact on Hungarian Jews, who lost their trust in the Western powers and became even more reluctant to report the atrocities to the entente mission in Budapest. The report vindicated the radical right, which had always denied the existence of the White Terror; it legitimized the national army as a political force, and turned its commander, Admiral Horthy, into a serious contender for power. Great Britain, which claimed the role of kingmaker in Hungary, was not indifferent to the plight of Jews: it merely subordinated the issue of anti-Semitic and political violence to its geopolitical interests, such as fighting Bolshevism and preventing French hegemony in Eastern Europe. Concerned about its reputation as a humanist power and civilized state, the British government continued to pressure Admiral Horthy to end the atrocities. On November 5, 1919, Horthy made an agreement, in the presence of the British mediator, George Clerk, with the leaders of the social democratic, liberal, and peasant parties. At the meeting, Horthy promised, among other things, that he would not introduce military dictatorship, would respect civil rights, and would not stage a pogrom after the entry of his troops into Budapest. It was on the basis of this agreement that Admiral Horthy was allowed to enter on his famous white horse and take possession of the capital on November 16, 1919.

The deal helped to prevent the outbreak of a city- or even nation-wide pogrom, which Prónay and his men had been dreaming about for months. The presence of entente diplomats and military representatives continued to have a restraining influence on the paramilitary groups, the main source of anti-Semitic violence, in the next two years.

---

3   See Maj. Gen. Harry Hill Bandholtz, AN UNDIPLOMATIC DIARY. http://mek.oszk.hu/08200/08202/08202.htm.

The second form of Jewish reaction to paramilitary and mob violence was anti-defamation: defending the honor and reputation of Jews as a religious community in the Parliament and in the press. The Hungarian Parliament had only a handful of Jewish representatives, as members of the liberal parties, between 1920 and 1922. Jewish leaders, such as Pál Sándor, did everything in their power to refute anti-Semitic propaganda and prevent the passing of the Numerus Clausus legislation. Since the Parliament was dominated by political parties in which fanatical anti-Semites represented a strong minority, it comes as no surprise that neither the liberal representatives' calm and rational arguments, based on statistics, nor their emotional appeal to compassion and decency could achieve much: not infrequently their voices were simply drowned out by the boos, jeers, and crude insults of their opponents.

The most important battle for the heart and soul of the Hungarian public was fought not in the Parliament but on the editorial pages of major newspapers and periodicals. The mouthpiece of the Neolog community of Budapest, the weekly *Egyenlőség* (Equality), fought hard to refute the most pernicious rumors about, and defend the honor of Jews. Lajos Szabolcsi, a poet and the editor-in-chief of *Egyenlőség*, even brought Dr. Elek Avarffy, anti-Semitic parliamentarian and one of the founders of the eugenics movements in Hungary, who claimed that only a few hundred Jews had fallen during the war, to court. The Neolog community of Pest collected statistical information to prove that the Jewish casualty rates surpassed, or at least matched, those of other ethnic and religious groups. In long articles, Jewish authors listed the names of people who had received high decorations for bravery during the war, and families who lost several members on the battlefield.

Beside the notion of Jews as shirkers of their military duties, it was the equation of Jews with Communism that patriotic Hungarians of the Israelite faith found the most insulting and dangerous. In the Parliament's chamber and in the press, Jewish leaders tried to convince the public that Judaism and Communism were incompatible. The Neologs did not deny that many of the leaders of the Council Republic had Jewish roots. Yet these Communists of Jewish descent, they contended, had long since cut ties to the Jewish community: they did not regard themselves as Jews; neither did the community accept them as such. With a few exceptions, *Egyenlőség* argued, Jews not only kept their distance from Bolshevism, they also counted among the most committed supporters of the counterrevolution. Jews were allegedly overrepresented among the victims of communism. It was mainly Jews who gave money to the counterrevolutionary government and the national army. "We can say this without exaggeration," *Egyenlőség* stated in early November 1919, "that without Jews there would have been no counterrevolution."

Anti-defamation meant questioning the credibility, motives and character of noted anti-Semites and perpetrators of anti-Jewish violence. Jewish publications sought to delegitimize anti-Semitic parliamentarians, such as Dr. Elek Avarffy, by exposing them as upstarts, swindlers, intellectual lightweights, and dangerous demagogues. They also drew attention to the hypocrisy of famous intellectuals, such as the playwright Dezső Szabó, the darling of the radical and anti-Semitic right during the counterrevolution, and the celebrated poet and novelist Dezső Kosztolányi, who declared war on 'Jewish domination of Hungarian culture' in the fall of 1919. The Jewish weekly was quick to point out that Szabó and Kosztolányi had started their careers in the "Jewish-liberal" camp, and that their first sponsors and publishers had been Jews.[4]

While intercessions, especially when they involved bribes, were often successful, the anti-defamation campaign seems to have produced meager results: parliamentary speeches and articles published in the Jewish weekly and Jewish periodicals failed to change the mind of the majority of the population. Jews were not the only ones to use statistics to prove their points; the anti-Semites were equality adroit in exploiting the potential present in numbers and charts to sway public opinion. The anti-Semites could afford losing individual arguments. Civilized debates had always been suspect in their eyes, and indeed, to large segments of the Hungarian public; rational arguments were doubly suspect when employed by Jews. The truth, many anti-Semites believed, had to be felt and grasped instinctively rather than demonstrated or understood through reason. Anti-Semites considered brashness, courage in the face of death, honesty, and simplicity as Hungarian characteristics; foresight, reason, self-control, on the other hand, were believed to be secondary and alien, German and Western virtues at best, and Jewish tricks at worst.

The anti-defamation campaign was a failure because Jews represented a small religious minority, because Hungarian society was largely hostile towards Jews, and because this hostility could not be dispelled by parlia-

---

4 *Egyenlőség*, November 4, 1922.

mentary speeches and articles published in an obscure Jewish weekly. The campaign proved to be a failure because it did not enjoy the full support of the dominant liberal conservative press. No major newspaper completely embraced Jewish interests during the counterrevolution.

Self-defense, like intercession, was both a national and local enterprise; yet it was practiced most effectively at the municipal and village levels by small groups and private individuals. As a response to the anti-Semitic riots in the spring of 1918, local Jewish communities set up self-defense units to provide protection against marauding soldiers. On July 6, 1918, Lajos Szabolcsi, the editor-in-chief of the Jewish weekly *Egyenlőség*, created an umbrella organization, the Self-Defense League (Önvédelmi Liga). In early November 1918, István Friedrich, then state secretary in the Ministry of Defense, urged Jewish cultural organizations to speed up the organization of independent self-defense units and promised financial and military support. In the next two weeks battalion-size units (between 1000 and 1500 men strong) had been set up. The moving spirit behind the organization of Jewish militias was the Zionist leader Ármin Beregi, who had served as a captain in the First World War. His subcommanders and the great majority of the rank-and-file also came from Zionist organizations, such as the National Association of Jewish University Students, the Makkabea. Simultaneously, Jews in many provincial towns, such as Pozsony and Pápa, set up their own self-defense units. These Jewish paramilitary groups helped in many places, especially in the western part of the country, to prevent pogroms; however they could not stem the rising tide of anti-Semitic violence. Self-defense petered out quickly. The poorly paid Zionist Guard met the same fate as hundreds of other paramilitary groups during the democratic interlude: its companies were disbanded and the members handed back their weapons to the state before the Communist takeover of power in March 1919. The radical leftist regime, which harbored totalitarian ambitions, jealously guarded its monopoly on the means and use of violence. Thus it not only proscribed dozens of Jewish educational, welfare, and cultural organizations in next two months, but it also snuffed out any attempt to revive the Jewish militias.

After August 1919, the new counterrevolutionary regime was intensely hostile to Jews and Jewish organizations. Before his entry into the capital in mid-November 1919, Admiral Horthy accused Jewish leaders in Budapest of incitement. He gave credence to the rumor, vehemently denied by the Zionist leaders, such as József Patai, that Jewish organizations had been distributing weapons among the members of the Makkabea to terrorize Christians. The charge was not completely baseless. Hastily created Jewish self-defense units guarded some of the synagogues, including the Neolog temple on Dohány Street, around the clock during the counterrevolution. Jewish athletes and university students patrolled Teleki Square and Lujza, Hollós, and Rákóczi streets in late 1919 and early 1920. Clashes between Jewish students and Gentile counterparts became so common that the academic administrators felt compelled to close the two universities in Budapest in the second week of August 1919 to prevent further bloodshed.

Jewish group resistance was heroic but ineffective. Hastily organized defense units, armed as they were only with sticks, knives, iron knuckles and whips, were no match for the university militias and officers' detachments, which normally carried guns, and who, as quasi-state employees, had the law on their sides. Rumors about the Awakened Jews planning to stage pogroms to exterminate all Hungarians were nothing but projections. Yet the real resistance was enough to justify harassment, illegal arrests, and even murders.

Individual self-defense ranged from dueling and resisting arrest to fistfights and armed confrontation between the *Pogromshchiki* and the male members of the targeted households. Since the turn of the century, the National Association of Jewish University Students, Makkabea, encouraged young Zionist men to defend their honor in duels, if necessary. As a sign of growing tension between the two communities, Jewish participation rose from 13 percent of people convicted of dueling in 1885 to 50 percent in the 1920s. The nature of dueling changed after 1919: while before the war, giving or accepting challenge was normally a response to verbal insult, during the counterrevolution and beyond, duels often followed clashes between individuals in university cafeterias, ball rooms, or lecture halls: i.e., they were responses to physical violence or the threat of violence.

Dueling was a preferred reaction of athletes, university students, and young Jewish middle-class men to insult and violence. Resistance to paramilitary and mob violence took many forms and mobilized the entire Jewish community. As we have seen, Jewish women moved heaven and earth to free their fathers, husbands, and sons from captivity: they visited Horthy, contacted politicians and ministers, wrote petitions and letters of denunciation, and gave depositions. They took known criminals to court. Elderly men tore down anti-Semitic billboards and removed flyers from their doors and windows. Both men and women and Jews of all ages and social backgrounds refused to leave their communities, and when forced to leave under duress, they returned to their villages and small towns at the first opportunity.

Middle-aged professionals may not have resorted to arms as frequently as students; however, this does not mean that they failed to resist, or that their resistance was always a failure. Generally, professionals, such as doctors and civil servants, who provided vital service and enjoyed the protection of the state were more likely to stand up to the militias than merchants. Individual resistance to militia aggression did not automatically lead to arrest and the intensification of violence. This was not true for group and armed resistance. There were several examples such as this: the Oblath family stood up against a mob, and one of them killed the man who led the charge. This resistance led to a full scale pogrom and the expulsion of Jews.

The civil war also widened the emotional, cultural, and political gaps between the Neologs and Orthodox, and between culturally assimilated Jews and Zionists, as well. During the parliamentary debate over the Numerus Clausus proposal in early fall of 1920, one of the Jewish members of the Assembly, Pál Sándor, confessed that he hated Zionists more than he did anti-Semites. The two groups did not see eye-to-eye on any issue. Zionists questioned not only the results but also the morality of emancipation and cultural assimilation. Zionists repeatedly appealed to international Jewish organizations and foreign governments to intercede on their behalf and help to end violence; they also welcomed the decision of the Western powers and the peace conference to recognize Jews as an ethnic minority. The Neologs, however, rejected foreign intervention and minority status as a threat to the survival of Judaism in Hungary. The idea of Jews as a separate ethnic group, they believed, played into the hands of anti-Semites, who had never accepted Jews as patriotic Hungarians.

The two groups drew radically different conclusions from the post-war events. The violence and discrimination that they had experienced reinforced the Zionists' conviction that Jews had no place in Hungary in the long run. The Neologs, on the other hand, believed that the only way to end discrimination was through greater social integration, complete cultural assimilation, and full identification with Hungarian national interests and goals. Zionists saw violence as a sign of widening and unbridgeable divides. On the other hand, the tribulations of the last two years only reinforced the Neologs' determination to prove their patriotic credentials and loyalty to the state. The Zionists had never fully trusted the Magyar political elite, and recent events only reinforced their distrust. The Neolog leaders, on the other hand, interpreted the reining in of the militias and the restoration of order by 1922 as a sign of the Hungarian political elite's continued commitment to liberal values and to the protection of Jews, as citizens, against their domestic and foreign enemies. The Neolog elite underestimated the conservative elite's opportunism and the danger inherent in their selective, and strong, but admittedly not genocidal, anti-Semitism.

In the end, the Neolog leaders tied Jewish survival to the survival of the conservative authoritarian regime and the traditional political elite. This strategy helped to avert genocide until the final phase of the war; yet its consequences became all the more serious after the German occupation of the country in March 1944.

The History of Military Chaplaincy

Rabbi Róbert Frölich

The topic that I'll talk about today is the reinstatement of military chaplains after the system change.

I understand that a scientific or scholarly presentation needs to keep a distance from its subject, and I also understand that the further we are in time from our subject, the easier it is to keep that distance. The truth of the matter is that I was an active participant of this process of reinstatement. This means that there is no objectivity that could be expected from a scholar, nor is historical perspective or distance present.

So, the idea of military chaplains is not an unknown concept in Hungary. Although the title of Jewish religious helpers was not exactly near to a chaplain, this position actually existed as early as in the times of the Hungarian 1848–49 revolution, and the father of Emmanuel Löw, Leopold Löw, was actually the first person to perform the task in Lajos Kossuth's army.[1] However odd it may sound, even until the beginning of the Second World War there were Jewish military chaplains in the Hungarian army.

I had a teacher in the Rabbinical Seminary, József Smideg, blessed be his memory, whose diary survived in the archives of the military rabbinate. In 1943 he was summoned for training as a military rabbi. The training of course was that he was forced to frog jump around a muddy courtyard—but formally it was called military rabbi training. And even after the war for a while there was a Chief Military Rabbi position, and it was filled by Dr. Ferenc Hevesi, who was my predecessor in many ways. He was my predecessor as the rabbi of the Dohány Street Synagogue and my predecessor as military rabbi.

---

[1] Lajos Kossuth (1802–1894) was a leading figure in the 1848 revolution against Austrian control of Hungary. When an Austrian backed Croat army invaded Hungary, Kossuth became head of the Committee of National Defense appointed by the Diet as provisional authority, giving him near absolute power.

At the beginning of the 1950s, the military rabbinate was basically diminished but it never officially ceased to exist. Soon after the system change, at the very beginning of the 1990s, the need or the desire for reinstating the military rabbinate emerged again, and interestingly enough it was not the Jewish community that first proposed it, but the then conservative MDF [Magyar Demokrata Fórum] government. All the churches or faiths in Hungary, including the Catholic, Protestant and Jewish denominations, appointed an expert that they sent to this new council to determine the future of the military chaplainship.

The legal bases of re-founding the military chaplainship was Law IV. 1990, which is about the freedom of conscience and the freedom of religion. But of course, the same law became the basis of debates about the military chaplainship, but that is the fate of laws. Perhaps it is not superfluous to mention the name of István Tabódy, one of the Catholic participants, who started his career as a lieutenant in Horthy's army. He was a very interesting figure. He courted Horthy's niece, then he became a priest, then in the 1950s, under the communist dictatorship he was sent to the forced labor camp, Recsk. He even features in György Faludy's famous 'My Happy Days From Hell', and eventually he was rehabilitated and became a member of this new military chaplainship.

The Ministry of Defence set up a board that consisted of lawyers, legal experts, military legal experts and foreign policy experts, who worked for three years on establishing this system. Our task as church experts was to try to somehow insert all the religious rules and church systems we represented into this state-run system. Of course, apart from István Tabódy, whom I mentioned earlier, nobody had ever seen a live military chaplain before, so we didn't have the foggiest idea of what we were supposed to do. That was the time when Hungary quit the Warsaw Pact, and soon after the Warsaw Pact ceased to exist—maybe not because of us—there was a slow movement closer to NATO, so we were getting experts from America and from NATO countries to advise us on this matter.

The task of these liaison teams was to tell us how these military chaplaincies worked in NATO member states. This was truly hard work for three years. The only question that was debated was whether the chaplain should be a military officer or not. As usual there were arguments in favor and there were arguments against why this person should be in the military. The state leadership—I think pretty wisely—decided that the chaplain should be a military officer, because military to military relations are truly different from military to civilian relationships. I dare to say that after having spent twenty years serving in the military.

The next big battle was about what rank we would have as soldiers. I, I mean not as Róbert Frölich but as the representative of MAZSIHISZ, had only one demand: whoever the Catholic and the Protestant bishops would be, they should have the exact same rank as the chief military rabbi. So, the first military chaplains were named. Let's mention their names, the Roman-Catholic one was Gáspár Ladocsi, the first military bishop of the Reformed Church was Károly Takaró, and the first chief military rabbi was someone I'm too modest to name.

I was a full 28 years old at the time. What happened eventually was that the two bishops became generals, and I became a colonel. That rank I had not deserved, considering that I only served three years, but I certainly served more than the two bishops. But the problem was that a general and a colonel are not in the same category. So, I summoned my courage and went to see Lajos Fürj, who was the defense minister at the time. His political state secretary was Ernő Raffay, who received a high state award last year and spent the last ten years of his life working on his global Jewish conspiracy theories. It was certainly not a love affair between the two of us. He had done everything he could to prevent a military chief rabbi from existing. Lajos Fürj later became one of the founders of the 'Hungarian Guard', the radical right wing—so he certainly is not a philosemite.

So, I went to see Lajos and I said, "Look, I'm sorry but something is wrong, that's not what we'd agreed". He said, "I hope Mr. Rabbi you do not believe that this is some sort of discrimination". "That's exactly what I think", I answered. He basically kicked me out of his office. Then he changed his mind and called me back, and he said, "Maybe it's not the right thing to do, let's talk about this, but Mr. Rabbi you are very young". And I responded: "Look, when Clemenceau first ran in an election campaign, he was often accused of being too young, and Clemenceau promised to get 365 days older each year". I also said, because I was really modest even back then, that Napoleon was already a general at my age. We didn't see eye to eye, but later the Socialist government kind of settled this matter.

In January 1994 the agreements between state and churches regarding the military chaplainship were signed. So, they signed it with the Catholic, the Reformed and the Lutheran churches, and with MAZSIHISZ. That's when the legal and organizational framework took shape, on the basis of which the military rabbinate is functioning.

Thank you so much!

"Nothing New Under the Sun…"

Tibor Pécsi

In this panel, I will speak about the forms of anti-Semitism in the post-Holocaust world. Although I believe that the title of my presentation "Nothing new under the sun…"—which is a Bible quote from the book of Ecclesiastes—explains what I'm about to say. I will be speaking basically in bullet points, because this is a complex topic and much more time would be required for me to fully elaborate. A person who thinks normally, like all of us here, would think that after the tragedy of the Holocaust anti-Semitism would cease to be. The world must have learned that we cannot exclude, discriminate against anybody, or be hateful towards anybody based on religion, race, and ethnicity. In my short lecture today, I try to refute that belief. In my opinion, what humanity has learned from the Holocaust is entirely different. What the world learned is that if there is somebody that we don't like for any reason then we are free to label, exclude, or even murder that person. My statement may sound too radical for you all, but I think that the past eighty years have proven that.

Let's start by looking at what happened just one year after the Shoah: across Eastern Europe pogroms awaited those who were returning from the camps. The most well-known example is the Kielce pogrom in Poland, while in Hungary we are talking about the Kunmadaras and Miskolc events. What happens? The survivors return and they would like to return home and get back their property. So, the biggest fear of those locals who have robbed the ones who have been deported materializes as they return. There are plenty of excellent books describing what the non-Jewish locals experienced at that time. For example, Jan T. Gross's book titled *Fear* is about that phenomenon, or János Pelle, the Hungarian public author also contracted to write a book recently about what happened at that time, or Pál Závada's novel which is also about the Kunmadaras events. This was just one year after the Holocaust.

The next critical point is the birth of the state of Israel. A state is created that is the home of all Jews, which defends those Jews whether they live in Israel or anywhere else. How dare those Jews to fight and not allow themselves to be slaughtered again? The image of the strong, armed Jew simply doesn't fit into the way of thinking of the anti-Semites. The Jew who can fight is not loveable to humanity. The next form of anti-Semitism is anti-Zionism that we've been speaking about today. This is not about criticism of a given Israeli government, because critiquing a government is allowed, what's more, it's necessary. Anti-Zionism actually questions the right to exist of the Israeli state and a national homeland of the Jews. This ideology is the one that replaced pre-World War II's anti-Semitism, and that is where all other ideologies depart from. It is critical of a Jewish state that can sustain itself, that can develop, progress, and defend itself.

Let's move on and look at left-wing anti-Semitism. This also emerged after World War II. There were socialist Zionist movements that made the Soviet Union hope that a Zionist state in the Middle East would be a bastion of state socialism. This view imagined the kibbutz movement as socialism or communism realized it. But Israel didn't become a socialist country, so as a result, the political left turned its back on Israel and started to support both politically and financially those terrorist groups that pledged to abolish the state of Israel. At the beginning of the 2000s, Israel was labeled as an apartheid state, and somewhat earlier Zionism was condemned as a racist ideology. You may say that these are only words, but these words have an important effect on the views of ordinary people. Of course, any sober person would not want to support a racist or an apartheid state. The purpose of this stigmatization is to make Israel lose the type of moral support that otherwise it would receive from the rest of the world.

The BDS (Boycott, Divestment, Sanctions) movement is also another new type of anti-Semitism. Labeling certain products simply because they were produced in parts of Israel that are not recognized by some countries? That somehow reminds me of what happened in the 1930s when Jewish business and Jewish-made products were labeled the same way. We're at a conference which would not have been possible to hold a few thousand kilometers from here, as we have Israeli and Jewish presenters here. This is scarily similar to how in Nazi Germany Jewish intellectuals were removed from public life.

Rewriting the history and heritage of modern Israel is also a form of new anti-Semitism. It's part of what we now call cancel culture. What is happening is the rewriting of our joint common history, past, and culture. It's manifested most strongly in questioning the right of Israel and the Jewish people to Jerusalem, the Temple Mount, and the Holy Land. It's a commonplace idea that those who rule the past rule the future. Let's be aware and conscious of what we write and say about our history.

Briefly we can talk about another huge problem, which is migration. This strengthens the Islamization of Europe and also the radicalization of those Muslim communities that are already living on the Continent. The primary targets of this radicalization are European Jews and Christians as well. The case of Sarah Halimi that we can read about in some European media is unfortunate proof that the situation exists.

I reserved for the end my maybe most outrageous thought: I believe that the newest form of anti-Semitism is limitless tolerance. We all would like to be good and nice persons, and therefore we would prefer to be able to accept all. But if we don't have the moral foundation and moral principles, this carries enormous threats and dangers. If we take this thought to the extreme, we might argue that the idea of limitless tolerance incapacitates people to act or even to resist. If there is no moral measure, we can't resist evil. So, what to do then? Learn, teach and let's try to influence our environment against these forces. Maybe the future will tell us whether we did a good job.

Does Anti-Zionism Equal Anti-Semitism? —The Satmar Rebbe's Extreme Orthodox Hungarian Ideology

Menachem Keren-Kratz

First, I wish to thank the organizers, the Danube Institute, and especially Professor Jeffrey Kaplan, for inviting me to this important conference.

Today I will address the question whether anti-Zionism is the same as anti-Semitism. To that end I will briefly discuss the Satmar Rebbe's Ideology, which is also known as Hungarian-style Extreme Orthodoxy. In 2016 the United States government, as well as other governments, adopted the definition made by the International Holocaust Remembrance Alliance. It stated that:

> "Anti-Semitism is a certain perception of Jews, which may be expressed as hatred toward Jews." It further stated that: "These manifestations might include the targeting of the state of Israel, conceived as a Jewish collectivity."

Because this definition refers also to the targeting of the state of Israel as a Jewish state, it indirectly implies that anti-Zionism, and especially the call to obliterate Israel, the Jewish state, may also be considered a form of anti-Semitism.

But is this really the case?

Let us look at the following pictures [PowerPoint presentation available at http://helenahistorypress.com/].

Here we see an Orthodox Jew meeting with Mahmoud Ahmadinejad, the President of the Islamic Republic of Iran and one of Israel's greatest enemies.

This picture shows a group of Haredi Jews meeting with Ismail Haniyeh, the leader of the Hamas terrorist organization in Gaza.

And this group of Haredim are attending a conference on Holocaust denial.

Here we see Orthodox Jews participating in a BDS (Boycott, Divestment, Sanctions) demonstration calling to boycott Israel.

These Haredi Jews are burning the Israeli flag in Jerusalem.

And here we see ultra-Orthodox Jews calling for the destruction of Israel, replacing it with an Arab-Palestinian one.

Viewing these disturbing pictures, we should ask ourselves: Who are these Jews that hate Zionism and Israel so much that they support its bitterest enemies? And what is the religious ideology that drives them? The answer to that question is Hungarian-style Extreme Orthodoxy.

To understand this religious ideology, we should first meet the man which promoted it the most in the twentieth century. His name is Rabbi Yoel Teitelbaum, and he is better known by his title—the Satmar Rebbe. Rabbi Teitelbaum was born in Hungary in 1887 to a Hasidic dynasty which was established there in the early nineteenth century. He served as a rabbi in several communities in Hungary, Czechoslovakia, and Romania. He abandoned his community during the Holocaust and was rescued by a Zionist initiative—the Kasztner train.

After the Holocaust he settled in New York and established the largest and richest Hasidic court. Seeking to give it a special character, he re-introduced the concept of Extreme Orthodoxy. This radical religious ideology was established in Hungary by his forefathers.

Rabbi Teitelbaum presented Zionism and the State of Israel as the greatest sin ever committed by Jews. He claimed that Jews should remain in the diaspora until God will redeem them. He asserted that Zionism was the reason why God punished the Jewish People with the Holocaust. He also said that anybody who cooperates with the Zionist state, even the religious and the Haredi, is as sinful as they are.

To better understand this ideology and the reason why it developed in Hungary, we should look at the development of European Jewry. In the late Middle Ages, the number of Jews was small. At that time, the religious communities had the authority to enforce a religious lifestyle. Consequently, the religious conduct of all the Jews was supervised by the community and most Jews adhered to the religious laws.

During the eighteenth century, there was a rise in the number of Jews. As a result of a decline in religious authority and with the rise of modernization, new trends spread among the Jews. This resulted in greater religious variability among the Jews.

During the nineteenth century there was a sharp rise in the number of Jews in Europe and their number grew fivefold from 2 to 10 million. New trends influenced the Jews which included enlightenment, religious reforms, acculturation, nationalism, socialism, and secularization. This greatly increased the religious variability among the Jews. Consequently, the more traditional and conservative Jews established their own inner camp, known as Jewish Orthodoxy.

In the last third of the nineteenth century, the Hungarian government allowed the Orthodox and the non-Orthodox to establish their own separate communities and organizations. In some ways they behaved as two separate Jewish denominations.

Since then, the Orthodox Jews in Hungary were not concerned with the non-Orthodox. Instead, they directed all their religious energy inwards. Consequently, a few decades later, a new group was established and became known as Extreme Orthodoxy. It claimed that it was superior to "regular" mainstream Orthodoxy which was too moderate and compromising. Because Extreme Orthodoxy existed only in Hungary, the title "Hungarian" became synonymous with religious zealotry and separatism.

In the twentieth century, following the establishment of the Zionist movement, the First World War, the establishment of Mandatory Palestine, and the Holocaust, it was Zionism which became the benchmark by which Jewish religiosity was measured. Consequently, the religious spectrum of Jews was as follows: The non-Orthodox, Zionist Orthodoxy (also known as Religious Zionism), ultra-Orthodoxy (also known as Haredi), and Extreme Orthodoxy.

The non-Orthodox regarded Zionism as a national idea, the religious Zionist regarded it a religious idea, the ultra-Orthodox Haredim regarded it as a practical means to advance their own interests, and the Extreme Orthodox regarded it the worst sin imaginable.

Their basic claim was as follows: 2,000 years ago, Jews had sinned. God punished them by ruining the Temple and by sending the Jewish people into exile. Jews are expected to remain in exile until God decides to redeem them.

The Zionists decided not to wait for Godly redemption and to redeem themselves. This indicated their disbelief in God's power to keep His promise to the Jewish people. This disbelief is the worst form of collective heresy. The Holocaust was the punishment God inflicted on the Jews because of this grave sin. The State of Israel is Zionism's greatest achievement and therefore it is the utmost sin and should be abolished.

In the PowerPoint slides we can see how the Haredim imagined the role of God in the redemption process, and we can see the secular concept of redemption. Here, it is not God but a man—Theodor Herzl—who is responsible for saving the Jewish people and for bringing it back to the land of Israel.

To conclude. Jews belonging to Hungarian-style Extreme Orthodoxy are also anti-Zionist and anti-Israeli. Yet, they are clearly not anti-Semitic. The reason this is difficult to understand is because this is a uniquely Jewish phenomenon.

With other religions, religious fundamentalism is almost always associated with nationalism. Consequently:

Radical Shiites will never attend a Sunni demonstration.

Zealous Sunnis will never burn the flag of a Sunni country.

Fundamentalist Christians will never openly support the Taliban.

Radical Catholics will never protest against the Vatican for being overly lenient.

Extreme Hindus will never wave a Muslim banner.

Consequently, it is only among the Jews that we can see such scenes.

Unfortunately, this type of religious fundamentalism is the main contribution of Hungarian Orthodoxy to the Jewish religion.

Thank you very much.

Modernity and Jewish Perceptions of Anti-Semitism

Jehuda Hartman

(This is a more detailed expansion of Prof. Hartman's presentation.)

The term 'anti-Semitism' describes the social phenomenon of hostility, prejudice, or discrimination against Jews. It was coined in the nineteenth century, but the phenomenon itself is much older. In Hebrew it was referred to as *Sin'at Israel*, Israelite-hatred or Jew-Hatred. Today it is called traditional anti-Semitism as opposed to modern anti-Semitism. Traditional anti-Semitism was focused on religion—Jews were 'others' as they had a different religion, a competing religion. As religion lost its centrality in Europe, a modern, race centered hostility emerged—Jews are 'others' since they belong to a different race, a harmful race. The two types are related and many other factors are involved.

Jewish tradition had well established percepts about the phenomenon of Jew-hatred long before the term anti-Semitism appeared. In pre-modern times the Jewish Diaspora (*Galut*-Exile) was conceived as a punishment from Heaven. Jews cited in prayer: "Because of our sins we have been exiled from our land and removed far away from our country". Prophet Isaiah said that God used powerful enemies to punish the Israelites for their misdeeds; "O Asshur, the rod of Mine anger, in whose hand as a staff is Mine indignation!" (Isaiah 10, 5). According to Isaiah, the Assyrian attack on the land of Israel was a divine punishment. The idea of 'Reward and Punishment' is a central principle in the Old Testament. Further, rejection and violence against Jews were always expected and accepted. In Passover Jews said: "In every generation they try to destroy us and God saves us from their hands."

These ideas not only provided an explanation and meaning for the reason of hatred but also included a layer of comfort and hope; Jews are not helpless in their plight—the key is in their hands—they can improve their situation by returning to their heavenly Father. This set of mind helped Jews coping with hostility and rejection over the ages.

On the other hand, if Jew-hatred is a divine punishment, one should not protest against aggression and refrain from questioning it. Since it is a heavenly act, Jews should not investigate the aggressor's motives, but rather examine their own religious conduct. They should repent and rectify their awkward ways. Thus, repentance, prayer and fasting were the typical responses of pre-modern Jews to hostile phenomena. Since Jews always expected hostility, they were not frustrated when it emerged. Jewish reaction to hostility was focused inwards but was passive outwards. No attempts were made to question it, search for possible reasons, and try to combat it. No attempts were made to address the general public and try to influence its opinion. Passivity characterized Jewish reaction.

In the nineteenth century, major changes occurred in Jewish worldviews; modernity, openness and attention to the surrounding world replaced traditional Jewish seclusion and withdrawal patterns. Jews became exposed to modernization and secularization trends, which were apparent in the society at large. Rationalism replaced mysticism. The new mindset significantly affected Jewish perceptions on anti-Semitism. Neolog Jews promoting integration and acculturation were first to walk in new paths.

In 1880, the chief Rabbi of the Neolog community in Budapest, Samuel Kohn, who was also a historian, devoted his Jewish New Year sermon to the issue of anti-Semitism. He opened his sermon asking, 'How should we face the assaults on us?' The mere questioning constituted a divergence from old habits.

Anti-Semites claim, said Kohn, that many Jews did not join the Magyarization process, but this is not true. There is no ethnic minority in Hungary that is Magyarizing faster than the Jews; furthermore, there are remote provinces where Jews are the only promoters of Magyarization. Kohn referred to rural northeastern Hungary, where many Hungarian-speaking Jews were scattered in small villages among local national minorities. At the same time, he encouraged Jews to deepen their acculturation and to select productive occupations. He identified possible faults and offered solutions. Kohn addressed the Jewish community advocating activity instead of passivity.

Salamon Schück, Orthodox rabbi of Karcag, went a step further, addressing the non-Jewish public. His point was that anti-Semitism is unjust and clashes with the Magyar spirit; a true Magyar cannot be an anti-Semite. According to Schück, the Magyars had a very long history of tolerance and noble attitudes towards Jews. This was a frequent assertion in his writings and repeated often by Jewish spokesmen. He thought that anti-Semitic feelings resulted from ignorance and tried to educate the general public.

Following the Tiszaeszlár blood libel of 1882, he published a booklet *A keresztények a zsidókról* (Christians about Jews), creating a virtual courtroom where anti-Semites sue the Jewish people. Their claims cover the typical range of anti-Semitic argumentations, and noted historical figures serve as defense attorneys. Each accusation is rebuffed by quoting a Christian historical figure—general, king, pope, etc.—rejecting the same accusation. The judge concludes saying: "Gentlemen, if you hold on to anti-Semitism you are not good Magyars"; the true Magyar spirit rejects anti-Semitism.[1]

Schück created a theater play where Christians are debating among themselves about the 'Jewish Question'; Jews are absent. Schück was among the first rabbis trying to influence public opinion.

Schück was a moderate Orthodox, but Chaim Sofer was not. He was one of the most prominent Talmudic scholars of his time, the Orthodox rabbi of Munkács and later Budapest. He was a fundamentalist leader of the emerging extreme ultra-Orthodox stream. In 1875 he engaged in an indirect dialog with the founder of the anti-Semitic political party Győző Istóczy; an unprecedented move in the Orthodox camp.

Sofer, like Kohn, realized that certain activities may create animosity. One of them was the acquisition of estates by Jews. In the last third of the nineteenth century Jews became involved in the growing economy, and some made big fortunes. Some Jews invested their funds in purchasing real estate from members of the nobility (gentry) that could not cope with the new economy. These acquisitions helped the Jewish buyers to achieve prestige and higher social status, but at the same time created anti-Jewish sentiments. The sellers, who lost family estates held for generations, became increasingly frustrated and turned against the Jews. Due to actions of individuals, the entire Jewish community was blamed. Sofer identified a reason for hate and proposed to issue religious rulings (Halacha) forbidding purchase of large properties by Jews. Further, he claimed that involvement of Jews in elec-

---

[1] Schück, Salamon. *A keresztények a zsidókról*. Karcag, 1882.

tion campaigns causes anti-Jewish feelings. Backing one candidate angers his opponents, who in turn develop animosity towards Jews; therefore he wanted to stop Jewish participation in campaigns. His standpoint was in-line with ultra-Orthodox seperationist tendencies; not to be involved. But he did have a point—modern anti-Semitism targeted the integrating Jews, and their political activity created growing rejection.

Sofer carefully observed the conduct of Jews and Gentiles, had insights and suggestions how to improve the situation. He rejected the old passive patterns and embarked on investigating the causes of Jew-hatred. For him anti-Semitism was not merely a heavenly punishment but a social phenomenon that may be rationally analyzed; an ailment that may have remedies. He observed that certain Jews may in fact provoke negative feelings against all Jews. Anti-Semites tended to generalize and blame the entire community for the deeds of individuals. Sofer left the passive path and requested Jews to be proactive. He certainly believed in the principle of 'Reward and Punishment', but maintained that Jews need also to take some responsibility. Unlike Schück, he thought that it is unrealistic to 'educate' the general public; instead he focused on possible remedies within the Jewish community. These rabbis deviated from the traditional mystical-theological patterns, adapting modern-rational approaches.

After the founding of the Dual Monarchy (*Kiegyezés*), Jews enjoyed for the first time equal civil rights, unprecedented economic prosperity, social mobility, and religious freedom; their condition was very good compared to most European countries. Jews were considered Magyars by the liberal ruling elite and counted as such in official censuses. Most of them developed a warm and sympathetic attitude towards the country, which gradually became a process of acculturation and identification with the Magyar nation.

Growing numbers of Jews joined the 'Magyarization Project'—adopting the Magyar language and culture and identifying with Hungarian national goals. Sociologist Victor Karády called it the unwritten 'Social Contract of Emancipation'—Magyarization for Emancipation.

Following the Emancipation Act of 1867, official Orthodoxy joined in. In 1868 a national society—the 'Guardians of Faith' (*Hitőr*)—was founded in Pest declaring Magyarization as one of its major goals. Magyar identification created additional motivation for active reactions to anti-Jewish initiatives. However, there were still conservative Orthodox communities, especially in the northeastern provinces, which strictly held on to withdrawal ideologies and did not change their lifestyle and attitudes.

In September 1920, the National Assembly introduced the 'Numerus Clausus' law, which stated that the proportion of members of various 'races and nationalities' (*népfaj*) within the higher education student population may not exceed their proportion in the general public. The attached instruction document stated explicitly: "Israelites are to be considered a separate nationality."

The law was a serious blow to the liberal Neolog stream that considered higher education a major key for integration. The Orthodox establishment saw higher education as a pathway to secularization and opposed it. Consequently, the number of university students belonging to the Orthodox stream was quite low.

The Neolog media, Jewish and non-Jewish liberals and social-democrat Parliament members protested the law. The Orthodox leadership tried to strengthen religion and promote traditional thinking; from their perspective the law served this purpose. Thus the Orthodox establishment remained silent. In contrast, the main Orthodox paper, *'Zsidó Ujság'* (Jewish paper), chose a different path; it conducted a consistent and lengthy campaign against the law. The paper wrote that, in spite of the fact that Orthodoxy is not directly affected by the law, any Jew should be concerned about it. At times it expressed criticism of the apathetic attitude of the Orthodox National Bureau.

Why did the *'Zsidó Ujság'* adopt a belligerent attitude towards an issue which essentially affected only its opponents, the Neolog-Liberal circles?

One important reason was the implication of the law that Jews constitute a separate race; a foreign national minority. Hungarian Jews considered themselves a religious denomination (*felekezet*) within the Magyar nation, just like the Catholics or the Calvinists. In their eyes, they were 'Magyars of the Jewish faith'. A senior Orthodox leader declared: "The new racial criteria for university admission are humiliating; we consider ourselves Magyars and not a separate race. Jews constitute a denomination; there is no Jewish race."[2]

Traditional standpoints, mentioned earlier, had an additional facet; Jew-hatred evoked in the past feelings of anger and resentment but not disap-

---

2   *Zsidó Ujság*, "Numerus klauzus, cionizmus, statuzskvó-szervezkedes" 25/11/1927.

pointment or insult. In pre-modern times Jews built virtual walls separating them from the surrounding society. These protection walls defended them not only from outside influence but also from shame and humiliation. The pre-modern Jew lived in an inner world, with his own set of values, detached from the environment and with a sense of uniqueness. A Jew lived largely in the world of Jewish concepts even when under the circumstances he was forced to live in solitude among Christians. The mental disconnection protected him from the contempt of the surrounding society and from feelings of insult and shame.

Theology provided reason and meaning to Exile and suffering; confidence in the Almighty helped the Jew bear his hardships and facilitated their acceptance. What was peculiar to pre-modern Jews was their immunity to shame reactions. They were detached from the values of the Gentile society so fully that outer humiliation could not easily penetrate the defenses of their culture. Hostility was considered an expected fate in every generation and any time and therefore was accepted. They did not feel disappointed or frustrated when it appeared.

Modern Jews, on the other hand, trusted and valued the seemingly enlightened society and wished to become part of it. The roles of religion and Church authority were declining, and this raised the hope that ancient antagonisms would gradually disappear. Jews felt that reason and enlightenment were replacing ignorance and prejudice. It seemed that finally they were being accepted into the surrounding society. But when they realized that anti-Jewish sentiments persisted, they felt frustrated. Neolog Jews were the first to express emotional hurt, disillusionment and loss of hope.[3]

Miksa Szabolcsi, the most prominent Jewish publicist of his time and the editor of the Neolog weekly *Egyenlőség*, complained: "They do not want us. We approach them quite willingly, and just when we think we've reached them, they push us back and deride us. We'll never win their favor. Whatever we do, in their view we do it badly. We cannot overcome their antipathy."[4] The general secretary of the Jewish Community of Pest wrote in 1912: "It is neither novel nor bold to state that equality of Jews is in fact a lie, and

---

3 Konrád, Miklós. "Jewish Perception of Anti-Semitism in Hungary Before World War I". *Jewish Studies at the CEU IV*, 2004–2005: pp. 177–190.
4 Ibid. in Egyenlőség 8/10/1912.

that no one even begins to take it seriously."⁵ In an article in *Egyenlőség* he declared in the same year: "Even if we stand on our heads and for two generations do nothing but contribute to Hungarian culture, for them, we'll still just be putting on a show, since for us Hungary is merely a place to live and not a homeland."⁶

As noted earlier, Orthodox Jews began their Magyarization after the Emancipation, but before the First World War they were much less involved in society. The vast majority of them had not yet tried to reap the fruits of emancipation, modern perceptions were less absorbed by them, and therefore it is difficult to find similar reactions. After the war, however, as Orthodox acculturation deepened and anti-Semitism spread, they also began to express themselves in similar ways. First emotional responses appeared in the context of the 'Numerus Clausus' law, which preoccupied the Orthodox press.

An article in the *'Zsidó Ujság'* from 1928 stated: "We are hurt by the 'Numerus Clausus' even though it may not directly concern us. The 'Numerus Clausus' is painful because it makes us second-class citizens. We are hurt because our homeland gets a bad name abroad; Hungary is portrayed in the world press as reactionary. We are hurt because it is more tragic for us than the troubles for Jews in Eastern Europe. Russian Jews have always seen their regime as an enemy supporting anti-Jewish tendencies. We Hungarian Jews have completely merged emotionally with the nation. We have already been educated that this country is our home and precisely because of this it is so difficult for us."⁷

The writer appears as a proud Hungarian patriot, concerned about the reputation of his homeland. The article emphasizes the emotional attachment to Hungary and the feelings of frustration and disappointment. The article emphasizes the gap between the fond feelings towards the state and the hostile attitude projected back. When Parliament members requested to renew the 'Numerus Clausus' after its abolition, the paper commented, "we are feeling insult and humiliation".⁸

About a week after the first anti-Jewish law (1938) was submitted to Parliament for approval, Dezső Korein, a noted Orthodox publicist,

---

5   Ibid. in *Hitközségi Szemle* September 1912, pg.189
6   Ibid. in *Egyenlőség* 9/6/1912.
7   "A diák-tüntetések hetében", *Zsidó Ujság*, 26/10/1928
8   "Még egy numerous clausus?", *Zsidó Ujság*, 28/8/1931

responded with frustration, protest, and insult to a law he called "a slap in the face to Jews and the equality laws of 1867 and 1895". He continued: "This law puts us, Hungarians of the Jewish faith, on the back bench… It puts us, patriotic Hungarian Jews, who are always willing to sacrifice for the homeland, into the shameful category of second-class citizens."[9]

Korein espoused a dual Orthodox-Hungarian identity, which is why he often uses in the article words like insult, shame and humiliation. The insult expresses a degree of recognition of the values of the majority society that also gave rise to anti-Semitism.

These emotional responses are the result of caring, of false expectations, of appreciation for the advanced world, of feelings of closeness, all of which appear to be unilateral love. The emotional response is perhaps the keenest response to anti-Semitism; it expresses a true emotion and has no utilitarian motives. Reactions of this kind attest, on one hand, to attachment to Hungary and on the other, to modern worldviews adapted by Western Orthodoxy. Historian Ben Halpern argued, "It is the most general sign that a Jewish community has become modern that it reacts with shame to insults and aspersions, as well as acts of overbearing oppression, addressed to it by outsiders."[10] Thus, we can state that Western Orthodoxy in Hungary has indeed reached modernity.

Many Jews assumed a dual Magyar-Jewish identity and affinity to Hungarian nationalism. They also adopted modern worldviews. All these reshaped their perceptions of anti-Semitism, replacing traditional approaches with modern ones.

---

9 Korein, Dezső, "Elsöosztályú zsidók legyünk!", *Zsidó Ujság*, 15/4/1938
10 Halpern, Ben. "Reactions to Anti-Semitism in Modern Jewish History". Pg. 6 in *Living with Anti-Semitism: Modern Jewish Responses*, edited by Jehuda Reinharz, (Hanover and London, 1987), pp. 3–15.

Part

4

Current Research & Contemporary Issues

Educational and Scientific Projects in a Changing World

Dr. Tamás Kovács

A warm welcome to our guests and audience. I will be presenting about the Holocaust Memorial Center and "Educational and Scientific Projects in a Changing World". Firstly a few words about the Center itself. The Center is managed by the Holocaust Documentation Center and Memorial Collection Public Foundation, which was created back in 2002 under the first Orbán government and has been operating ever since. Our Charter Foundation document has all our activities listed. They are commemorations (especially on April 16), research, collecting the names of victims, creating exhibitions, publishing, and holocaust education for teachers and students. So basically, our memorandum includes all activities that are related to the Holocaust and its memory. The memorandum also includes the fact that on April 16th the Hungarian government holds its official commemoration at our Center. The government also represents itself at a high level at the Center on the International Day of the Victims of the Holocaust, which is January 27th. Now a few dry facts that I would like to share with you. First, our budget is small and modest, and generally people don't know that roughly ninety-five percent of our budget comes directly from the Hungarian government and the remaining five percent comes from our other revenues, mainly from selling tickets. On our website, you can find our bank account, and if somebody feels that after that, they would like to donate, feel free. We have a relatively small staff, all included 21 people work here.

Now some key dates from the history of our Center: Firstly, 2002 was when the Center was funded, 2003 was when the actual exhibit building was finished, and 2006 is when our permeant exhibit was inaugurated that still can be visited today. Its title is: From Deprivation of Rights to Genocide.

As I mentioned, we keep collecting names of victims continuously, which is a more complex and complicated process than we've imagined; that's why we only have 200 thousand names so far. Since 2002–2003 we hold all these important commemorations on January 27th, which is the International Memorial Day, and on April 16th, which is the Hungarian Commemoration, and August 2nd which is the Roma Holocaust Memorial Day.

We've had several permanent and temporary exhibits between 2002 and 2019. I chose this 2002–2019 period to talk about because this period represents the history of the museum for me, as I have only been the director here since 2019.

I would like to highlight that since 1995 there is an intergovernmental accord between the Hungarian government and Israel regarding a teachers' training program in Israel in cooperation with Yad Vashem. This is coordinated by the Hungarian Holocaust Documentation Center, which means that it's our committee that selects the 23 educators and we have the largest voting bloc. Not only history teachers can apply, in fact recently we've had more non-history than history teachers. We've taken physical education teachers to this training as well.

Since 2012 we also had our education program for teachers, titled "Lives gone in the smoke". It's very popular among teachers for two reasons: it's online so people from the countryside don't need to travel to Budapest, and teachers get a large number of points in the Hungarian Public Education grading system that all public teachers need to collect during their career. With this program, they can gather fifty percent of the points needed. Now we've also included the requirement that only those can go to Israel who first complete this program. So, the number of applicants has been increasing from year to year. Now even the directors' list of duties includes correcting applications.

Since 2019 as I mentioned I've been the new director of the Center and I have made plenty of changes. I used to teach police officers at the University of Public Service, and that influenced the new work order that I created, which is based on planning. So instead of having these ad hoc ideas and shards of thoughts, we want to plan as much as possible. Right now, we have three program series which are prominent. First are round table discussions which are dedicated to specific historical issues, and excellent lecturers are featured, like Béla Bodó who is one of our speakers here. Second is the so-called Library Evening, which looks at the literary-historical perspective, and the third series is the film club, which is self-explanatory. Our visitors learn about the Holocaust through movies. We've organized plenty of conferences since 2019, which I will list now: the first was titled "Once upon a time there was a countryside Jewry," then we had "Jewish fates under the Arrow Cross period", the third one was "What's next? Jewish families in Hungary after the war," which specifically looks at who ended up in orphanages after the Holocaust.

We focus a lot on memory issues, which was the theme of our last three conferences. The first international conference about this issue is titled "Holocaust Memory: Recent Challenges in Research and Representation". (These conferences were published in book formats as well.) The last two conferences, concentrating on authentic locations, were titled: "What locations in Hungary have an important role in Holocaust memory" and how these can be included in education or what the local population can remember and knows about the past. The Komárom fortress, which is an iconic location in Hungary, is a good example. By the way, unfortunately locals in these places don't know or remember anything.

For this year we have two more large conference plans. One will be looking at the Kamenets-Podolsky mass murders, which have an anniversary this year and is important to know about, because it was the first deportation of Jews from the territory of Hungary. We'll have an international conference on the ghettoization in Hungary, which we will organize with the help of Eötvös Loránd Research Network.

We have another exhibit that has nothing to do with the Holocaust. It will present the oeuvre of Lipót Baumhom, which is important because he was an architect who designed the Páva Street synagogue and a large number of synagogues in Greater Hungary. This exhibition will be done in collaboration with the Hungarian Architectural Museum and Art Documentation Preservation Center. We have another two large temporary exhibitions. Last year we opened the "Liberation of Auschwitz" exhibit together with the Russian Holocaust Center. It was opened by the Russian ambassador on January 27th last year. In cooperation with Yad Vashem, we have a temporary exhibition called "Art during the Holocaust," with a separate pedagogical program that goes with it. Lastly, we have an independent work titled

"Córesz and Mázel Tov," an exhibition in the Páva street building, which looks at the history of Páva Street synagogue and its district. It took us two years to develop this exhibit from scratch.

About some present and future plans: we've published a book by Aron Shneyer about the history of the Trwaniki concentration camp, where the guards of the camps were trained. Our plans include launching next year a large research project on forced labour in Hungary. Of course, our plans include doing everything better and continuing our work. We hope that the future holds a lot of good things for us and that the prime minister will continue to support us.

Thank you for your attention!

Old and New Anti-Semitism

Tamir Wertzberger

There are two problems to being the last speaker. The first one is, those who survived are very tired. The second one is that most of the things that you plan to say have been registered by previous speakers. So, my challenge is to be short and interesting, and I will do my best to do that. So, I will speak about the new anti-Semitism, from my perspective, and my understanding. First of all, when someone feels some pain, you understand that he has a problem. So, you go to the doctor and ask for a diagnosis in order to get the right treatment. The world is still dealing with the COVID virus which influences our life, and we already know that the virus has variations. So as long as the body creates immunity against the virus, the virus starts to develop and creates different variations to escape the immunity. And this is exactly what's happening was anti-Semitism. Anti-Semitism today is recognized or identified by three different types. The first type is historical anti-Semitism, which is mainly based on religion and religious elements. The second type of anti-Semitism is the one we know based on race, which is known as modern anti-Semitism. In the last few years, there is a new type of anti-Semitism starting to get more and more attention in public life, which is known as the new anti-Semitism, and this is what I want to speak about.

I want to start with the study case of Sarah Halimi. However, I want to speak about it in order to try to emphasize how the international community understands the problem called new anti-Semitism. Or more precisely, how there is a lack of diagnosing and identifying the new anti-Semitism. So, the story of Sarah Halimi to those who are not really aware of it: In 2017 a Jewish woman, 67 years old if I'm not mistaken, Sarah Halimi, was murdered by her Muslim neighbor after a long period of anti-Semitic attacks by the same guy. It took a while until the French authorities admitted that this attack had an anti-Semitism background, and that happened only after very, very large and intense criticism by the Jewish community about the silence of the authorities. But it came out in 2019 and later on, after appeal to the Supreme Court. A few months ago, there was a decision by the Supreme Court, which actually says that the attacker who murdered Sarah Halimi was under the influence of drugs, and therefore he is not responsible for his actions. So, this case can teach us the gap between the reality that we're experiencing and the way the international community and the government are understanding the problem. We all understand that there is a problem. We all feel the pain. We all want to go to the doctor or in this case, the government or authorities to diagnose the problem and to give us some treatment, but it all falls apart at the point of diagnosing. The international community is not able yet to identify new anti-Semitism as anti-Semitism, and this is the main problem that we're facing now. So how should we actually recognize the new anti-Semitism? But before we speak about that we need to understand what new anti-Semitismis and where it comes from.

If historical anti-Semitism is based on religion and modern anti-Semitism is based on race, there is an understanding that new anti-Semitism is based on nationality. We can say that it started on the day the State of Israel was founded, because as I say, anti-Semitism as a virus didn't disappear after the Second World War and the Holocaust; it just became illegal. Anti-Semites didn't disappear, anti-Semitic views didn't disappear, but they had to develop their hatred, they had to develop their agenda in order to make it accepted. So, this is where we see how the State of Israel, as the Jewish state, became a target for anti-Semites and anti-Semitism. I think that the best example of that is what we saw in the last decade. So many terror attacks against Jews here in Europe. I can mention the terror attack in Toulouse, France, where three students, three kids, and one teacher were murdered. I can mention the Hypercacher kosher supermarket terror attack in Paris [in 2015]. I can mention the terror attack in Brussels and the Jewish Museum in Copenhagen—the synagogue attacks. All those cases are actually cases that cost lives. And every time, the excuse for those attacks was that this is happening because of what's happening in the Middle East and what Israel is doing to the Palestinians most of the time. So, first of all, we must recognize that there is a problem in order to understand that there is a problem.

And now, we should see how we can identify and where should we draw the red line between legitimate criticism toward Israel and anti-Semitism.

Because this is actually the question that made the space for anti-Semites to express their hatred, because if there are no red lines or everything is legal and everything is within the law, even if you call for the destruction of Israel it can be accepted under the name of freedom of speech. We saw just last month in demonstrations against Israel, how people shouted "from the river to the sea Palestine will be free." People must understand what stands behind this sentence, because the river is the Jordan River, the sea is the Mediterranean Sea, and in between is the state of Israel. So, when they call from the river to the sea Palestine will be free, they call for the destruction of Israel. This is a very pure anti-Semitic statement, but it's still accepted, because people don't understand the meaning or it is on behalf of some values, or democratic rights. Governments and authorities allowed such expressions to happen. And this is the main challenge of our generation, first of all, to identify the problem, then to diagnose the problem and then to give the right treatment in order to fight it, because anti-Semitism will not disappear.

Back to the question of how we can recognize it, I say, first of all, there are some visible elements that light some red lights. We must give attention to these cases because they are maybe anti-Semitic. The first one is double standards. When we are talking about the double standard, we mean the way international community organizations or governments are treating Israel differently from how they treat other countries. I can give several examples, but the UN is the best example. If you want to understand how new anti-Semitism appeared on the international stage, you have to take a look at how the UN works, because Israel is the most condemned country in the UN institution. When I say institution, I'm talking about the UN General Assembly, the UN Security Council, the UN Human Rights Council. So we see the way the UN discusses Israel and the resolutions adopted against Israel. And on the opposite side, when we see how the UN treats, for example, other conflicts around the world like the civil war in Syria, we understand that there is a problem of double standards. If you have one standard for a few houses that Israel built in the West Bank, but you say nothing about chemical weapons used by Bashar Al Assad against these people, there is a problem of double standards. So, this is the first element that triggered the red alarm for us.

The second one is disproportion, and I come back to the UN, because in the UN Human Rights Council, for example, Israel, every year, is condemned more than all the countries in the world put together. So, when you see such a gap between the way a country or institution is focusing on the Jewish state in contrast to how much time and energy they spend on all the rest of the world, you can understand its agenda, its values or principles. This is an obsession. And if you are obsessing about the Jewish people and about the Jewish state, there is no other way to see it besides anti-Semitism.

The last element that I will talk about is justification of violence. For me, in my world and according to my values, violence is a red line, there is no justification for violence, no matter what is the case. As someone who was born and raised in Israel in the 80s, I remember the times of the Second Intifada, and the terror attacks before the 90s, and whenever we experienced such terror attacks, we immediately got a response from the international community that started with "we are sorry but"... There is no but. Innocent people were killed, there is no but, there is no reason for that. And the moment that you say or think that there may be some justification to murder innocent people, you must reject yourself. So, those are the three elements that should be an alarm for us to try to understand when anti-Semitism appears.

The question is, what are the sources nowadays for this new anti-Semitism. In this case we must be very straight and clear, because if we will not recognize the problem, we won't have any ability to fight it. And yes, we must say that the alliance of progressive forces and radical Islam is the main source today for the new anti-Semitism. And there is a reason why we don't see the new anti-Semitism appearing so much in the eastern countries in Europe, but we see it is very, very intense in the western countries. So, if we will not recognize the problem, if we will not identify the problem, we won't have any ability to fight it. This is what we are trying to do as well. This is my message in the short time that I have to speak here: that the main goal of every organization that deals with anti-Semitism should be to identify it, and say clearly and loudly what is the problem, how shall we recognize the problem, and who shall we be warned off of.

So, this is my message. Thank you for listening.

The Work of the Action and Protection League

Kálmán Szalai

My name is Kálmán Szalai, I was appointed to set up and develop an organisation that combats anti-Semitism in Hungary nine years ago. Thank you to Jeffrey Kaplan and the Danube Institute for the opportunity to be here and introduce our organisation, results and future plans of our activities.

Our organisation's new name is Action and Protection League, 'league' referring to a much bigger and much wider organisation than the local Hungarian foundation. It means Action and Protection Foundation became a European organisation operating in seven countries, with the goal to be present in all 27 Member States. Action and Protection League was also founded by Slomó Köves, Chief Rabbi of the Unified Hungarian Jewish Congregation (EMIH).

The activities of the Action and Protection Foundation were based on three major pillars: legal activity, research and monitoring, and education. Education, as Rabbi Köves mentioned in his introduction, is the most important part of our activities. Naturally, this is a long-term investment, which will yield results in the long run. The legal activities include legal aid given to victims of anti-Semitic incidents in Hungary (we had 55 legal cases). We combat Holocaust denial; during the nine years of our operation, we initiated legal proceedings in 97 cases due to Holocaust denial. Most of the perpetrators were punished by the court, and the highest penalty was almost HUF 1,000,000 (approximately USD 3100) imposed on a Jobbik politician. We are preparing documents to submit to the lawmakers and representatives of Hungarian assemblies. We act on Section 332 of the Criminal Code, which protects the community's dignity and provides a safe environment.[1] Obviously, we

---

1   Section 332 of the Criminal Code: Incitement Against a Community. "Any person who before the public at large incites hatred against: a) the Hungarian nation; b) any national, ethnic, racial or religious group; or

were also involved in the drawing up of the Fourth Amendment to the Fundamental Law of Hungary as an advisor.²

With regard to our research and monitoring activity, we have been publishing monthly anti-Semitic incident reports in Hungary since 2013. We prepare annual reports of anti-Semitic incidents which are also used by the OECD—we are the only Hungarian NGO that provides such data. We have also been preparing and conducting anti-Semitic prejudice surveys in Hungary, and now we do so in other European countries as well. Of course, we have other research too. For example, we are trying to find out about the connection between George Soros and the Jewish community in Hungary; whether there is a correlation if someone blames Soros that refers to the entire Jewish community, or whether the mention of Soros's name evokes the notion of Judaism, or is the name of George Soros merely related to the interpretation of the political sphere and only refers to his political activities and not to his Jewish origin.

With respect to our educational activity, we have a program for primary and secondary schools. We developed a curriculum for university education to prevent hate crimes, and we revise the representation of the Jewish people, community and religion in the textbooks used in the Hungarian education system. We are the organisation that develops and conducts the research and monitoring, the surveys that are the basis for statistical data. Naturally, there are communities, human beings behind these numbers, but still, they are crucial key indicators that need to be considered in the related discussions.

Let's take a look at identified anti-Semitic incidents in Hungary in the past few years. Let me detail the data from 2019. Among the 35 cases, there was only one that included attempted physical assault, most of the cases were just painting a swastika or Star of David on Jewish buildings, and 27 cases were about hate speech, mostly in social media. Let me introduce some comparative data on the international level. As Rabbi Köves already mentioned in his speech, the number of the anti-Semitic incidents referred to are

---

c) certain societal groups, in particular on the grounds of disability, gender identity or sexual orientation. is guilty of a felony punishable by imprisonment not exceeding three years.

2 The Fourth Amendment of the Hungarian Basic Law is a complex document dealing with everything from the crimes of the communist regime to the treatment of national minorities. For the full text, see https://www.boell.de/en/2013/04/02/some-factual-notes-fourth-amendment-hungarys-fundamental-law.

per one million, in different countries. If we take a look at the numbers we can see the dynamic of the increase, for example in the United States, Great Britain or the Netherlands, or for that matter in any other European countries except in Hungary with only three and a half cases per million capita. The data in the United States is 6.4, and 22.7 in Great Britain.

We use the OECD's methodology recommendation to identify anti-Semitic incidents. For example, the previous data came from the ADL, which is our strategic partner in this field. It means that the data is comparable. You can see there are no significant differences in anti-Semitic prejudice between the different governments ruling in Hungary, but in 2010, when the Jobbik party entered Parliament in Hungary, the numbers of moderate and strong anti-Semites became higher than in previous years.

The data of 2011 shows a slight and slow decrease in the number of anti-Semites in the following years. The survey was conducted in 2019 and 2020 as well, but the data is not yet evaluated. We plan to present our newest research data later this year. The three major pillars of the Action and Protection League's activity is almost identical to that of the Hungary-based organisation Action and Protection Foundation: legal activity, education and monitoring and research. The order of the main three areas is changed due to shifts in priority: the importance of education is much higher on the European level, having realised the situation in Europe in the past few years.

We try to use all legal instruments to identify and handle anti-Semitic incidents on the European level, and we wish to support decision-makers by providing the basic data. Naturally, the first step is to map all legislative and law enforcement procedures in the European countries. Monitoring and research are increasingly important in our activities, therefore, we have slightly changed our activity in this field on the European level, because a different national aspect has to be of concern when we prepare a monitoring methodology or any other prejudice survey methodology for each country.

We conducted anti-Semitic prejudice surveys in Europe in the past two years, the results of which will be presented later this September. Several European countries were involved and the market research firm Ipsos conducted the survey, which included random walks and face-to-face questionnaires. A thousand people were queried in each country, and altogether the answers of 16,000 people were collected and are shown. The Action and Protection League's work so far includes the conducting of this survey, cooperation with almost 50 Jewish organisations in 17 countries, the creation of anti-Semitic indicators on the European level, and the elaboration of comparative indicators with more aspects of the anti-Semitism surveys together. We plan to arrange conferences jointly with the European Jewish Association, whose representative, Ruth [Daskalopoulou-Isaac], is here, and I hope to hear her speak at this conference too. Moreover, we have just opened an office in Brussels which will coordinate our activity in the involved European countries. We plan to be active as advisors to political decision-makers, to arrange conferences and workshops all around Europe, and to share our monitoring and survey results as widely as possible.

And of course, we set up a European education project. What is the representation of Jews and Judaism in the schoolbooks of European countries? We are just at the beginning of this enormous work, but hopefully, with the experience we gained in Hungary in the past nine years, our cooperation with lots of international organisations, NGOs and Jewish organisations, these initiatives will be Europe-wide, and combating anti-Semitism will be a success. I truly hope and strongly believe that this conference, like all conferences, will share these initiatives and the news, because anti-Semitism is not only a Jewish issue, it has to become a social issue in all of Europe. There shall only be a result if there is cooperation between Jewish and non-Jewish organisations.

Thank you very much!

Part

5

Media and Popular Culture

Personal Experiences with Anti-Semitism

Ruth Isaac

Good morning, it is an honor to be here with you, being together with such a distinguish panel. The first thing I wanted to say is that I'm very happy that this event is held by a non-Jewish organization. I think this is the most important and key aspect, that the issue of anti-Semitism is not a Jewish issue, it is an issue that affects every single one of us. I am going to expand a little bit on that. First of all, I want to introduce myself. My name is Ruth, and I have two surnames, one in Greek and one in Hebrew. So, my name is Ruth Daskalopoulou Isaac. A little bit long, but they are both mine. I work for the European Jewish Association, our partners here in Hungary are Action and Protection. You heard about them previously, and I going to talk a little bit about their work and what we are doing together.

The first thing I wanted to say is that the first time that I experienced an anti-Semitic attack I was 13 years old. I was 13 and people wanted to hit me. They said that they wanted to hit me, they told me why, and my friends told me to be careful of them. Basically, because my name is Ruth they just assumed that I was Jewish. So, all my life, I had a lot of hate against me and I'm going to tell you later what happened with my life, and that was all because people assume that I am Jewish.

Today I work for the European Jewish Association. When I tell people that I'm Greek, they don't believe me. They just assume that I'm hiding my identity. I have people three doors away from my house telling me that I'm an Israeli spy. I lived in a community that unfortunately had a lot of elements that are very hostile to Israel. So, I experienced different types of anti-Semitism, and when I was 13 years old, that one was from one neo-Nazi stupid young man who thought that it was a cool thing to do. But later in my life, inside of the European Parliament, I have not met with one neo-Nazi or far right person, so, anti-Semitism seems, at least to me, to be coming from different directions, which is mainly from the anti-Zionist perspective. Again, I'm going to touch on this very briefly later.

So, as I said, I'm very happy to see that other non-Jewish partners and friends are involved in this work. I wanted to say about Hungary that I was pleasantly surprised by the amount of work that has been done in this country. I think that it is important that we all know the past, we all know what happened, but we also all know that things don't have to be like they were in the previous generation. Humanity has come a very long way. What today we call human rights, it's almost like a miracle. Today the value of life, the value of women, the value of right is respected in such a degree that it is really a miracle. And we can work on those things to become even better.

Together with our partners, Action and Protection here in Hungary, we work specifically on the issue of education, because we believe that this is the solution, and looking forward we believe that we will offer more solutions. If we involve more partners, more and more people can be educated about this issue. Specifically, I wanted to say that in Europe today the reality is that we see a very big commitment when it comes to dealing with anti-Semitism, and not only with anti-Semitism but also with valuing Jewish life, valuing the contribution that Jewish people made not only today but through history.

But sometimes we see this commitment at the top, at the level of the president of the European Commission, the vice president, the committees, and for example of the government of Hungary, but that doesn't necessarily translate to everyday life and doesn't necessarily translate to the ordinary or maybe the average person's life. So it's not the same priority. But change does take time, it's not an overnight thing.

The other thing that I wanted to say, is that when you are working in education and you have long term goals, you know it is going to take one generation maybe. The young people in schools have to become adults and make better decisions.

The reality is that the average European person today is not exactly anti-Semitic, it's just that for most of them, the reality is that they are maybe ignorant of this problem. Even for me, who was aware that anti-Semitism is a very big issue and a very big part of the past of my own country. Unfortunately, yesterday I read a lot of other different statistics, that anti-Semitism in Hungary has a very big percentage. Unfortunately, in Greece it is even worse, the highest in Europe, which is a very unfortunate thing. But I do have hope, and I've seen in the last 20-30 years that there is a difference between attitudes and understanding. And there is definitely a big commitment by the government of Greece, both from the right and the left.

As I said, the majority of people are not aware. For me personally, I was aware that anti-Semitism is a big issue, it was almost like a background noise in my life. I could hear the noise, I could see that it was an issue, that there was a very specific and very distinct hate when it came to the Jewish people. But later in my life the background noise became so loud that I couldn't ignore it any more. And I decided to do something about it. And this is how I've got involved, and I think I was doing such a good job.

Today I'm inside the European Parliament and I'm advocating on these issues. I had the privilege of meeting with the EU Parliament vice president, the EU Commission vice president and members of the Parliament, ambassadors, the ambassadors of Hungary (both the the ambassador to Belgium and to the EU). Both of them were really wonderful. I also had the privilege to meet with the commissioner from Hungary, his excellency Mr. Olivér Várhegyi, who is a very strong friend of Israel and the Jewish people. The commitment that I've seen from him, obviously this was coming from the government and from him personally... I couldn't lie, I couldn't stand in front of you saying that it wasn't genuine. That was definitely genuine, and for that I'm very grateful for sure.

The one thing that I want to touch, that I mentioned earlier, is about how anti-Semitism has changed. A couple of days ago I was speaking to a major NGO, one of the biggest political think-tanks in Europe. I was talking with them about cooperating together on a project. They said, yes, we would like to cooperate on the issue of Israel, because there are a lot of anti-Israel feelings and voices in Europe. I said, OK, but what about the issue of anti-Semitism, can we do something specific on that? They said, "I don't think that anti-Semitism is a big problem, we don't have as many neo-Nazis today." So, for them, it was obvious, to minimize the problem they just associated neo-Nazis with anti-Semitism, like that is the only aspect of anti-Semitism. The anti-Semitism that I see today is very much from the left-wing, very much linked to anti-Zionism and the situation in Israel. Which is not very different, because it's still anti-Semitism. Very much so. It is a deadly anti-Semitism, because terror attacks come from that also.

One of the other points I wanted to make is that whether it is anti-Semitism from the right or the left, whether this is religious or non-religious, or whether it is national or both in this sense, I don't differentiate between the two. I just think that there is a solution. The solution is education, as we said before. We had the privilege again to meet with the Ministries of Education from around Europe and with ministers themselves. They are willing to work on this, that's a priority on their agenda, they are even willing to change the text in their books. It is a major thing for a country, for a minister and for a government to go as far as to change the old textbooks and revise them, and being able to give us the privilege of working with them. For me this is huge and really shows a clear commitment.

Now, this commitment doesn't always translate down. We don't see the same commitment from teachers. Teachers sometimes… they have very strong thoughts on Israel or on other issues, so it seems that in education even before we reach the childrens, sometimes we have to work with teachers themselves. In all of these meetings as I said… I also have the privilege of bringing to Israel about 200 people.

I had a delegation and I took them to Auschwitz. The first time I went there, I didn't go alone. Actually I went with 200 people. Some of them were politicians, including from the European Parliament. I was just an individual who cared about this sort of problem. I thought that I was important and I felt that it was my responsibility to do something. By the grace of God I have the opportunity to do these things. In November we had a second delegation, specifically with Ministries of Education from countries which have a very small Jewish community, but still have such a commitment to come and learn and work with us.

So this is the short message I want to say to you: solutions are available, there are wonderful people just like this panel and our friend Virág [Gulyás], and maybe they are not Jewish but they are getting involved. They take this issue very seriously and they are willing not only to raise awareness but also to work on solutions. Those things really make a difference.

Thank you.

The Culture of Hungarian Anti-Semitism

László Kürti

Thank you for the invitation. It's very nice to be here today, especially since I met Jeffrey Kaplan 25 years ago, and I have never seen him since. So today I discuss popular anti-Semitism, a topic that permits me a closer examination of a number of intersecting undercurrents. I argue broadly that for anti-Semitism to be taken into account, it has to be understood first, not as a once in a lifetime happening, coming and going from the outside, but as an ingrained, super organic phenomenon. It's not like treating a cold; there are no ready-made homemade remedies for anti-Semitism. It is an uphill battle through and through.

The main reason being that anti-Semites may hate Jews, but not only them. And understanding anti-Semitism may help us to understand the nature and structure of human evil. As an anthropologist who grew up on Franz Boas and his insightful essays on race, culture, relativity, and social theory, I am against all forms of prejudice stemming from racism, eugenics, or xenophobia or any kind of orthodoxies of today.

Popular sentiments about race, skin, color, genetics, and power of heredity are pervasive both among the elites and among the uneducated, especially those harboring extremist views of various persuasions. I want to stress the name and scholarship of the early pioneer anthropologists the Austro-American Franz Boas, who almost 100 years ago, wrote about these topics. It is with reason that I cite him, for I hold the view that at the base of popular anti-Semitism is a primordial racism, the widespread view of the genetic difference and inferiority of the Jews.

In contrast, Boas and his liberal minded followers claim that culture, upbringing and socialization together with environment, including diet, determine our shapes, forms, how we look, how we speak, and how we think. But it also determines our believes in gods, the supernatural and afterlife.

Popular anti-Semites reject Jewishness, because they reject the culture of Judaism. They see worshippers as different people and, in their mind, this difference has to be marginalized, or even eliminated.

Unlike Michael Billing's notion of banal nationalism, that is, the mundane in an everyday form of nationalism, anti-Semitism has its two major forms: an everyday routine form of anti-Jewishness that often goes unnoticed; and also the extreme, vigilant anti-Semitism. You all know that from the daily news, ranging from desecration of Jewish cemeteries, painting swastikas, to physically attacking Jewish citizens. What is new and often comes from the left, and Islamic extremism, or even Protestant churches, is the hatred of Israel.

I do want to make a point about the connection of official political anti-Semitism and popular anti-Semitism, the latter being historic and permanent. Unlike popular anti-Semitism, political anti-Semitism is more or less cloaked as secular.

From time to time, resentment of Jews and other pariah groups by the populace flares up as a symptom of social problems that states attempt either to diffuse, or, in the worst-case scenario, even to exacerbate. In turn, policies often result in mistakes and unintended actions because they find willing groups and communities already harboring resentments against Jews, or in certain instances, like in Hungary, against gypsies or foreigners. So as a social scientist, I have been concerned with the underworld, the underbelly, the things that often are hidden and go unnoticed. That is why I focus on popular culture. Films, literature, theater, or even Jewish jokes are well known and profusely discussed by academics. But we seem not to give enough weight to them among the people.

As the American philosopher and social critic Cornel West points out, and I quote, "The culture of mass distraction generates indifference towards the things that really matter." This is the problem with popular culture in general, and Hungarian popular culture in particular. It plays both cards. On the one hand, it maintains virulent attitudes towards issues of race, ethnicity, and religion. Yet it promotes stereotypes of various groups and subcultures by spreading hatred, bigotry, and majoritarian superiority on the other.

For example, the Hungarian television program depicting gypsies or the Romas. I focused earlier on the media depiction of Gypsies. Hungarians will know the most ridiculous one is the *Győzike show*. The sitcom has been ongoing since, get this, 2005. It was the first year when it was aired on RTL

Klub. This depicts scandalous everyday actions of a Roma family. And yet Hungarians laugh at this just like they find anti-Roma jokes funny. But what's terrible is that they also think that this is true.

Interestingly, while Jewish jokes are staples of popular culture, blatantly anti-Semitic tropes are rarely if ever in Hungarian films or television programs, not counting of course, the extremist channels and radio stations. In these extreme right media, anti-Semites express a worldview recently, with labels like this: ugly liberals, urbanites, cosmopolitans, leftist Bolsheviks, henchmen of George Soros, or simply just the enemies or foreigners. *Idegen* in Hungarian.

Since George Simmel,[1] we know who the strangers are. As recently as a few days ago during the current European Championship match between Germany and Hungary, German police arrested a few Hungarian football fans for the swastika tattooed on their arms. This is what Michael Billig paraphrases as the banal form of anti-Semitism. But he clearly points to several disturbing factors. It is widely known that this white, urban, working-class male subculture is openly racist and anti-Semitic. Anybody who watches football or goes to football matches knows this, but you can also hear it on television programs. They regularly sing the anthem, "The trains are leaving for Auschwitz." This is part of the FTC Nationals, the so-called FTC club's anthem (*Zöld sasok* - green eagles), which also has the line "destroy the stand", or perhaps better translated as "ravage the bleachers".[2] "*Pusztítsatok a nézőtéren*" in Hungarian.

It's not very difficult to see the connection between destroying the bleachers and the trains leaving for Auschwitz, and it recalls Nazi ideology or the fascist hymn of Ferenc Szálasi, the leader of Hungary's notorious Arrow Cross of World War II fame. And it has exactly the same line. Long live Szálasi and Hitler, beat up the Jew with a bully stick. This anti-Semitic folklore, of course, is well known to scholars. But what's less well known is that these are regurgitated constantly in popular culture and the new anti-Semitic songs. For example, I looked at some of the irredentist songs of 1940–1944. And it's very, very shocking that many of the so-called

---

1   Donald Levine, "The Stranger." In Georg Simmel: On Individuality and Social Forms, Chicago: Univ. of Chicago Press, 1971, pp. 143–50.
2   For the song see, https://m.zeneszoveg.hu/m_dalszoveg/33589/naksi-vs-brunner/fradi-himnusz-zene-szoveg.html.

popular irredentist song of the early 1940s were also very anti-Semitic songs at the same time.

One of the songs that that is actually also sung today by the National Socialist punk bands in Hungary is the so-called "Sweet Transylvania" song, which was translated into anti-Semitic labor camp songs for the Jewish labor camp conscripts. In Hungarian there was a sweet shovel instead of sweet Transylvania. It's very interesting though, when you look at how, for example, the Jewish communities related to some of these songs and how they felt about being Hungarian during that time, even though they were rejected by the state as Hungarians.

It was Bob Cohen who researched some of the Transylvanian Hungarian folk music, and he wrote about one of the songs that he collected from survivors of Auschwitz. It's very interesting that he wrote the text about the yellow star, the Jewish yellow badge. In the work camps, the laborers were singing the song in Hungarian, not in Yiddish, because the German soldiers would understand the Yiddish. So instead, they decided to sing it in Hungarian, so the Germans wouldn't understand. So, the reason I'm mentioning all these songs is because what is totally mind boggling is that today, we still have these things, and they are still circulating on the net and being played in underground clubs in Hungary. And what's more, there is plenty of anti-Semitism in Hungarian popular culture and Hungarian folklore. Dozens of anti-Semitic proverbs are known still today, and people are constantly referring to them. It is interesting that in Hungary there are more anti-Roma proverbs than anti-Jewish proverbs, which is completely the reverse in Poland. In Poland, there are more anti-Roma proverbs, and fewer anti-Jewish ones. But even in Hungarian folklore you have anti-Semitic dances. The obvious message is clear: ridicule and rejection of Jewish culture and Jewishness. And of course, we can go back even to the late 19th century to see how this continues even today.

Taking the example from the Tiszaeszlár blood libel case,[3] which is today used by the NS [National Socialist] bands, for example, Blood Libel, Natural Born Killers Division ADA, Healthy Skinhead, and the Final Solution. They all constantly play on this anti-Semitic trope.

---

3   For English readers see, Edith Stern, *The Glorious Victory of Truth: The Tiszaeszlár Blood Libel Trial, 1882–1883; A Historical-Legal-Medical Research* (Jerusalem, 1998).

By the way, I have to mention that the line "beat up the Jew" is not really connected to 1944 and Ferenc Szálasi.[4] It was already used in the 19th century, as a slogan as part of a political campaign in Hungary, which was, of course, the time when the anti-Semitic party was also in the Hungarian Parliament. But what is more disturbing is the fact that the beating of the Jew is a staple of folklore traditions all over Europe. The flogging or burning of Pontius Pilate is part of Good Friday, Easter celebrations all over Catholic Europe, even in Hungary today, where a straw dummy of Pilate sometimes called Judas is burnt and thrown in the river.

So obviously, there's a very fine line between symbolic, or you can call it banal anti-Semitism and verbal and actual atrocities, such as beating up the Jews. Hungarian popular anti-Semitism never lost its hold and a big question is why? I think one simple answer is that as long as education remains the same, and as long as the state allows its myriad forms to thrive, it is clear to me that the rejection of Jews and their way of life will continue to inflame bigotry and remain a feature of racist ideology. Racialization as well as the dehumanization of the Jewish people, or even branding Israel as a fascist state, are currently staples of anti-Semitic rhetoric.

And of course, governments do not necessarily author openly anti-Semitic slogans or rhetoric. But isn't it enough if they simply celebrate certain people who are openly nationalist, racist and populist? And of course, you all know living in Hungary that the cult of Admiral Miklós Horthy, Albert Wass, or József Nyírő are all cases of this celebration.[5] And of course, currently, awards given to far-right politicians are also supportive of this trend.

Here I want to briefly note one of the mainstays of anti-Semitism found in populist neo-folk music and take a brief detour there. For his part, Anthony Smith has realized that Hungarian populist nationalism, "seeks inspiration from the communal past in order to link the past, present, and the future together". This reification and homogenizing attempt places the neo-folk music and the dance house cultures on a tightrope. They highlight aspects of a mythologized peasantry. It truly attempts to connect national community

---

4   See, László Kürti, " The Arrow Cross," in C. Blamires, and P. Jackson eds., *World Fascism*, A-K. Vol. I. Santa Barbara: ABC-Clio, 2006, p. 58.

5   Krekó, Péter/Mayer, Gregor (2015): "Transforming Hungary—Together? An Analysis of the Fidesz-Jobbik Relationship," in: Michael Minkenberg (Ed.), *Transforming the Transformation? The East European Radical Right in the Political Process*, London: Routledge, pp. 183–205

with the highly skewed notion of the past as exemplified by one particular social stratum, the peasantry, especially the Hungarian peasantry of minority culture, as in Romania.

I just want to call your attention to the disastrous event of 2015, which was unprecedented in Hungary, when the revival folk music band Muzsikás was pressured to withdraw from the popular Jewish culture week in Budapest. What created quite the major uproar was the participation with the band of the ceramicist and singer Mária Petrás. She is the wife of a well-known right-wing poet who openly declared his anti-Semitic ideas. She also had participated together with him in right wing events. The opposition of the Association of Jewish Hungarian Congregations resulted in making the singer persona non grata at the Dohány Street synagogue. What this case amply illustrates is that populism and anti-Semitism are strange bedfellows indeed, while for example, the early American populist movements of the 1930s were not anti-Semitic.

About a decade later, it all turned anti-Semitic. And in Europe, from the very beginning, it was based on anti-Semitic and fundamentalist Christian nationalism. This anti-Semitism has been anchored to the notion that national culture and its essential peasant tradition must not be lost to foreign elements. In the extremist populist mind, peasants and the culture, whatever that means, have been continually under attack. The destruction of their way of life is the result of industrialization, urbanization, and liberalization of the entire society caused by certain groups, and of course, you know who they have in mind.

In addition to these globalizing forces, a recent trend has emerged, which is the Muslim foreign invasion, which is, of course, all crystallized into this conspiracy theory about the international economic interest groups and urban elites and foreigners who appear as our enemies. Obviously, this entails a penchant for over simplifying identity and socio-economic processes and scapegoating just about anyone who is placed outside the Hungarian nation.

After posing the question "Whose Auschwitz", as he does in the title of his crucial essays in 1998, Imre Kertész[6] does not hesitate to provide an outright answer. Auschwitz must belong less to the generation of the victims

---

6   Imre Kertész, "Kié Auschwitz?", https://konyvtar.dia.hu/html/muvek/KERTESZ/kertesz00032/kertesz00047/kertesz00047.html.

but to those still to come. And we must claim it, and I think this is the real stress here. A proper example of how to claim it, and of what examples we can give to claim it is a favorite film of mine called the "Music Box", you have probably seen it. It was a 1989 Golden Bear winning film, directed by Costa Gavras, which tells an important story, an important Hungarian narrative of an immigrant father living in the US who has to face his daughter by admitting that he was an officer in the Hungarian army, an army that was responsible for the heinous crimes committed against Jewish families during World War II.

The message of this cinematic revelation is so shocking because it highlights the secret Hungarians have and what, for the most part, they tried to hide and deny. For a long time. They claim it was the German army and the Germans and the German fascist state who were responsible for the horrors committed against the population during 1940–1945. The father in the "Music Box" however, has to face the truth that the Hungarian army as well as the compliant civilians in the hinterland were all part of the monstrous plan to send Jews to the gas chambers.

But look at what happened. It took about 20 years and Hungarian cinema grew up. We produce such incredible films as "Son of Saul", "1945", and "Sunshine". What these cinematic productions really reveal is simple; unless you are willing to face your actions in the past, feel remorse and repent, you will carry the burden of insidious secrecy and communal complicity. Today the Jew, the Jewish man has many faces. He is still a boogeyman; in this, anti-Semitism, popular culture and political culture coalesce. Think of the giant anti-Soros posters dotting the Hungarian landscape few years ago.

Another Jewish boogeyman today is Sacha Baron Cohen. The guy who is famous for the "Borat" films in Great Britain. Of course, Borat can be questioned because it is based on ethnic stereotypes. It is funny, but it's also a question of mockumentary; its characters belong to a larger fictional community of Gypsies and of Kazakhs. But what happens? What happens is that there is an organization in Hungary called Turanic Nations who think that Borat is the liberal West, destroying Hungarian ancient Turkic identity. And they actually wrote a letter to Hollywood, to various organizations rejecting this liberal provocation and attack on the Turanic nations, including the Kazakhs obviously. This is a kind of a mythic and remote contested identity about the ancient Hungarian Turkic language and prehistory. And of course, you can always say okay, well, this is totally ridiculous. It is a film, just like few years earlier, when there was a whole series of South African films called "The Gods Must be Crazy". And now there are four or five of these films that madly ridicule tribal African people.

So, I want to conclude my presentation by stressing that with all the political, scholarly and artistic projects describing various forms of prejudice, racism, and Jew baiting, there are many more steps we have to take. We are not finished. We are just at the beginning of confronting anti-Semitism. I want to rephrase an expression introduced in 1900 by an American scholar and thinker, the activist W. E. B. Dubois, who wrote that the problem of the 20th century is the problem of racism. But I rephrase it to say that the problem of the 21st century is the problem of anti-Semitism. We live the memory and the consequences of what took place in history. As Kertész argued, Auschwitz is everywhere and it belongs to all of us.

Thank you very much.

The War of Public Opinion—Social Media & Influencer Marketing

Virág Gulyás

Thank you very much. Good morning, everyone. So, I am sure you know that we have an eight-second attention span, so I have a lot to do in the next twenty-five minutes to keep you awake and listening. And I know that it's not too ladylike, but I'm a curser, but I promised Professor Kaplan that I won't curse here, so I'm calling on social media to do that for me. Every talk I gave is in memory of our friend, a friend of mine Ari Fuld, who was killed just because he was a Jew, so our presentation is dedicated to him. And now back to the topic at hand. (The slide presentation is available at http://helenahistorypress.com/) Not long ago in New York City, restaurant goers were being attacked. There have been several atrocities, Jewish people got attacked, people at demonstrations (such as the Dyke March in Chicago) were carrying anti-Jewish and anti-Israel signs, were waiving the Palestinian flag, etc. And yes, it is 2021 and not 1933.

Primarily, I was asked to talk about digital media and social media and influencer marketing when it comes to anti-Semitism. There are so many angles we could approach it from, but I'm trying to bring you something of an added value. Nowadays my primary location is in New York City, so that's where I live and I help Jewish nonprofits to make rallies and hold digital campaigns, and help them fight anti-Semitism. None of them are really important in Hungary or needed in Hungary. Would that mean that Hungary is perfect and we don't have anti-Semitism? Obviously not. I mean, let's not kid ourselves. I also don't believe that we can stop anti-Semitism in any form or eliminate it at all. But I mean, we cannot undo human nature. It is there. But what we can do, and I think what Hungary is doing pretty well is minimize the level of anti-Semitism.

Hearing the speakers yesterday, there is this battle of statistics and numbers, which is very important as well, but one thing we do not touch upon, the quality and the type of anti-Semitism. There is a huge difference between someone in a village in Hungary at a pub telling Jewish jokes. That for me equates with blond girl jokes. There is no difference in terms of ignorance. And there is this kind of anti-Semitism that I just mentioned, where actually Jewish people are attacked for being a Jew.

I have the honor to serve on a board in Hungary at a nonprofit which is doing something of a media watch activity. What we do is we are checking the media in Hungary, how they are covering Israel-related issues, especially in war situations. So, without polarizing the audience here, I need to break the news: in Hungary, it's the left-leaning media who is somewhat biased towards what's happening in Israel, starting with the very, very important thing that it's legitimizing Hamas, a terrorist organization. That's a big problem when the media is picturing them as freedom fighters. That's where you go all wrong.

So why is it important? Because if in the media very educated, skilled, "credible" people are able to write this down and without presenting any balanced view, then what do we expect from social media platforms where basically everyone and anyone can be a reporter? So, let's see what happened during the month of May, when Israel had some heated situations, as we know. Social media yet again failed to offer facts, and what it did create was a very perception-based "reality" on social media and platforms and amplified a false narrative.

Again, we can just shrug our shoulders, and say, who cares, whatever, let's move on. But the moment there is one person who dies because of what happens on social media, we realize that we have a huge problem. And it happened, Jewish people were stabbed because of the narrative that was being spread on social media. And that is extremely important.

There is a clear connection between online anti-Semitic hatred and the racist, hateful comments and images and what happens offline. This is not a theory; this is a fact. Combine that with an increasing level of ignorance and a lack of regulation when it comes to social media and you arrive at a very catastrophic situation: that, in 2021, is what we are facing. But again, what I just said in the beginning, there are really, really big differences not only between the offline world and the online world, but also between countries. So, when it comes to Hungary and to the EU, we are way more regulated than the other side of the ocean, the free world, the United States of America.

So here are, for example, some numbers, like twenty-one percent of Americans between the ages of eighteen and twenty-nine know nothing about the Holocaust. Still, the same people have zero issues creating a hashtag on Twitter that says "Hitler was right." Sixty-three percent of generation Z and millennials in the U.S. do not know that six million Jews were killed, but the very same people don't shy away from sending me messages that "I should die in a gas chamber with the Jews." In New York City, twenty percent of the same generation believes that the Jews caused the Holocaust, and if you ask them, they also do not see any problem with the statement. They don't think that's racist or anti-Semitic or whatever. So, when people ask me whether I have any cultural shock over there being a Hungarian, well, the number one culture shock is the First Amendment right in America. That is a huge difference from Hungary and the EU. First Amendment rights give you so much freedom of expression and freedom of speech that basically I need to check my sanity sometimes. How is that actual freedom of speech and not hate speech? That is a really fine line.

For example, we celebrated Israel's birthday in Washington Square Park, which is a big center in Manhattan, and the pro-Palestinian people were burning up Israeli flags and American flags right in front of me with three police officers here. And I asked them, how is that allowed? They said that it is free speech. And I was like, sure. Teachers in Florida openly say, "I cannot teach you Holocaust because I'm not sure it happened". That person in Florida was fired, then rehired then fired and now rehired again. There were zero consequences for his Holocaust denial. Jewish kids on college campuses are attacked every day. There is something called *Nakba* week. *Nakba* is the expulsion of the Palestinian people. I can make a comparison, basically, it would be like Romanians would have a happy Trianon Day, where they are burning Hungarian flags and wiping out Hungary from the map of the world. So, that's what it equates to when you go to *Nakba* week. That is horrendous. You don't feel safe. And why do I need to get death threats every day just because I'm a Zionist? Obviously, I'm not alone, but I can talk from my experience.

So, the differences need to be emphasized, and here is some comparison. Hungary is way more regulated. Some would say, "Yeah, we don't have freedom of speech." Well, let's be very honest. This conference could not come to fruition if we did not have freedom of speech, because we have heard some absolutely anti-government speakers. So, in a country where there is no free speech that could not happen. So, let's be very realistic here. We have zero-tolerance for anti-Semitism, and I'm going to compare it to the U.S. because of the First Amendment rights you do not have. There are so many videos when I'm doing my research that I can access in America, but I cannot access in Europe because of mainly Holocaust denial and incitement for violence.

There is mandatory Holocaust education in Hungary. Yes, we were taken to the Holocaust Museum as 16-year-old kids. And yes, I went back to my history book now as an adult and I checked how it was portrayed. And no, I haven't found a sentence that would deny Hungary's responsibility in the Shoah. So, again, it is mandatory to know about the Holocaust. Whereas in the states, only 15 states actually require some kind of Holocaust education. This is why many Americans think that Hitler was a cool guy. Denying the Holocaust in Hungary is a felony, whereas again, in the U.S. it is absolutely not. Hungarian people don't wake up with the Israeli-Palestinian situation. Right. It's not our daily lives. There are some people who are interested in it, some people have an opinion, but most people are actually very ignorant or oblivious about it. Whereas in the US there are protests every day, especially when there is some action going on in Israel.

And here's my eight-second check on you guys, so do you know that the United Nations have no definition of what terrorism is? It's a bit of a cognitive dissonance here when an organization was created to sustain peace but we do not define what the opposite of peace is. Imagine if they would actually have a definition, maybe China, Cuba, Pakistan, Russia would not sit on the United Nations Human Rights Council. Why is this a problem? Because we have the same situation with anti-Semitism. Actually, we do not have a definition that's accepted. I mean, we have the IHRA [International Holocaust Remembrance Alliance] definition that nobody seemed to mention here yet, which is very important. Especially because Hungary is a member of the committee that came up with this definition. You can see that it says "Anti-Semitism is a certain perception of Jews, which may be expressed as hatred towards Jews. The rhetorical and physical manifestation of anti-Semitism is directed towards Jewish or non-Jewish individuals and/or their property, toward Jewish community institutions and religious facilities." This definition, in my opinion, is pretty correct and a minimum benchmark base that we need to use. But so many people, including some fellow Hungarian academic people, are targeting this definition, saying that this is against free speech and this definition would stop you from criticizing Israel. That's a really far stretch, if you ask me.

But how actually does anti-Semitism translate in practice? I'm talking about social media purely in practice, it looks like a call to violence. So, there are these posts that are going all around social media, for example, "how to stab a Jew". That was called a digital intifada in 2015, when there were images of 'how to stab a Jew' circulating on Facebook. You can still find it. But it was so precise that it showed you in the picture how to make sure that the Jew actually dies. That is when Ari Fuld was murdered, the person that I talked about in the beginning.

Holocaust denials like "Jews invented the Shoah to get a state" are also very common. How convenient. The anti-Semitic conspiracy theories: when COVID broke out, there was a trending hashtag *#Covid1948*, basically the creation of Israel. Zionism is a replacement word for basic Jew-hatred.

When people actually rant on the streets "from the river to the sea", who knows where it is from? Because it's a peaceful social justice protest, right, to help the Palestinian people? Let me break the news "from the river to the sea" is in the Hamas charter. Hamas is a designated terrorist organization. And the moment you say that that's okay to go on the street and chant "from the river to the sea", that basically means that you eliminate the whole Jewish state. That is why anti-Zionism is anti-Semitism. Yesterday we talked with my colleague from NGO Monitor and the question came up, why is it problematic to say that anti-Zionism is actually anti-Semitism without mentioning the word Jew in it? It's because, as we discussed, being a Jew is not simply a religion. It's a race. It's being part of a nation. So, we could easily say that anti-Zionism is basically anti-Jewish. And sometimes I do think we need to reclaim certain narratives for people to understand, such as we need to reclaim the definition of Zionism, which is a beautiful word in and of itself. Especially as a patriotic Hungarian, I need to tell you; it's nothing less than that I have the right to my own country. The Jewish people have the right to their own country. It was perverted and we let it be perverted, and that's a problem.

But let's go back to the media, because there are some very dangerous things happening there. Contents glorifying the Palestinian militant groups can fly without deletion. Full-fledged stabbing intifada, as I said, and digital pogroms can totally fly without deletion. Why? Because neither Twitter nor Facebook, YouTube, or Instagram actually signed up for the IRA definition. They are all saying, "oh my God, yeah, we are fighting hate speech", but they let these anti-Semitic posts easily go on for four weeks. They have groups for terrorist organizers and 4.2 million anti-Semitic tweets were counted two years ago. I understand that on a big scale it doesn't look so big, but when it comes to death threats and those people go on the street and attack Jews, then that's a huge, huge problem.

On the other hand, Zionist and conservative voices are all the time deleted. My personal Facebook account was deleted after nine years without any warning signs, I wasn't in Facebook jail like everyone who knows what it means nowadays, I was just deleted, eliminated just like that, and I don't even understand why. I don't know why. And here again, there are big differences between countries, because I don't know how much you know about how it works, that you post something and then the technicalities behind the scenes and the algorithms are tracking your words, what you use. But it's so important you cannot use Jew, but you can use Jewish. 'Jew' is a trigger word, 'Jewish' is not. When you post something Zionist in it, you cannot boost meaning, you cannot market it on social media, because it's going to be blocked.

But then again, these things that I showed you before can fly without a problem. So, in America, it's very computerized because America is huge. But there are also people who are assigned by Facebook to check what is hate speech and what is not on their social media platform.

So, it's very interesting that in Hungary, anyone who is a journalist, we all know who is that one person in Hungary hired by Facebook who is checking what we post. And I know it's a sensitive topic to say censorship because I was born in 1985, and I still know what actual censorship really means. I know what my parents had to go through during the regime, but I'm not using this word just for the sake of triggering. It is censorship when I get death threats for being a Zionist. But how to kill a Jew can easily be promoted. I have been working in this field for a decade. I helped huge campaigns, so what I'm saying is really not a subjective opinion. Our last rally that I had the pleasure and the honor of organizing was during the month of May, we named it *Unite Against Terrorism*. Christians and Jews were coming together in solidarity with what was happening in Israel, and also in solidarity with all the Jews being attacked in New York and in Los Angeles. Facebook deleted the event on the spot, we were blocked because we use the word terrorism. I understand it's a triggering word, but still...

There are groups on Facebook that when the war was happening in Israel, all the people whose names indicated that they were Jewish were kicked out of the group. So, these things are a very dangerous game. The bottom line here is this Twitter post that is still going on: "Hitler did nothing wrong. His only failure was he didn't finish the job." Seems very innocent, right? If we look at the removal rates for anti-Semitism (traditional, new, Holocaust denial etc.) in social media we can see a scary picture. And I think Twitter is way more hateful than Facebook, and YouTube is definitely a dangerous platform. But if anyone has young kids, then watch out for TikTok, because TikTok is a dangerous game to play. The recent challenge was "how to hit a Jew?" That's why you saw people in Jerusalem going around and hitting Jews randomly because it was fancy and it was trendy, it was a TikTok challenge, and who doesn't want to be part of a TikTok challenge and be cool?

Before I get to that, something very important to mention, and this is a little off-topic from the presentation, but you need to understand the big picture and that is a sociological issue of this generation of millennials, so my generation and the generations after. This generation is continuously seeking meaning in life. Most of this generation was born into comfort, in peacetime to free democracies. They have zero idea what communism really means, inasmuch that at Columbia University when I presented there, those kids tried to convince me that communism is a good thing. It was a really ambivalent situation to be in. I needed to tell them that that's not a free bread for all kind of situation. But the point I'm trying to make is that this generation is in a way very lost when it comes to meaning, and social media is their first source of news.

In another presentation I gave I asked college kids, "What do you want to be when you graduate?" And the answer was, "I want to be famous." There are human resource studies about this, that whereas our parents' generation wanted to be doctors, lawyers or do traditional jobs, fame was somewhere down at the bottom. Our generation just wants to be famous and famous by tomorrow. Social media is the perfect tool for that. It's very easy to become someone overnight. You find the hashtag is trending, you ride the waves, the next day you can be on the cover page of the *New York Post*. Who doesn't want that? And that's the problem, because when the hashtag "Hitler was right" is trending, there comes a person who doesn't even know who Hitler was but seizes the opportunity to become someone who will ride that wave.

Well, let me remind you of something else. The threshold level for this generation needs to be triggered. When there was a terrorist attack in Austria during the pandemic, I'm sure you remember there was a video that was taken from a window which showed basically one person killing the other person, and that video went viral. Why could it be posted by default? Like the moral question is there, how can we post someone killing another person? Because this generation has zero boundaries. They just want to go viral. And you need to understand that when it comes to social media, they are living off of influencers.

So, for example, Malala. What comes to your mind when I say her name? Oh, social justice warrior, right? She suffered so much, she was at the U.N., she's someone very peaceful. And then she writes "The violence in Jerusalem—especially against children—is unbearable. This long conflict has cost many children and their lives and their futures. Leaders must act immediately—there is no peace when children and civilians are not safe." Sure. Basically, a kid died in Jerusalem, it probably was an Israeli kid being stoned by an Arab, like let's be honest again.

Here is another one. I loved Pink Floyd when I grew up, I love *The Wall* you know, I grew up on that. But today, Roger Waters is the poster boy of the BDS campaign, the Boycott, Divestment, and Sanction movement. He enjoys that. I mean, he got all the fame he wanted, he can be drunk and have videos going viral. So, his acts are actually nothing new under the sun.

Then we have Susan Sarandon, who just posted that what's happening in Palestine "is settler colonialism, military occupation, land theft, and ethnic cleansing." If she said so, it must be true. And it's really, really like this, I can't emphasize that enough.

There is an influencer called Bella Hadid. She has four times more followers than the whole Jewish population. So, imagine the impact, I call it in my jargon "clout", the kind of influencing factor she has. She actually poses as a

Palestinian refugee. I mean, who minds that actually she is a millionaire and her father is a millionaire? She's still a refugee because the United Nations said so. Palestinian refugees' status is the only inheritable status. So, she lives in New York, she is extremely rich and still a refugee and talks on behalf of the refugees. And she participated in most of the rallies in New York that are extremely violent. So, whatever she says, these kids are eating it up. On the other hand, when you are Jewish and you post something, the second after it's identifiable that you are Jewish, you get the "free Palestine, stop killing the kids, stop the genocide" kind of hashtags. You didn't talk about Shabbat; you didn't talk about a bar mitzvah. You are a Jew who, I don't know, posted some happy sunset pictures, but the moment someone knows that you are Jewish, this is the response you get. So, there is some dichotomy here as well.

Social media is definitely the reason why Jews are being attacked more and more. And if you ask me, BDS and the pro-Palestinian movements are absolutely winning this public relations war by influencer marketing, they nailed it. They really invested in it. They really know how to trick people. And the only difference between the Nazi and the Arab boycotts and the current online BDS and pro-Palestinian campaign is simply branding. Back then it was the Nazis, now "we are human justice warriors, we just want good for everyone", except when it comes to the Jews. Extremely good branding, really.

And this is where the Jewish community absolutely fails. There are so many different [Jewish groups that I] like and, I am working with wonderful clients, but what I'm seeing is how the competition is always there between the Jewish communities. And I understand we all need the funding and we all need, you know, the help, but what the BDS is doing when they go on the street, they have one enemy and they focus on that one enemy and that's why they become actually very strong. Facts do not matter anymore at all. Emotions do. Because after all, like when I talked to you about the Dyke March with the Palestinian flags, do you think that the LGBTQ community could march in Gaza for two seconds before they are lynched? Yet they are there with the pro-Palestinian flags. Basically, we are building up a world of perceptions forced on us. This is why it's very important what I said in the beginning, how the Hungarian media justifies terrorism, or certain parts and elements of the Hungarian media, and they do not spell out that Hamas is a terrorist organization. It is a huge disservice to everyone.

Let's speed up a few things because I'm running out of time. The situation in Hungary is actually not horrible, regardless of what we have heard. It's really not horrible. There are so many ignorant people in Hungary, let's be honest, and that's the problem. So, yes, when the foreign minister is going to Israel, if you go through his social media platform, you're going to see a lot of ignorant anti-Semitic comments. There are also pro-Palestinian marches in Hungary and there are also anti-Israel groups in Hungary, but a little trick if you actually check who these people are, most of them are not Hungarian people. They're foreign students who are generating some kind of sentiment that otherwise is not necessarily the daily agenda of the Hungarian people.

As a proud Hungarian and as a Zionist, I have kind of like a double edge goal. Number one is to kill the misperception of Israel and the Jewish people. But on the other hand, when someone slanders my country, I get really angry. So, when the foreign media is picturing my country as the dark spot for the Jewish people in Europe, and we are the worse people ever, inasmuch as someone told me that anti-Semitism is in my DNA and in the Hungarian people's DNA. Those are not happy moments, actually.

So, here is my thing. The ADL [Anti-Defamation League] put out a report that shows that the actual violence against Jews in Hungary is very minimal, like almost nothing. We have stupid stereotypical jokes, but it stops there. And yet the ADL also put out a press release just a couple of months ago saying how European countries use anti-Semitism to further their political agendas. I was very interested in that. Hungary was the second one in line and guess what was mentioned there? Why we are again, so horrible? Because of the Soros campaign from 2015; six years ago and the Soros campaign is still a topic. Again, my problem with this is not that Hungary is mentioned regarding that, but when we make a partisan issue about how we report about anti-Semitism, we've got a credibility check to make, because the ADL should report about the anti-Semitic situation in Hungary, but then name also those left-leaning politicians or the far-right wing politicians who are actually in the European Parliament even, and yet they want to count the Jewish people in the House of Parliament in Hungary. No, it's only about the current government, the only government in Hungary that for the first time ever apologized for our responsibility during the Shoah. So, yes, let's talk about the problems, but don't cherry-pick what the problem is. And the same is palpable in America, where during the last four years, every anti-Semitic attack was because of Trump, obviously every anti-Semitic attack. Now, the number of attacks is up by 500 percent. 500 percent! But it's obviously not President Biden's problem and on his account. So, I really care for nobody's politics here, but the moment we make anti-Semitism a partisan issue, we fail the Jewish community. And remember that.

So, I'm getting to the end of my presentation, I want to give some thoughts to ponder in reference to the conference title, which is Anti-Semitism in Hungary, Perception, and Reality. So, as I said, why many, many Israeli, primarily left-leaning media outlets and also American mainstream outlets are picturing Hungary as the devil. Let's be very honest here. Did you see any tanks when you came to this conference? Did you see any police, helicopters, choppers? No, there are no tanks in front of Jewish institutions and events. Whereas in Brussels, where I lived for six years, the Jewish schools need to be protected by two tanks. Jewish kids need to be collected by a special bus to be taken to their kindergarten or school.

None of this is actually happening in Hungary. In the US it is the same, wherever you go to a Schul, you are a target. There are really no violent attacks against Jews in Hungary, and I want you to remember that, because it's one thing to say stupid jokes, yes, okay, it's sad, nobody likes that, but it ends there. That person who is in the village in Hungary and is going to tell a Jewish joke will not go out and stab a Jew. But on the other hand, what Tamir [Wertzberger] yesterday mentioned, the Sarah Halimi case in France, that's huge. An elderly French woman was tortured in her home and then thrown out of the window because she was Jewish. The moment this happens in Hungary, call me back, and I'm going to make a very, very different speech. In Western Europe, there are zero consequences for Jew-hatred, but in Hungary, there is zero-tolerance for Jew-hatred. And I understand that there is a minority group in Hungary who still are filled with hate or prejudice and so on, but the minority doesn't represent a country. Also, there is no BDS pressure against artists, academia, and businesses. Jewish businesses here in Hungary do not need to be afraid that tomorrow they are going to be shut down just because they are Jewish businesses. That's not the case in New York right now in the Lower East Side where I'm getting calls from people saying, "Please help me with your organization because we are afraid." And also, I'm never actually getting death threats for being a Zionist in Hungary, but I do get them when I'm in Brussels or when I'm in America.

Again, Western Europe and America, very different situations as I've said in the beginning with some statistical points. So, I try to be very, very objective towards my country, I really am. Nobody's perfect and we don't need to be perfect, because otherwise there's no reason to wake up tomorrow. Right? So, we need a goal and mission in life. So, we have anti-Semitism, but it's extremely important to distinguish between the anti-Semitism that comes from ignorance, which is primarily present in Hungary, and the anti-Semitism that is conscious Jew-hatred.

One of the organizations I'm working with is End Jew Hatred. And basically, the goal is to arrive at the situation that the BLM [Black Lives Matter] and LGBTQ community could achieve. Which is what? That if you are saying something that's slightly racist, you are canceled, you feel ashamed, you feel guilty because you feel you did something wrong. Today, when you make a comment that is absolutely Jew-hater, anti-Semitic, there are zero consequences, business as usual, life goes on, nothing happens. And that has to be changed. Whoever is anti-Semitic needs to feel ashamed about that. Whoever says anything against Jews in that negative connotation should feel ashamed. We are really far from that yet, but we are getting there.

Actually, a little anecdote as I'm closing. As Hungary is so horrible, when I came back from New York now three weeks ago, I made a little social experiment and put on a t-shirt every day, something different that was either in Hebrew or IDF shirt or saying End Jew Hatred or like Shabbat Shalom or something that is a visibly Jewish or pro-Israel. I was waiting for someone to harass me because that's what the news says, that I should be harassed. After two weeks, thank God I'm still here, nobody harassed me. So that's that. The same cannot be said when I'm in New York, or in Brussels when I go to an underground rally I need to take off my necklace. Sometimes I, for journalistic purposes, go for undercover missions where you need to put on a wig, otherwise, you would be lynched. And I'm not kidding, the violence in these anti-Israel events is really, really palpable.

Freedom of speech, last sentence on that before I conclude. There is a woman called Leila Khaled, I'm not sure if you are familiar with her name. Poster girl for freedom fighters, but I would translate it; she's a terrorist. She hijacked two planes. She then transformed her face so that she's not recognizable. She's a terrorist, right? She was invited by San Francisco State University last October to give a speech. Because of social justice and she's a freedom fighter. They did it because, again, freedom of speech is allowed, right? There is one tiny problem. This woman, as a terrorist and as a member of a terrorist group, officially cannot enter the United States. But online, it's a whole different story because it's a very unregulated market, unregulated business. So, with the movement End Jew Hatred, we actually put pressure on Zoom not to allow this lecture to happen and we used legal knowledge to do that. So eventually Zoom canceled because they said it incites hate. So, the organizers very quickly went to YouTube. So, we started to pressure there. Thank God, also YouTube canceled. But let me emphasize again, it's a state university hosting a terrorist to educate the next generation. I hope this is never going to happen in my country because then I will be back for sure.

My conclusion and your take-home message are that online media platforms are way more dangerous than we think. The content you can disseminate at such a fast pace, absolutely free, and the most dangerous thing, you can do it in a very funny way with all the memes and gifs. So basically, it becomes a game. What starts online doesn't stop online, people radicalize themselves online, then they go to the streets and kill a person. So, this is absolutely no joke. Freedom of speech here and there, inasmuch as I thank God every day that I grew up in freedom and not under the regime, it cannot be that it happens on account of inciting to hate. So, freedom of speech needs checks and balances. Nothing can be so free that it actually costs lives. So that is why I would very much welcome all the social media platforms either to sign up for the IHRA definition and have that as a basic benchmark or come up with their own definition. But have something, because all those influencers, when they go on the platform, they are not facing any kind of consequences for spreading Jew hatred. So Cyberhate must be prosecuted, there must be absolutely zero tolerance for online terrorism in all forms.

There is some cognitive dissonance here again. Profit-oriented companies should not self-regulate. I mean, you know, the saying is follow the money, right? How dangerous is that, that these profit-oriented social media platforms are self-regulating as to what is hate speech, what is anti-Semitism? So, they are basically a village in a village, and that's not okay when it costs life.

Many people mentioned education here and I agree with that. Education is super important, but I have a very different approach. What we need is exactly what I said before, to educate, like the BLM educates, as BDS educates, like LGBTQ+ whatever they advocate. Meaning every day, they tell you why it is racist what you are saying, why it is homophobic, what you are saying. So, they educate the other side who is not in their community as to what constitutes racist, what constitutes homophobic. The Jewish community often assumes that the other side actually knows what blood libel is. Ask an average Hungarian what a blood libel is, and they will look at you like, what are you talking about? And that's totally normal. We don't need to know everything about everyone, but that's where education comes in. So that I, as a Jewish person, hypothetically explain to you what blood libel is and why when you say that, it's actually anti-Semitic. This is the education that we need, what is really anti-Semitism.

So, to conclude right now, I do believe that in Hungary the situation is not horrible. Really not. But it doesn't mean it cannot be, because we are living in a big, globalized village. So, it's very, very hard to stop what information comes in. I really thank you for your attention, and I hope I could serve you some added value here today.

Thank you.

Part

6

International Perspectives

Is Anti-Semitism a "Problem" in America Today?

Shaul Magid

(This article is a more detailed version of Prof. Magid's presentation.)

The problem of anti-Semitism has once again emerged in today's America. Or is it the rise of anti-Semitic acts? And is there a difference? Part of the challenge of deciphering what is happening in America today is that the very term "anti-Semitism," or what constitutes anti-Semitism, is a hotly debated issue, something I will return to below. In fact, the question of *definitions*, that is, what defines anti-Semitism, seems to have taken center stage in this new decade. The prime illustration of this is debates around the IHRA (The International Holocaust Remembrance Alliance) document or the Jerusalem Document, both articulating definitions of anti-Semitism rather than the thing itself. In fact, defining anti-Semitism may be the central issue in regards to anti-Semitism in America today. What has dominated the American landscape is (1) reporting anti-Semitic acts; and (2) debating the definition of anti-Semitism, which is largely focused on the relationship between anti-Israelism or anti-Zionism and anti-Semitism. If we would—if we could—remove Israel from the equation, it is arguably the case that neither of these documents would have been necessary as both focus on the complex nature of criticism of Israel's half century occupation as trafficking in oblique or tacit anti-Semitism, what Bari Weiss erroneously called "a left-wing anti-Semitic conspiracy."

But let us set aside the knotty question of Israel and look at the rise of anti-Semitic acts in America today to examine whether these acts constitute a "problem." Much has been written about recent anti-Semitic acts, the most horrific being the attack on the Tree of Life synagogue in Pittsburgh, Pennsylvania, in October 2018 when eleven Jews were murdered by a single gunman during Sabbath services. But even given this unspeakable tragedy, the most murderous anti-Semitic act in American history, we should consider, and I would argue, distinguish between this act and others like it and the rise of a so-called "problem" of anti-Semitism in America. This is not to suggest the attack on Tree of Life synagogue was not an anti-Semitic act, it certainly and obviously was. Rather, it is to suggest that there is an important distinction to be made between an anti-Semitic act, or an anti-Semite who acts out hatred of the Jews, and anti-Semitism as a societal problem.

In the 1970s Jewish historian and rabbi Arthur Hertzberg wrote that "for all intents and purposes there is no anti-Semitism in America." And half a century earlier in the 1920s, constitutional lawyer Louis Marshall wrote, "We do not recognize the existence of a Jewish Question in the United States." The Jewish Question, of course, formally arose in the wake of Jewish emancipation in Europe on whether Jews were assimilable into European society (the more theologically inflected Jewish question, which was more about the very existence of Judaism, extends back into the Middle Ages). In his book *Race: A Short History*, George Fredrickson puts it quite succinctly. "In Germany, 'the Jewish question' arose initially when the German 'nation' was only a cultural and linguistic community and not yet a unified state. The question of how Jews would fit in when cultural and linguistic identity became the basis of citizenship, and the *Volkgeist* was embodied in the *Volksstaat*, could be answered in one of two ways. Either Jews had to surrender their Jewishness and become good Germans or there would be no place for them."

The case in America was quite different in, large part because religious toleration and separation of church and state (disestablishment) made official discrimination on matters of faith, illegal. While both Hertzberg and Marshal certainly acknowledged anti-Semitic acts in America, they distinguished that from the societal "problem" of anti-Semitism. Below I would like to examine and in fact justify both of these statements, with some important qualifications, by trying to distinguish between anti-Semitic actors and anti-Semitism as a societal, even systemic, problem that requires radical intervention.

To begin, I think much of what is being written today, certainly in more popular venues by both scholars and non-scholars, about "the problem" of anti-Semitism in America today is misguided, precisely because the "problem" in these studies is determined by lone actors, egregious as those actions may be. In many of these studies, the *problem* of anti-Semitism is judged by the existence of anti-Semitic acts or actors, be they violent, verbal, or silent; for example, a Jew being verbally accosted on the street or anti-Semitic graffiti on subways, buses, and thoroughfares, which are still fairly rare and certainly not tolerated. Books have appeared recounting anti-Semitic events, a kind of Greatest Hits of Anti-Semitism throughout history, claiming these contemporary acts prove the problem, linking contemporary America to much more precarious times in Jewish history.

I want to pose a question that underlies much of the present discussion about anti-Semitism in America: What exactly is the *problem* of anti-Semitism today? That is, if the problem is that there are anti-Semites, what do these authors who call out these acts seek to achieve? Is the intended goal of anti-anti-Semitism to eradicate the existence of anti-Semites? That would be as futile as aspiring to eradicate racism. Groups will always hate other groups for all kinds of reasons. The great American writer and essayist James Baldwin remarked when asked about "black anti-Semitism" in the 1960s, "Everyone hates everyone, the only question is power." I don't care, Baldwin continued, if Barry Goldwater hates me. I do care, however, if he prevents me from getting a job. In his book *Notes of a Native Son* published in 1955, Baldwin opined, "I imagine one of the reasons people cling to their hates so stubbornly is because they sense, once hate is gone, they will be forced to deal with pain." In other words, there is no real way to eradicate hatred. It is no surprise to anyone that like all haters, anti-Semites will always exist. This is not to say marking anti-Semitic acts is not important, it certainly is. But more deeply, what is the goal of anti-anti-Semitism if we conclude that the eradication of it is impossible? We can say that anti-anti-Semitism seeks to curtail social tolerance of anti-Semitic acts, and that is a noble goal. But then the operative question is: What is the social tolerance for such acts in American today? That is, in what ways do these acts threaten American Jews as a community?

That which divides "acts" from a "problem" arguably rests on the question of social tolerance. In that case, the Pittsburgh massacre was both an *act* of anti-Semitism and a tragedy that showed why there is so *little* tolerance for it in America. Communities in America from the far left to the right (the far-right may be an exception) reached out to help the families of Pittsburgh's victims and sympathized with their loved ones. For example, Muslim activist Linda Sarsour, an American of Palestinian descent often considered an anti-Semite (falsely in my view) because of her critique of Israel, raised money from the American Muslim community to pay for all the funerals of Pittsburgh's victims (she also raised money to repair a desecrated Jewish cemetery in Colorado). In addition, President Biden recently nominated professor of Jewish history Deborah Lipstadt from Emory University to be his special envoy to fight anti-Semitism. Such an appointment gives governmental sanction to address anti-Semitic acts, but its very existence also speaks to the lack of social and political tolerance for anti-Semitism. For example, Minnesota representative Ilhan Omar recently urged President Biden to appoint a special envoy to fight Islamophobia in America. In a letter to Secretary of State Anthony Blinken, Omar and 23 other Democrats urged the Biden administration to appoint such an envoy the way he did to fight anti-Semitism. As of this writing, the White House has not responded.

This, I think, is what Hertzberg meant when he said in the 1970s that there is essentially no anti-Semitism in America. That is, there are anti-Semites who act, but there is little or no social tolerance for those actions. I think he was right in the 1970s and he is right today. A politician in America today who makes an openly anti-Semitic remark will be castigated and his or her political career will be in peril. Subtler remarks such as Trump saying he wants men with yarmulkes counting his money are harder to judge, as are comments, say, about how blacks can jump or that Asians are good at math.

Jewish sociologist and activist Earl Raab (1919–2015), long time director of the Jewish Community Relations Council, referred to negative stereotypes of Jews in the 1970s as instances of "folk anti-Semitism," part of that which permeates all societies, and not just about Jews. There is a distinction to be made between those who hold such stereotypes, and arguably we all do to some extent as they are part of social conditioning, and real racists, anti-Semites, or bigots, those who castigate minorities verbally or physically. These stereotypes, often held by people who would never support anti-Semitic polices, for example, legislation that would prevent Jews from employment, do not according to Raab constitute the *problem* of anti-Semitism. The problem arises when folk anti-Semitism crosses over to the realm of the political. When negative stereotypes become the source for exclusionary legislation, policies, or social tolerance that limits Jews from participating freely in society.

Some years ago a friend returned from Prague and told me of the serious problem of anti-Semitism there. "You wouldn't believe it," he said, "there were Czech police officers at the gates of the synagogue checking the bags of all who entered." "That is not a *problem* of anti-Semitism," I replied. "There would be a problem of anti-Semitism if there were *no* Czech police there to protect the Jews." One historical example to illustrate this point can be viewed in the shift in political alliances of Otto von Bismark, chancellor of the German Reich from 1871–1890. The emancipation of the Jews in Germany occurred when Bismark was chancellor when he was aligned with the Liberal party, even though anti-Semitism in Germany existed. When Bismark repudiated his ties to the Liberal party in 1897 and aligned with more conservative elements in the Reich, the situation of the Jew deteriorated precipitously and we witnessed governmental policies against the Jews, that is, Germany saw the rise of political anti-Semitism.

In his essay "The Black Revolution and the Jewish Question," published amid the race and culture wars in America in a volume provocatively entitled *Black Anti-Semitism and Jewish Racism* (1970), Earl Raab further notes that, "There are three obvious conditions that coincide to produce a period of political anti-Semitism: the kind of political and social instability which makes anti-Semitism useful; a political leader who is willing to use it: a mass population that is willing to embrace it." This suggests yet another distinction that merits mentioning; that being complicit in anti-Semitic policies as a political reality needn't require one to be an anti-Semite. Hannah Arendt noted that ironically the "normalization" of Nazi polices made it such that complicity in anti-Semitic polices does not necessary mean the individual was an anti-Semite, just as complicity in American "white supremacy" doesn't make every individual a racist. In her essay "Nazism" in the collection *Key Concepts in the Study of Anti-Semitism*, D.L. Bergen writes, "A German solider did not have to be a fanatical anti-Semite to help herd Jews into a ghetto." This is behind some of the criticisms of Jonah Goldhagen's 1996 *Hitler's Willing Executioners*. Were German or Polish citizens who went along with anti-Semitic polices *necessarily* anti-Semites in the same way as those who legislated those policies? They certainly held negative stereotypes of Jews that made it relatively easy to morph their "folk anti-Semitism" into "political anti-Semitism," but to use Raab's terms, the shift from the folk to the political was not necessarily their initiative but the decisions of others.

The complicity of the populace is certainly remarkable, disturbing, even horrifying, but openly opposing such views was exercised at considerable personal danger, which many undertook to save Jewish lives. The Christian theologian Dietrich Bonhoeffer, executed for his open protest against Nazi policies toward the Jews, is the classic victim of that danger. When "folk anti-Semitism" becomes law, as it did in Germany, Poland, and other countries, negative stereotypes and social tolerance becomes a legal mandate for discrimination and worse. Keeping "folk anti-Semitism" in check is thus an important element in insuring it does not extend into the realm of the political. But mistaking "folk anti-Semitism" as the *problem* is, in my view, misguided. As Kenneth Stern, director of the Bard Center for the Study of Hate noted in his critique of the IHRA document's attempt to too easily silence critics of Israel with the accusation of anti-Semitism, such overuse and politicization of the term threatens to devalue anti-Semitism and make real acts of anti-Semitism less prominent.

At any rate, returning to Louis Marshall's comment about the absence of the "Jewish Question", which in post-emancipated Europe had been considered the engine that generated the rise in anti-Semitism (a term invented in the wake of emancipation), the American context for Jews never quite had the same texture as it did in Europe. Jews never fought for emancipation in America; they arrived on its shores emancipated. It is true that Peter Stuyvesant wanted to refuse entry of Jews to New Amsterdam, later to become New York, but his resistance failed.

Perhaps the history really begins not with Stuyvesant but with George Washington's gracious letter to the Jews of Newport, Rhode Island, in 1790 where he wrote, evoking scriptural imagery, "The citizens of the United States of America have a right to applaud themselves for having given to mankind examples of an enlarged and liberal policy—a policy worthy of imitation. All possess alike liberty of conscience and immunities of citizenship...May the children of the stock of Abraham who dwell in this land continue to merit and enjoy the good will of the other inhabitants—while everyone shall sit in safety under his own vine and fig tree and there shall be none to make him afraid."

By and large America has lived up to Washington's aspirational comment, at least regarding its Jews. Of course "everyone" in Washington's letter referred only to white people. There were certainly times when the elasticity of America's embrace of Jews was tested, as in Henry Ford's publication of the four-volume pamphlet *The International Jew* in the 1920s, and the anti-Semitic radio broadcasts of Father Charles Coughlin in the 1930s. And with the Cold War battle against communism marked by the Rosenberg trial and their execution in the 1950s. But in each case, and there were others, the political realm held firm, helped by constitutional rights and the courts. One can't say the same, for example, of anti-Black racism that required an internal war to eradicate slavery and then a century later congressional legislation to outlaw political racism. And even then, incarceration polices and legal loopholes such as redlining (the Federal Housing Authority refusing to grant mortgages in black neighborhoods) extend that systemic political racism to this day. Open anti-Semitism, on the other hand, never became public policy in America.

In addition, the impact of social tolerance for anti-Semitism never quite took hold in America. Militant rabbi Meir Kahane, for example, in his book *The Jewish Stake in Vietnam* (1967) and elsewhere predicted that if America pulled out of Vietnam suffering humiliating defeat, the Jews would be blamed and a rise in anti-Semitism would ensue. This is because he believed that anti-Semitism was endemic to Americans, like all other gentiles, and it would just take a destabilizing act, the first of Raab's criteria, to evoke it. He was mistaken. In the early 2000s when Joe Lieberman was chosen to be Al Gore's running mate for VP, there were murmurs that his Jewishness would become a political issue. It didn't. And in 2016 when Bernie Sanders ran on a ticket of democratic socialism, Jews feared an anti-Semitic backlash. There wasn't. Or we can cite the convictions of Bernie Madoff for his Ponzi scheme, Harvey Weinstein for sexual assault, or Jeffrey Epstein for sex trafficking. All horribly embarrassing for American Jews but they did not result in increased social tolerance for anti-Semitism. In short, these events or figures never moved folk anti-Semitism, which has always and will always exist, into political anti-Semitism, which would actually threaten Jews.

Recently, a number of important things have changed, three of which are worth mentioning. First is the question of Israel, especially after 1967. The second is the distancing of the Holocaust as an event that evoked tremendous sympathy from many Americans such that there was support in the late 1970s initiated by President Carter to establish a Holocaust Memorial Museum on the sacred American landscape of the Washington Mall. One should not underestimate the significance of that decision; not the museum itself, many countries have them, but its place on the Washington Mall buttressed by the Washington and Lincoln memorials and the Smithsonian Institute. The National Museum of the American Indian only opened in September 2004, and the National Museum of African American History and Culture opened its doors in September 2016. And finally, third, is the new articulation of and discussions about, race, or perhaps better put anti-Blackness, and in particular, Jewish whiteness, that has emerged in light of Critical Race Theory.

The individual who murdered eleven Jews in Pittsburgh, whose name I will not even mention, chose that synagogue because it was a center of HIAS [Hebrew Immigrant Aid Society], a historic progressive Jewish organization that today helps facilitate immigration from countries in Africa and the global South. This is to say that this anti-Semitic act illustrates the complexity of anti-Semitism and racism in America in ways that often go unnoticed. Pittsburgh was not *only* an anti-Semitic act but a racist one as well. It sought to stop immigration from non-white countries, in this case being facilitated by Jews. And if we take this back to 1961 and Freedom Summer, it is no accident that two of the three Freedom Riders who were murdered by white supremacists in Mississippi in June 1964, Michael Schwimmer and Andrew Goodman, were Jews. But they were not killed because they were Jews, they were killed because they were helping blacks.

Regarding Israel, perhaps the first formal iteration of a shift was a locution added to the proceedings of the New Left's New Politics conference in September 1967 in Chicago, a mere two months after the Six-Day War. The New Politics conference was a national conference of the New Left that included Students for a Democratic Society, the Black National Caucus, and many other leftist groups. Martin Luther King gave one of its keynote addresses. On the recommendation of the Black Caucus a statement opposing "Zionist colonial exploitation" was added, to the consternation of many Jewish New Leftists at the time. King also claimed he did not know of this addition and would not have agreed to speak had he known it.

This was in many ways a first salvo of Black Nationalist Third-Worldism against Israel and also American imperialism in places in Africa, that would continue to have an impact in later decades as the occupation grew into its present state of de-facto annexation. It is not without irony that prominent blacks such as W.E.B DuBois as well as Marcus Garvey referred to their respective ideas for black liberation as "Black Zionism." It is also interesting to note that James Baldwin visited Israel in the early 1960s and was immensely impressed, even considering moving there to get away from American racism (he later moved to France). But by the late 1970s Baldwin soured on Israel as the occupation grew more oppressive and the settler project began to dominate the landscape. Suffice it to say that the anti-Israelism of Baldwin is not identical to that of Black Nationalists. Black anti-Israelism thus cannot easily fit into conventional definitions of anti-Semitism.

More recently, especially after 9/11 and the rise of negative attitudes toward Muslims in American in its wake, now known as Islamophobia, evangelical Christians increasingly saw Israel as the front-line in the global fight against Islamist terrorism. This has moved from a political into a theological realm whereby Israel increasingly became viewed as a necessary phase in the second coming of Christ and the fulfillment of the prophecies in the Book of Revelation. This can be seen even before 9/11 in Jerry Jenkins and Tim LaHaye's *Left Behind* series, a pulp fiction depiction of Christian dispensationalism, and later John Hagee's evangelical Christian Zionist movement. This ostensible philo-Semitism, or philo-Israelism, comes at a theological price—the Book of Revelation does not end well for the Jews—but Israeli officials, especially in its dominant right-wing government, have cynically deflected dispensationalist theology and are willing to pay that price, as it gives them much needed leverage and financial support. It is no accident that Hagee was invited to give the invocation at the new US embassy in Jerusalem where his mention of Jesus during his invocation was quietly tolerated by noticeably uncomfortable ultra-Orthodox rabbis sitting in the audience.

Thus the progressive left, increasingly viewing Israel as an extension of white American imperialism in its treatment of Palestinians, and the white nationalist right, increasingly viewing Israel as the stepping stone to its own ethnocentric project (see for example white nationalist Richard Spencer's positive views of Israel)—sometimes called "Judeo-Christian" but in reality not Judeo in any sense of real Jews—in addition to its theological aspirations of Armageddon, has made Israel, and Jews, and thus anti-Semitism and anti-anti-Semitism a wedge issue in today's polarized political climate. Some white nationalists applaud Israel because they see in it an ethnonationalist state they want to produce in America. And many of those same people think American Jews should move there and allow America to be the white Christian country it was meant to be. On the other hand, progressives are anti-Israel because they view that ethnonationalism as a source of its racism against Arabs. The issue for me is not to judge whether in fact white nationalists or progressives are correct in their assessment, only to describe the contours of the ideological map and its implications.

It may be because of the contentious debate about Israel that the main issue in America today regarding anti-Semitism is more about definitions of anti-Semitism rather than anti-Semitism itself. And the debate about definitions is not really about anti-Semitism *per se* but about the relationship between anti-Zionism and anti-Semitism. That is where the IHRA and Jerusalem Document differ most sharply. The crux of the debate about anti-Semitism in America today is thus not about anti-Semitism—we all know what that is, the unmitigated and unwarranted hatred of, or animus against, the Jew qua Jew. The debate, rather, is the extent to which criticism of Israel falls within that orbit. It is not about social tolerance of anti-Semitism but social tolerance of anti-Israelism, for example, tolerance of BDS, of which there is very little political tolerance as we see by the many states who have legislated anti-BDS laws. It was curious, for example, that the summer 2021 Washington rally to fight anti-Semitism listed among criteria for sponsorship that the organization must be "Zionist." Why would Zionism be a condition to sponsor an event fighting anti-Semitism? Are non or even anti-Zionist Jews not also subject to anti-Semitism?

It is quite easy, and convenient, to say anyone who is against Israel is against the Jews. In some cases, this may be true. But why should one assert this is true *by definition*? If you say that Israel is not only a "Jewish" state but the state of the Jewish people, even though more than half the world's Jews do not reside in that state, one can arguably say that to be against Israel in principle, and that itself requires considerable clarification, is anti-Semitic. And Israel often defines itself as the state of the Jewish people, even though most Jews are citizens of nations other than that state. When Benjamin Netanyahu or Naftali Bennett claim not only to be the prime minster of the citizens of the state of Israel but of the Jewish people, they feed into that anti-Semitic claim. By conflating Jewishness with Israel we leave open the connection that opposing one is opposing the other. And here, ironically,

Zionists and anti-Semites share a similar assumption. But many Jews, even many who support Israel, do not want their identity as Jews to be inextricably intertwined with a country they choose not to live in.

On the other hand, many Jewish progressives who are highly critical of Israel but want to retain a commitment to Zionism in some form often find it difficult to secure a place in the progressive world, in part because progressives have in some way bought into the narrative that Israel and the Jews are one thing. If you are a Jew, it must mean you support Israel, and thus you are not welcome here. And white evangelical supporters of Israel have done the same. Their ostensible philo-Semitism is based on the same principle, thus Jewish critics of Israel are viewed by them as "bad Jews" and justifiable targets of animus one might call anti-Semitism. Here then, anti-Semitism is arguably directed at Jews who support Israel by progressives who view Israel as an arm of white imperialism, and by Christian Zionists who view Jews who don't support Israel as preventing the unfolding of the second coming of Christ.

In this way, while Israel claims it is a nation-state of all its citizens in principle, in practice some of its polices do not reflect that, as the National State Law in 2018 makes clear in defining Israel as primary "the nation state of the Jewish people," about half of whom do not reside there. This has created a confusing paradigm on the question of anti-Semitism in America, as elsewhere in modernity, anti-Semitism was mostly about Jews in the environs where they lived. Louis Marshall claimed there was no "Jewish Question" in *America* because Jews' inclusion in the American project never posed a political problem. And Arthur Hertzberg claimed there was really no anti-Semitism in America, that is, no *problem* of anti-Semitism, because while anti-Semitic actors exist and sometimes act on their hatred, there was, and remains, little social tolerance for such behavior in America. The question of Israel confuses the calculus because it both widens and narrows the definition of the Jew. It widens it by suggesting the Jew is *also* defined by affiliation with a state. And it narrows it by defining the Jew *only* through affiliation with a state.

Finally, a word on the present debates about Critical Race Theory (CRT) or the "1619 Project", an educational curriculum to teach about slavery from the black perceptive in public schools (that is, history told from the perspective of its victims). This is perhaps the latest iteration of a clash between racism and anti-Semitism. Some prominent Jewish leaders have come out against CRT in part because it implicates Jews as "white people," and thus part of the systemic racism in America, that is, part of "white supremacy." Setting aside the complex conversation about Jews and whiteness, some Jews feel threatened by such an implication, especially when it exposes Jewish participation in the slave trade and Jewish "white privilege" denied to people of color. Recently, Jewish historian Henry Abramson published an essay "Banning critical race theory will gut the teaching of Jewish history" (*Jewish Telegraph Agency*, July 8, 2021) where he argued that structurally CRT is precisely how Jews teach Jewish history and banning it would make teaching Jewish history impossible. Teaching Jewish history is often about teaching from the perspective of history's victims. Yet when CRT does that with blacks as its subject, sometimes placing Jews as white on the side of the persecutors, Jews quickly become suspicious of anti-Semitism. The same can be said of the Jewish reception of Edward Said's *The Question of Palestine* (1979), which tells the story of Israel from the perspective of its victims and was castigated by some as "anti-Semitic" in effect if not in intent. This illustrates another aspect of the confusion between implicating Jews of wrongdoing, whether it be Israel's actions as a hegemon toward its victimized subjects (Palestinians), or implicating them (Jews) in white supremacy. If African Americans can't tell their story (a story which may in part implicate Jews) without being accused of anti-Semitism, how can Jews tell their story of victimization without a similar accusation?

It may be impossible today to separate the question of anti-Semitism from the question of Israel in America, or the question of Jewish whiteness and Jewish success, and that itself is a *problem*. This is in part because American Jews cannot figure out what to do with Israel in relation to their identities as Jews, and in part because Americans more generally, progressive and conservative, have allowed Israel to become the barometer by which it understands the American Jew. In addition, Jews have benefitted from white privilege and yet when they are called out as its beneficiaries, they become offended and too easily use anti-Semitism as a shield against any such accusation.

And finally, the American Jew has not quite figured out how to relate to anti-Semitism; is it circumstantial, is it historical, or is it ontological? Is it a problem that can be resolved, or is it endemic to the nature of human civilization? That is, American Jews often remain mired in the question, "Why the Jews?" Too many, I submit, act as if anti-Semitism is rooted in the former two (historical and circumstantial) but believe that it is that latter (some form of ontology). And if the latter, meaning if anti-Semitism is a form of ontology, there is nothing save divine intervention that can accomplish anything except managing Jewish anxiety about anti-Semitism. But rabbinic teaching tells us that it is forbidden to rely on a miracle. And so we remain entangled in the unfortunate state of self-serving categories that prevent us from even getting to the crux of the problem of anti-Semitism which, at least in America, may not be a systemic societal problem as much as an anxiety of the past combined with struggling with the increasingly complex nature of the present. That complexity itself may raise anxiety for some American Jews. That, however, is another problem altogether.

Anti-Semitism in Poland

Marek Kucia

Hello, welcome everyone, I'm very glad to participate in this conference and thank you very much for inviting me. Special thanks to Dr. Kaplan for extending this invitation to me.

I have been requested to speak about anti-Semitism in Poland, which is a pretty wide topic. So I've chosen to discuss just some aspects of that phenomenon. I will not discuss various anti-Semitic or philo-Semitic acts which take place in this country. The focus of my talk will be anti-Semitic beliefs of Poles.

Most of us are familiar with the survey research on anti-Semitism carried out by the Anti-Defamation League (ADL) in over 100 countries in recent years. One of the conclusions of this research is that Poland features as the worst among countries covered in Eastern Europe, alongside Hungary. In my talk, I'm going to discuss survey results. These will not be the results of the ADL surveys. I shall present results of anti-Semitism questions from a survey representative of Poland's population, whose questionnaire I and my team designed. The survey was carried out in autumn of last year. The questions whose results I shall present dealt with agreement and disagreement of Poles with various anti-Semitic beliefs.

Before I discuss the survey results, let me give you some background about the Jews of Poland and the Polish population in general.

We all know that there was a huge Jewish community in Poland before World War II, over 3 million people, that was nearly 10% of the country's population at that time. That was one of the largest Jewish communities in the world. At present, there are only a few thousand Jews living in Poland. We can use various sources to document this. I'm using the census of Poland's population carried out 10 years ago. Another census is going on right now in the country. So, we shall see in a couple of months, when the census is over and the data is published, what the present situation is.

Here is the census data from 2011. In the questionnaire, there was a question about self-declared identity. The census allowed respondents to choose up to two national or ethnic identities. 7,500 individuals self-declared Jewish identity: 1,600 of them Jewish only and 5,400 Jewish and Polish. There were also some declaring Jewish and some other identity—Jewish people from other countries living in Poland. In the census, there was also a question about religious affiliation. In response to that question, 764 individuals declared themselves as belonging to the Jewish religion. But according to other data, which are provided by the Jewish religious organizations, they should be twice that many. That's the Jewish population of Poland.

Regarding the overall Polish population, I would like to discuss it referring to some stereotypes. I would like to address them, using various statistics. One of the stereotypes, which happens to be true, is that Poland is ethnically almost homogeneous. According to the census from 10 years ago, 95% of the population of the country declared to be exclusively of Polish ethnicity while 2% declared themselves Polish and another ethnicity. There are hardly any countries in the world that would be ethnically as homogenous as Poland.

There is another stereotype about Poland: that all Poles are Catholic. This belief is not true. Not all Poles are Catholic. According to the data provided by the Roman Catholic Church and published in the Statistical Yearbook of Poland, 85% of the population in Poland were baptized in the Roman Catholic Church. However, according to the count which the Church does once a year—of those who attended holy masses on Sunday in 2019—only 37% of obliged Catholics practiced their religion. If you compare those results with ones from earlier years, you will see that fewer and fewer people are baptized in the Catholic church in Poland and fewer and fewer Catholics attend church.

So that's the background.

Now, I would like to talk about what the Poles think and believe regarding various anti-Semitic views, according to our survey. When listening to those results, it's good to bear in mind what sort of respondents we had. Most are ethnically Polish and many of them are Catholic, but very few of those Catholics practice their religion. In the survey, whose main subject was on the memory of Auschwitz and the Holocaust, we asked a couple of items about anti-Semitism. Some of the items we designed ourselves. Others we just cut and pasted from other surveys to have data for comparison. For every item, we asked our respondents whether they agree or disagree with the statement in the item.

The first item was: "Today the Jews in Poland may feel safer than in any other European country." It corresponds with the view of the safety of Jews living in Poland or coming to Poland which the Jews themselves have. The European Union Agency for Fundamental Rights (FRA), which has been referred to by some of my co-speakers in this panel, asked questions like this of members of the Jewish community in various countries. The members of the Jewish community in Poland, some four hundred of them were questioned, did not report many anti-Jewish incidents at the time the FRA's survey was done. This does not mean that there are no such incidents in Poland, but they are fewer than in other countries. The perception of this by the ethnic Polish population is more or less similar. [The presentation can be found at http://helenahistorypress.com/]

The next item we asked about was: "It annoys me when someone talks about crimes committed by Poles against Jews." We designed and included it because the main subject of our survey was the memory of Auschwitz and the Holocaust. We wanted to know the perception of the discussion of the crimes committed by Poles against Jews during the Holocaust. Almost two-thirds of Poland's population gets annoyed when they hear this view.

Another item which we designed ourselves was "Jews cannot change their bad national characteristics, because that's how they are." We included it because we wanted to know what is the general perception of the Jews by the Poles, whether the Jews are an evil people in the Polish perception or not. We found that Polish society is divided on this issue.

Further we also enquired, as other surveys did, about whether our respondents agree or disagree with the following statement: "Jews have too much influence in the world." Surveys of anti-Semitic opinion use this as one of the markers of anti-Semitism. The result of our survey was that more than half of Poland's population harbor this anti-Semitic view.

Now we can determine how those views change over time, because we have the data from other surveys.

You can see that the agreement with this statement was almost always high, except in 2010—when it was 10% lower. The data show that belief that Jews have too much influence in the world is more or less constant in Poland.

We also asked whether Jews in our country have too much influence on political life. This is a question that sociologists in Poland ask quite a lot. We found this unexpected result: the majority of Poles disagreed with that anti-Semitic statement.

The agreement with this statement was much higher in the previous surveys. That's the comparison of the adult parts of our sample with the adults asked in previous surveys.

You can see an increase in disagreement and a slight decline in agreement, as compared with the survey carried out 10 years ago. We can see the influence of the current government on the perceptions of the population in this country. As you know, Poland is ruled by a right-wing populist nationalistic government and also a right-wing populist nationalistic president, who won a second term last year, using among other things anti-Semitic propaganda in his campaign. The government is perceived by its supporters, who are at a level of 30-40%, as a very Polish government. Perhaps this accounts for the change of opinion between 10 years ago and now.

We also included an item pertaining to religious anti-Semitism: "Jews had so many troubles during the war because God punished them for the crucifixion of Christ." Similar items were asked in other surveys. In our survey, we deliberately put religious anti-Semitism in the context of World War II and the Holocaust. Only 11% of the respondents agreed with this statement, which happened to be similar to the results of other surveys.

We may interpret this as a low level of religious anti-Semitism in Poland, but it's still frightening that 11% of the country's population would agree with the view we asked about. Particularly since the majority of Poland's Jews lost their lives in the Holocaust. At least 2.7 million Polish Jews were killed in the Holocaust, and also because of the Holocaust other Jews from other countries were killed in Poland. So, this sort of view is still quite widespread in the country.

The next item ("The war was a terrible thing, but it is good that as a result of it there are not so many Jews in Poland as there used to be.") Researchers are afraid of asking, but we weren't too afraid to do so. I would say that this result is even more terrifying than the previous one. To have 1 in 5 of the Poles agreeing with this statement is utterly frightening. And I believe that the effort to conduct Holocaust education in Poland, to invite people, the ethnic Poles to discuss what happened to the Jews in this country has been very inefficient.

In our survey, we also asked a question about competition in suffering between Poles and Jews, something that has been very much debated in Poland over the past decades. We found that 51% of the respondents believed Jews and Poles suffered the same, and only 26% said it was the Jews that suffered more. I think it's good to see this result in a diachronic perspective. Since this question was asked for the first time in 1992, we have had a huge decline in the belief that it was the Jews that suffered most during the war. At the same time, we had an increase in the view that the Polish nation suffered more and in the view "both suffered the same". The latter is now held by a majority of Poles. You may interpret it in various ways. A standard historical discourse on this matter has been in Poland that 6 million Polish citizens were killed in World War II: 3 million Poles and 3 million Jews. This standard historical narrative would justify the 53 percent level of answers that both suffered equally. But if you look critically at the historical data, the 6 million number proves inaccurate, and the 3 million ethnic Poles killed is also inaccurate. Recent research by historians, including the Institute of National Remembrance, proved that the number of citizens of prewar Poland of other nationality than Jewish who lost their lives during the war at the hands of the Germans was 2.77 million, that is, 9%. This number includes not only ethnic Poles, but also Belarusians, Ukrainians, and members of other minorities living in prewar Poland. The number of Jewish citizens of prewar Poland who lost their lives during the war is put at 2.7–2.9 million, that is, 77–88%. These figures do not support the belief that both ethnic Poles and Polish Jews suffered the same. Considering, that the total loss of Jews in the Holocaust was almost 6 million, the belief in equal suffering is not at all substantiated. However, it is held by the majority of the Poles today. Unfortunately, this is not the only belief that is widely shared despite the facts. All beliefs that I and my team researched and I have discussed in this presentation are such. We may only counter them through education.

This is all I have to say. Before I finish, I should give credit to members of my research team who designed the questionnaire with me and also to the funding institution, the Polish National Science Center, which funded the research whose results I could show to you in this presentation.

Thank you very much for your attention.

The items and data from 2020 came from the national representative survey of a random stratified sample of 1,522 inhabitants of Poland aged 15–79 years conducted through computer-aided personal interviews, internet self-completion questionnaires and computer-aided telephone interviews by CBOS on 21 September—25 November 2020. Questionnaire design by M. Kucia and Katarzyna Bisaga, Marta Duch-Dyngosz, Maciej Koniewski, Katarzyna Odrzywolek, Sylwia Sadlik, and Katarzyna Stec.

This work was done as part of the research project titled "Auschwitz in the social memory of Poles 75 years on: in the context of changes of the memory of the Holocaust and World War II and the politics of memory in Poland, Europe and the world," financed from the resources of the National Science Centre, Poland, grant no. 2018/29/B/HS6/02133. The project has been carried out at the Jagiellonian University in Kraków, Philosophical Faculty, Institute of Sociology.

Sources of other survey data:

1992 and 2002—Krzemiński, Ireneusz. Ed. 2004. *Antysemityzm w Polsce i na Ukrainie: Raport z badań.* [Anti-Semitism in Poland and Ukrainie: A research report.] Warszawa: "Scholar". 2010—Kucia, Marek. Ed. 2011. *Antysemityzm, Holokaust, Auschwitz w badaniach społecznych.* [Anti-Semitism, Holocaust, Auschwitz in social research.] Kraków: Wydawnictwo Uniwersytetu Jagiellońskiego.

Sources of statistics:

Census 2011: GUS, Struktura narodowo-etniczna, językowa i wyznaniowa ludności Polski. [Central Statistical Office of Poland. The national-ethnic, language, and religious structure of the population of Poland.] https://stat.gov.pl/spisy-powszechne/nsp-2011/nsp2011-przynaleznosc-narodowo-etniczna/

Church's statistics 2019: ISKK, Annuarium Statisticum Ecclesiae in Polonia. Dane za 2019 r. [The Institute of Statistics of the Catholic Church. The statistical yearbook of the Church in Poland. Data for 2019.], http://www.iskk.pl/images/stories/Instytut/dokumenty/Annuarium_Statisticum_DANE_2019_FINAL_KOREKTA_26012021.pdf" http://www.iskk.pl/images/stories/Instytut/dokumenty/Annuarium_Statisticum_DANE_2019_FINAL_KOREKTA_26012021.pdf

Polska 1939–1945. Straty osobowe i ofiary represji pod dwiema okupacjami. Poland 1939—1945. Personal losses and victims of repression under two occupations.] Wojciech Materski and Tomasz Szarota (eds.), Warszawa: IPN, 2009.

Anti-Semitism in Central Europe

Sebastian Rejak

Hello—*Jó napot kívánok*! Thank you for your invitation. I'm really honored to be part of this panel. I would like to offer what I think would be a bird's-eye view of the situation in Central Europe when it comes to anti-Semitism. So, I will focus on this part of Europe, but at the same time, I want to make reference to what Prof. [Shaul] Magid has said, and I basically would like to ask the same question, "Whether there is acceptance in Central Europe for anti-Semitic views and anti-Semitic acts?"

Let me start with briefly analyzing the very title of the conference. We are supposed to focus on appearance and reality when we talk about anti-Semitism in Hungary, but also from a wider perspective, a Central European perspective. So, what I see in the very title is some sort of tension, maybe even juxtaposition. To what extent is appearance reflected in reality, to what extent does reality confirm appearance? What is the appearance, to start with? I think there are at least two kinds of appearance—they are opposed to one another.

One is that Central Europe has been historically, traditionally anti-Semitic; anti-Semitism is a visible characteristic of Central Europe's culture. This is what people in Central Europe very often think that the West thinks of them. So, in Central Europe a lot of people fear that this the image Western Europeans have of them when it comes to anti-Semitism.

The second thing is like an automatic reaction to that in Central Europe. That reaction is very often about trying to prove that anti-Semitism today is just a marginal phenomenon. Specifically, if compared to Western Europe, or recently also to the U.S., the reactions we often hear would be "there are no burning synagogues here, Jews are not being murdered on our streets, Jewish schools do not need to be guarded by heavily armed police". This is actually a fair point, a fact that is hard to deny, but it's definitely not the full picture. So, what's missing in the picture? What's missing in this self-perception of anti-Semitism in Central Europe, including among decision-makers?

What is missing is just all the rest of the picture, and that is an important part of reality. It's the media, the social media, the political discourse, as well as political and administrative decisions. Let me give you a few examples or rather allude to certain aspects of that. We have seen over the last couple of years people sharing anti-Semitic views or using dog-whistles in a way that makes it clear they are talking about Jews. These people are sometimes employed by government or local government agencies. They are appointed to mid- and high-ranking positions in the government or in scholarly institutions, including institutions that deal with, let's say, broadly understood cultural, historical issues.

Then we have people who belong to political establishments who publish op-eds or make public statements that include anti-Semitic tropes or allude to anti-Semitic stereotypes. For example, calling someone a rootless Hungarian and a rootless American. This is a kind of language that everybody in Central Europe, but beyond Central Europe as well, understands. When you hear this, you know that this is an allusion to Jews; a very popular and widespread stereotype of the Jews.

Then the media. I know the topic on the media and popular culture has already been covered, so I'm not going to go into too much detail. What I want to underscore is the question of state-funded media. I think we would all agree that this is a major challenge today in at least some Central European countries. Let's take the language that state-funded media is using when talking about minorities, and Jews in particular. Again, quite often there is dog-whistling—Jews may not be called by their name, there may be references to Zionists (let's remember Zionism is an ideology), you can hear the media talk about international bankers' groups, lobbying groups. Well, of course, sometimes media also engage in spreading messages which use traditional folk anti-Semitic tropes.

This is something that we have seen in Central Europe particularly frequently during elections campaigns, including in Poland last year. That is very concerning because a lot of people tend to shape their worldviews based on what they see in the media, what they are fed by the media. That is why this is such an important issue and such a big challenge.

So, I have mentioned the media as an instrument of communication that reaches the masses. I talked about people holding mid- to high-ranking public offices, but there is also the grassroots level which is no less important. Sometimes that's where the problems are coming from, sometimes the grassroots level is on the receiving end—when people respond to or echo what they see in the media. What we keep seeing, what we keep witnessing on this basic level is there is still a lot of disrespect for Jewish heritage and a lack of proper inclusive education that would help our citizens understand that portraying Jews as the menacing other is plain wrong and is hurtful.

I have to admit at the same time that there is a growing number of NGOs, activists and individuals who are sensitive to Jewish or other non-majority cultural heritage and there has been a growing number of initiatives. They consider helping preserve that heritage. I want to make sure that this is not overlooked—this is a phenomenon that was not part of the landscape thirty years ago, or it was to a much lesser degree.

That being said, NGOs exclusively are not capable of taking up on their shoulders the whole burden of reaching hundreds of thousands of school children, let's say. They are unable to reach thousands of school children with their programs. However superb those programs may be there are simply not enough people doing that. Of course, the governments themselves have that on their shoulder, so we should not even expect NGOs and civil society to replace governments or take over from governments the important task of doing that educational work.

When we witness incidents that involve vandalism, when the Jewish heritage is being destroyed or anti-Semitic graffiti is being sprayed on walls, then of course governments have to respond in a proper way. But those responses not infrequently go in the direction of saying "let's send a positive message." That positive image is about the scale of financial support, or how much governments are involved in preserving, restoring, securing maintenance of synagogues or Jewish cemeteries. That, of course, has to be appreciated, it's a super important task, and I couldn't imagine anyone saying it's not important. But that is not enough, and putting that in the spotlight in a way deflects our attention from the ills that have to be addressed.

Let me reiterate: the financial support that Jewish communities in Central Europe are receiving is something that definitely has to be appreciated, but it has to be matched by educational efforts. Those efforts need to be made by governments. And this a topic for a separate discussion: how governments are handling the question of education about their Jewish communities, about World War II, etc. In Central Europe this is still a sensitive issue, an issue that both governments and whole societies are grappling with. It's going up and down, it's not a smooth process. I could not say that Central Europeans have been steadily moving upward and forward toward becoming more and more capable of facing even the most difficult chapters of their history.

Bur there are noteworthy exceptions. We recently heard from the Lithuanian prime minister [Ingrida Šimonytė] something that I'm not sure most political leaders and decision-makers would be able of saying out loud. The prime minister said that only a mature society is able to face its painful past: "I tend to believe that the maturity of a society is also measurable as to whether it can accept from historians truth which can at times be awkward or which can call for revisiting or rethinking of what has already been established, or it wants that the historians weave one or another collective narrative or mythology, where our side involves only heroes, victims or observers, at worst, but, God forbid, certainly not executioners or collaborators."

In Central Europe, the most painful part of the history is definitely World War II and the Holocaust. The question that has to be asked is whether governments are willing to address the challenges of their education systems when it comes to countering anti-Semitism and providing knowledge about the Jewish community to school children. And what kind of knowledge would be provided—honest, research-based or a narrative that voters would like to see? I'm asking a question—not saying that this is impossible. But again, what are we witnessing today in many Central European countries? Unfortunately, I have to say there is too much sugar-coating and glossing over in what schools are teaching. And it's not something that started very recently, it's a long-standing issue. The quality of educational materials when it comes to World War II is not satisfactory. True, there have been successful attempts at trying to help children face the difficult World War II history, but much of that was outside the classroom activities offered by NGOs. So, that is still—I have to say—an exception rather than the rule.

Of course, we can see examples of those deficiencies in the process of education not only in Central Europe but the world over. Recently, there was a case where 12-year-olds destroyed more than sixty Jewish graves because they wanted to build a fortress. It only testifies to a horrible lack of education not only with the children themselves, but also with their parents and teachers. It's also about education against hatred, inclusive education about respect for other people. We have seen Central Europe's Jewish graveyards vandalized—even those untouched during World War II, which was, of course, a rare case. Those cemeteries were vandalized just recently, a few years ago, not by German soldiers or the SS, or any military or occupation forces. This is happening almost as we speak. And again, it's not only in Germany or the Netherlands or other parts of Western Europe. It's a problem that remains a challenge in Central Europe. And it's undoubtedly a sign of deficiencies in the respective educational systems.

The last major issue I want to focus on is the condoning of anti-Semitism. Professor Magid talked about the degree of acceptance for anti-Semitism, and I think this is a crucial question. There is hardly a place under the sun that would be totally immune to anti-Semitism, a place where there would be no anti-Semitic incidents or anti-Semitic hate speech. The key question is: What's the reaction on the grassroots level and what's the reaction among decision-makers?

I will focus exclusively on the top level, the decision-making level. Violent, hateful language has become accepted in our societies, including by the political elites. It has become part of what is "OK to be said in public." It was not always so. It's a negative shift from what we call political correctness. It used to be politically incorrect and outrageous to use anti-Semitic tropes. Now you can hear that even from active politicians. Of course, political correctness can be criticized and it sometimes is a mechanism of censorship. But it can also serve as a filter, let's say, that helps distinguish between what can be said in public and what shouldn't because it might hurt somebody or a group. So, this tool that spares others from being labeled in a negative, humiliating way seems not to be working. Maybe in Central Europe it actually never worked perfectly, but what we are seeing now, I'm afraid, is that it has become okay to use in public negative stereotypes pertaining to whole groups: Jews, Roma people, or non-heteronormative people. Somehow, the public arena has become used to this kind of language.

And again, we have to ask the question of responsibility. Whose responsibility is it to react or on whose shoulders does the responsibility fall for not reacting or not reacting in an effective way? One of my predecessors, I think, mentioned the EU's Fundamental Rights Agency survey conducted in 2019. One of the questions asked was "Do you think your country's government is doing enough, or it is being successful in addressing the question of anti-Semitism?" Poland and Hungary for example, the only two Central European countries to be in the survey, fared really poorly in the whole survey, but in particular answering this question. Between 18 and 19% of Poles answered "definitely not or rather not". This is the answer to the question of whether the government is effectively combating anti-Semitism. But it's not only about politicians and those who make decisions on the top level. It's also about any elected officials and law enforcement institutions and police officers. It is up to them, facing an anti-Semitic incident, to send a clear message: this is a violation of the law, this will not go unpunished. Unfortunately, sometimes the only reaction we hear in our part of Europe is "things look much worse in Western Europe." Well, this is not an answer, it's an excuse.

Why is it so important to react to hateful words and not to point fingers at others? It's true that synagogues are not burning, Jews are not being killed on the streets of Central European cities. But you never know when hateful words will be translated into active violence. What we do know—we know that from history—is that words do have consequences, and words do lead to actions. The fact that physical violence vis-á-vis Jews is not a major problem for Jews in Central Europe does not mean that this may not change in the coming years. This is of course something that we all would like to avoid, but it's always better to prevent something than to try to react after things have already gone wrong. And when lives are lost. That's why hateful language should not be taken lightly by governments. That is why we would expect governments to be more proactive in countering anti-Semitism in the public arena. Before hate speech turns into attacks that harm not only our sensitivity, our identities, and our dignity, but before these attacks become an actual threat to our physical safety.

So, to close my remarks, when we talk about anti-Semitism in Central Europe, it's a bittersweet story. It's definitely not a one-dimensional picture. On the one hand, we do see governments being involved in supporting Jewish communities, including financially. We see considerable help offered to the restoration of Jewish cemeteries. But governments have to take care not only of dead Jews but first and foremost of the living Jewish communities—and that is always best done by actively and effectively countering anti-Semitism even when it's seen "only" in words and language.

I think we will have questions—I will be happy to answer them. Thank you for your attention.

Part

7

Concluding Remarks

Anti-Semitism in Hungary: Appearance and Reality, Concluding Remarks

Jeffrey Kaplan

Over the last two days, we have heard a variety of voices from the Hungarian Jewish community, from Hungarian and foreign scholars and NGOs, and from the Hungarian government as well. There are some common themes that have emerged, as well as some disagreements. Before turning to these however, I wanted to say a few words about how this conference came about.

Some months ago while the lockdown was still in effect, there was a discussion at the Danube Institute Research Center about what research, under the circumstances, was really possible. István Kiss offered the suggestion that anti-Semitism in Hungary would be an interesting topic. I was immediately sold on the idea and began to do some preliminary research which brought to light how unique the Hungarian situation in many ways really was. This was followed while I was in the US by some Zoom interviews, most notably with Rabbi Andrew Baker of the AJC in New York and Professor Jehuda Hartman in Israel. Both are a part of this conference today.

The original idea was to publish a report, but as the research went on, I thought that we should organize an international conference on the topic—a suggestion that the Institute accepted in principle, though planning a non-virtual conference seemed quixotic at the time. But with the support of the Batthyány Lajos Foundation, we went ahead with planning and hoped for the best. The rest, as historians are fond of saying, is history.

Background of the Conference

The subtitle of the conference, Appearance and Reality, was a reflection of the perceptions that I brought to Hungary from the US as juxtaposed with the complex realities that emerged from interviews with the Hungarian Jewish community and a more thorough study of academic and popular sources in Hungary.

The perceptions I brought to the study were largely gleaned from Western media and think tanks. The tropes that were most prevalent were that Hungary, and in particular the Hungarian government, were deeply anti-Semitic and so opposed to democracy that the Parliament had been shut down to allow for dictatorial power even before the first wave of the pandemic had reached Hungary. To my surprise, when I arrived the Hungarian Parliament was in fact open for business, while even a cursory statistical examination suggested that contemporary Hungary conspicuously lacked the kind of communal and anti-Semitic violence that has become all too common place in other EU states, and indeed in the United States itself.

The reasons for this dichotomy between appearance and reality constitute a major subtext of this conference, which we will examine in greater depth presently.

Interim Report

In 2020 the European Parliament, in agreement with the Pew Research Center, noted that the Jewish population of Europe is declining, with the primary factor being emigration to Israel in response to anti-Semitic violence in member countries. Hungary is currently little affected by this trend, with the Jewish population estimated at 47,000–65,000, with a MAZSIHISZ estimate ranging as high as 100,000. But the real question is who is doing the counting and who is being counted.

An interview with Prof. András Kovács, who could not be with us at the conference unfortunately, shed a good deal of light on the problem. In the aftermath of the Holocaust, with Orthodoxy nearly destroyed and remnants emigrated, no more than 10% of Hungarian Jews aligned with any religious communities, while long standing assimilationist tendencies reasserted

Anti-Semitism in Hungary: Appearance and Reality, Concluding Remarks

themselves. In terms of measurables, in 2020 only 12,000 Jews paid the voluntary tax to Jewish groups and only perhaps 1% of Jews actually attended synagogue regularly. Thus while the Jewish population of Hungary is quite large, the number of active Jews is really quite small.

From cold statistics emerge remarkable, and remarkably Hungarian personal life stories that are at the core of our research. But before turning to these, another statistic is of note. Genetic research indicates that Hungarians have a greater degree of Jewish blood than the people of any other country in the world save Israel. This hidden fact helps to explain the surprising number of Hungarian Jews who were unaware that they were Jewish until quite late in life.

Anti-Semitism in Hungary, an Interim Report

In the interviews and background research we have done so far, some areas of broad agreement have emerged.

First and foremost, anti-Semitism is much less prevalent in Hungarian public life today than it was a decade ago with the rise of Jobbik and the call for a 'Jewish list' in the Hungarian Parliament. A part of this perception is the increasing sense of physical security reported by Hungarian Jews, with only one violent incident reported in the last two years nationwide.

At the same time, many do report that they have been subjected to, or overheard, anti-Semitic remarks or jokes. And for some, a sense of potential insecurity remains, with Holocaust memories a part of this. "We seemed fine then, too…"

History is thus important in a number of ways. During the early communist period, a number of surviving Jews, believing the promise of a classless society no longer divided by ethnicity, faith and creed, joined the Communist Party and raised their children without ever telling them of their Jewish heritage or the horrors of the past. Some of these children never learned of their heritage, while others learned often quite by accident.

This aspect of history is a double edged sword, playing into anti-Semitic tropes internationally that blamed Jews for communism. How deeply rooted this canard actually is was brought home to me only a few weeks ago. I collect Soviet era propaganda posters, and while at the flea market in Budapest I stumbled on a poster that I had to have. It was Russian in origin and used the typical artistic motifs of the Stalinist era. It depicted a peasant and a worker, yoked together and under the whip of a Soviet Commissar. The poster reads: Peasants and Workers/ This is Soviet Freedom. I thought great, a rare piece of *Samisdat*. Only after I took it home and studied it more closely did I see that the lock on the yoke constraining the peasant and the worker bore the Star of David. The meaning was clear enough.

But if many Hungarian Jews feel that overt or public expressions of anti-Semitism are declining, proscribed both by law and by popular opinion, how to explain the depiction of Hungary as dangerously anti-Semitic from the outside?

The View from the Outside

The case against Hungary which can be found in the Western press and in elite discourse follows two primary tributaries. In Israel, the collective memory of Hungarian Holocaust survivors remains strong and continues to shape popular perceptions of Hungary. The close diplomatic relationship between Israel and Hungary, and the even closer relationship between Prime Ministers Orbán and Netanyahu play exceedingly well on the Israeli right, but in the slightly more than 50% of Israelis who detest the former Israeli prime minister, the imagery is less sanguine. The Israeli view will of course change and evolve over time, but archetypal beliefs change more slowly than ongoing political trends.

In the US, the case is much more complex. There is little or no popular awareness of Hungarian Holocaust history. Rather, the view of Hungary is shaped by the memory of the Cold War. 1956 is the dominant theme and it is reinforced by the many Hungarian refugees who came to the West in the wake of the Soviet invasion. Hungarians are seen as the brave freedom fighters who stood against Soviet oppression.

The evidence presented against Hungary in the Western media is therefore much more contemporary in nature. The *causus belie* in this indictment centers on the George Soros campaign. The short lived poster campaign and some of the more extreme rhetoric did seem to have an element of classical anti-Semitism.

What has come out of this research, however is that, in contrast to the Western press, very few Jews we have interviewed believe that the Soros campaign was in fact anti-Semitic either in intent or execution. With only a few exceptions, the Soros campaign is seen by those we have interviewed as entirely political, and that, moreover, neither he nor the rhetoric surrounding his activities is seen as having any connection to the Jewish community in Hungary.

This view though was lost on the Western media, or simply ignored. Rather, the charge of Hungarian anti-Semitism became an element of a wider critique of what has come to be called *illiberal democracy* and could thus be rolled into an indictment of conservative parties in Europe, which could then be equated with fears that the Trump administration constituted a threat to American democracy as well.

This media driven view of Hungary as anti-Semitic and anti-democratic however has not taken deep root in the US, and after the events in Washington on 6 January has drawn increasingly little public interest. Rather, a joke heard in Europe has become increasingly prevalent in the United States. America has always been a missionary culture. Over the years, America has exported Protestant Christianity, free trade, briefly anti-colonialism, anti-fascism, and most of all anti-Communism from the end of World War II until 1989. Underlying all of this however, is the core American faith in democracy as a panacea for all social and political ills. The observation that America has exported so much democracy that they kept little for themselves is all too telling. And with that realization, the media focus and the elite discourse which it represents have turned inward, and fears of anti-Semitism and the dangers to democracy in Hungary have thus faded from the public square.

It is hoped that this conference and the publications to follow, will offer Western readers a more nuanced, fieldwork based view of anti-Semitism in contemporary Hungary that encompasses both perception and reality.

Finally, it is customary to close a major conference like this with a name check of all who were involved. Given my inability to pronounce Hungarian this is a perilous but necessary task. What made the conference and the research that it reflects possible was the knowledge and enthusiasm of the researchers who did most of the work and much of the conceptual design. For the passion that they invest in this research, I want to thank:

> Tamás Orbán
> Dávid Nagy
> Zsófia Tóth-Bíró

Lidia Papp, and
Sáron Sugár

Once we had the idea and the grand design, the researchers soon came to the collective realization that we had no idea how to make the conference a reality. The organizational details, and the ability to solve each crisis as it arose, are what has made these two days possible. I would therefore like to thank:

Orsolya Belányi
Rebeka Illés
Dorina Dósa, and
Ágnes Berei

Finally, a very special thanks to the man with the phone numbers of seemingly everyone in Budapest when needed, and for sponsoring my stay in Hungary, Prof. János Besenyő of Óbuda University. And another very special thanks to Istvan Kiss, who was the genesis of the study, and John O'Sullivan, president of the Danube Institute, as well as the Batthyány Foundation who make all that we do possible.

But most of all, I want to express my deep sense of gratitude to the Hungarian Jewish community, who opened their institutions and shared their lives with us in the course of this research.

Thanks to all. Be safe and goodbye.

Part

8

Supporting Articles

Can Jews Be Anti-Semitic? The Case of Neturei Karta's Extreme Orthodox Anti-Zionist and Anti-Israel Ideology

Menachem Keren-Kratz

In 2016 the United States government, as well as other governments, adopted the working definition made by the International Holocaust Remembrance Alliance (IHRA) which stated that: "Anti-Semitism is a certain perception of Jews, which may be expressed as hatred toward Jews [...] These manifestations might include the targeting of the state of Israel, conceived as a Jewish collectivity." The working definition also stated that one example of anti-Semitism was "Denying the Jewish people their right to self-determination, e.g., by claiming that the existence of the State of Israel is a racist endeavor."[1]

Because this definition refers also to the targeting of Israel as a Jewish state, it implies that the call to obliterate Israel, the Jewish state, may also be considered a form of anti-Semitism. Since then, many public bodies which fight anti-Semitism denounced the expression of anti-Zionist and anti-Israeli stands as a form of anti-Semitism.

But what can be said of such anti-Zionist and anti-Israeli expressions when they are voiced by Jews? Clearly, simply claiming that Jews, because of their Jewishness, cannot be anti-Semitic is a racist statement. Such a claim either assumes that Jews are better than non-Jews or that Jews are unable to make statements which offend their collective identity. This is all the more so considering the long history of objection to Zionism by several Jewish camps.

Since the dawn of history Jews immigrated to *Eretz Israel*. Yet, following the destruction of the Second Temple and the expulsion of Jews by the

---

1 https://www.holocaustremembrance.com/resources/working-definitions-charters/working-definition-anti-Semitism

Roman Empire, the number of newcomers was very low, and their socio-economic status was poor. This began to change in the mid-nineteenth century. Although the Zionist movement was established in 1897, the yearning for a collective immigration and settlement in *Eretz Israel*—Palestine—began a few decades earlier. A few rabbis who were disturbed both with the spreading of anti-Semitism and by the decline in religious observance, particularly among the young, felt that a collective return of observant Jews to Zion may present a good solution to both challenges.[2]

Since the 1860s this nationalistic notion was known as *Yishuv Eretz Israel* (The settlement of the land of Israel), and by the early 1880s a new organization titled *Hibat Tzion* (the love of Zion) sought to direct this theoretical agenda into a more practical framework.[3] The period between 1882-1903 is known as the first *Aliya*, namely the first wave of immigration of Jews who were motivated by nationalistic rather than purely religious reasons.[4] To put things in perspective, while the total number of newcomers to Palestine in that period was some 25,000 Jews, over 1.5 million Jews made their way from Eastern Europe to the "true" promised land—America.[5]

Yet, although the number of Jews who settled in *Eretz Israel* was negligible compared with those who preferred to immigrate to other countries, and even before the Zionist movement was established, the settlement of *Eretz Israel* was condemned by religious Judaism's two major camps: the Orthodox and the Reform. It should be remembered that the objection to Yishuv Eretz Israel and later to Zionism was present mainly among Ashkenazi Jews, which until the Holocaust comprised some ninety percent of the Jewish People.[6]

---

[2] Jacob Katz, "The forerunners of Zionism," *Jerusalem Quarterly*, 7 (1978), pp.10-21; Monty Noam Penkower, "Religious forerunners of Zionism," *Judaism*, 33, 3 (1984), 289-295.

[3] Yosef Salmon, "The emergence of a Jewish nationalist consciousness in Europe during the 1860s and 1870s," *AJS Review*, 16,1-2 (1991), 107-132.

[4] Mordechai Eliav (ed.), *The First Aliyah*, Jerusalem: Yad Ben Zvi, 1981 (Hebrew); Yossi Goldstein, *We Were First: A History of Hibat Zion, 1881-1918*, Jerusalem: Bialik Institute, 2015 (Hebrew).

[5] Samson D. Oppenheim, "The Jewish Population of the United States," *American Jewish Year Book*, 20 (1918-1919), 31-74.

[6] Many other Jewish camps objected to the settlement of Eretz Israel and later to Zionism. These included the acculturated, the socialists, and the secular anti-Zionists. On such movements see: Haim Avni and Gideon Shimoni, *Zionism and its Jewish Opponents*, Jerusalem: Bialik Institute, 1990 (Hebrew).

The Early Objection to the Zionist idea

Although the Zionist movement itself was only established in 1897, ideas which were later titled Zionist were expressed by several Jewish leaders, both religious and secular. Until the last third of the nineteenth century, "old style" Orthodox immigrants came to *Eretz Israel* seeking to practice a fully observant lifestyle and intending to spend most of their time in prayer and in the study of the Torah (namely the Talmud). Many of them were elderly people who came to spend their last years in the Promised Land so they could be buried in its holy soil. It was these immigrants who eventually became what was later known as "The Old Yishuv" (the old settlement). No one objected to this type of immigration, even after the 1870s when a second sort of newcomers began to arrive.

These immigrants, most but not all were observant Jews, sought to lead a different, a more productive way of life in the land of Israel. They usually came at a younger age, accompanied by their families. They also brought some capital with them, which they used to open a business or to buy land in one of the new Jewish colonies, hoping to become farmers. This type of settlement became known as "The New Yishuv," which attracted firm objection from the right and from the left.[7]

The rabbinical figures who expressed their support of the New Yishuv conditioned it only as far as observant Jews were involved. They justified their stance by both pragmatic and religious reasons. They believed that given the rise in anti-Semitism, and especially following the early 1880s' devastating pogroms in the Russian Empire, Eretz Israel might become a safe haven for many Jews. Moreover, because by that time some of the immigrants were non-observant Jews, they considered it essential to maintain a majority of Orthodox Jews in the Holy Land. In addition, because there are many *mitzvoth* (religious commands) which are only applicable in *Eretz Israel*, it was important for Jews to practice them so they will not be forgotten.[8]

While these arguments sounded reasonable to many East-European rabbis, others objected to this type of Jewish settlement even if carried out by

---

7   Israel Bartal, "'Old Yishuv' and 'New Yishuv': image and reality," *Cathedra*, 1 (1981), 215–231; Yehoshua Kaniel, "The terms 'Old Yishuv' and 'New Yishuv': problems of definition," *Cathedra*, 1 (1981), 232–245.
8   Yosef Salmon, "Akiva Yosef Schlesinger: a forerunner of Zionism or a forerunner of ultra-Orthodoxy," *Journal of Modern Jewish Studies*, 15,2 (2016), 171–187.

fully observant Jews. Their objection was based on three major arguments. First, unlike the Old Yishuv, this type of settlement was a new phenomenon and this contradicted one of Orthodoxy's main principles, which asserted that "Everything new is forbidden by the Torah." Although originally referring to a completely different topic, Rabbi Moshe Sofer, also known after his book's title *Hatam Sofer*, used this expression to encapsulate his stance against any expression of modernity.[9] Although until his death in 1839 Hatam Sofer supported Yishuv Eretz Israel in its old-style version, his followers used his statement to condemn the movement's modern manifestation.[10]

A second argument was based on eschatological reasoning. According to Jewish tradition and based on the Talmudic verse known as "The Three Oath Midrash," Jews are expected to stay in exile even under harsh conditions and they are not allowed either to "rebel against the nations" or to "hasten the redemption." The opposing rabbis claimed that the call for many Jews to settle in *Eretz Israel* is a violation of these two binding oaths.[11] Moreover, because a growing number of the Jewish immigrants were non-observant, they desecrated the Holy Land and made it unsuitable for redemption.[12]

The third reasoning was practical. The objecting rabbis claimed that because the Ottoman authorities as well as the local Arabs were hostile, the new settlers were risking their life and their money, which was also forbidden by the *halakha* (religious law). They further claimed that in any case the number of Jews who could settle in *Eretz Israel* was limited, the New Yishuv did not offer a true solution to the problem of anti-Semitism. Moreover, because it was clear that the settlers of the New Yishuv would not be able to support themselves and would ask the support of other Jews, this would diminish the funds collected to support the Old Yishuv, which was almost totally dependent on these donations.[13]

---

9 Charles S. Liebman, "Orthodoxy faces modernity," *Orim: A Jewish Journal at Yale*, 2,2 (1987), 7–21; Israel Bartal, "Responses to modernity: Haskalah, Orthodoxy, and nationalism in Eastern," in: Shmuel Almog, Jehuda Reinharz, and Anita Shapira (eds.), *Zionism and Religion*, Hanover, NH: Brandeis University Press, 1998, 13–24.
10 Yosef Salmon, "The Hatam Sofer and the land of Israel," *Jewish History*, 33 (2020), 437–459.
11 On the Three Oaths Midrash see: Aviezer Ravitzky, *Messianism, Zionism, and Jewish Religious Radicalism*, Chicago: University of Chicago Press, 1996, 211–234.
12 The third oath was imposed on the Gentiles who were sworn not to overly enslave and oppress the Jews.
13 Yosef Salmon, "Zionism and anti-Zionism in traditional Judaism in Eastern Europe," in: Shmuel Almog, Jehuda Reinharz, and Anita Shapira (eds.), *Zionism and Religion*, Hanover, NH: Brandeis University Press, 1998, 25–43.

The objection from the left, namely from the Reform movement, carried a different character. Part of this movement's agenda was the narrowing of the gap which separated Jews and gentiles. For example, seeking to resemble Christianity, the Reform movement abandoned all the practical religious commandments, even those considered the most basic ones. The Reform houses of prayer were named "temples" rather than "synagogues" and were built to look like Christian churches, and the ceremonies they held in these institutions were also modeled after those which took place in the churches.[14]

As part of this general trend, the Reform movement also discarded certain Jewish concepts which it considered no longer appropriate for modern Jews. They, for example, omitted or altered the prayer sections which mentioned the sacrifices made in the Temple.[15] Seeking to present themselves as loyal citizens, they also cancelled or altered the prayers calling for the return of the Jews to Zion. For them, even the symbolic yearning for the return of the Jews to the land of Israel was considered disloyalty to their homelands as well as a misinterpretation of Judaism's true mission.[16]

The rejection of Zionism was even greater among the Reform rabbis in the United States. In their 1885 Pittsburgh Platform, which became the almost official agenda of this movement, the fifth clause stated:

"We recognize, in the modern era of universal culture of heart and intellect, the approaching of the realization of Israel's great Messianic hope for the establishment of the kingdom of truth, justice, and peace among all men. *We consider ourselves no longer a nation, but a religious community, and therefore expect neither a return to Palestine, nor a sacrificial worship under the sons of Aaron, nor the restoration of any of the laws concerning the Jewish state.*"[17]

Only in 1937, more than half a century later, as anti-Semitism was rampaging through Europe and America, did the Reform movement adopted a more nuanced endorsement of Zionism, noting that:

---

14 Michael A. Meyer, *Response to Modernity: A History of the Reform Movement in Judaism*, New York: Oxford University Press, 1988.
15 Stanley F. Chyet and Norman B. Mirsky, "Reflections on circumcision as sacrifice," in: Lewis M. Barth (ed.), *"Berit Mila" in the Reform Context*, New York: Berit Mila Board of Reform Judaism, 1990, 59–68.
16 Michael A. Meyer, "Liberal Judaism and Zionism in Germany," Almog et al, *Zionism and Religion*, 93–106.
17 https://www.ccarnet.org/rabbinic-voice/platforms/article-declaration-principles/

"In all lands where our people live, they assume and seek to share loyally the full duties and responsibilities of citizenship and to create seats of Jewish knowledge and religion. *In the rehabilitation of Palestine, the land hallowed by memories and hopes, we behold the promise of renewed life for many of our brethren. We affirm the obligation of all Jewry to aid in its upbuilding as a Jewish homeland by endeavoring to make it not only a haven of refuge for the oppressed but also a center of Jewish culture and spiritual life.*"[18]

In conclusion, while in hindsight ideas about the Jewish People's return to Zion and the birth of the Zionist movement turned out to become a major Jewish issue, this was not the case in the nineteenth century. The fact that some 98 percent of the Jews who emigrated from Europe chose to settle in other countries shows that the debate over *Yishuv Eretz Israel* was greatly theoretical and bore almost no practical meaning.

Jewish Orthodoxy's Objection to Zionism in the early Twentieth Century

Once the Zionist movement was established, and particularly after it declared itself a secular movement, the Orthodox objection to Zionism intensified. Several Orthodox activists published anti-Zionist polemic texts,[19] and a new Orthodox newspaper published anti-Zionist articles.[20] While many Orthodox Jews and rabbis who formerly joined the movement reconsidered their position, a few rabbis established the religious-Zionist wing and named

---

18 https://web.archive.org/web/20120313101700/http://www.ccarnet.org/rabbis-speak/platforms/guiding-principles-reform-judaism/.

19 Shemuel Ya'acov Rabinowitz, *Ha-Dat Ve-Haleumiyut*, Warsaw, 1900; Arye Miller, *Bein Or Le-Hoshekh*, Vilnius 1901; Dobrish Toresh, *Bar Hadiya O Halom Herzel*, Warsaw 1901; Ya'acov Lifshitz, *Ma'amar Devarim Ke-Khtavam*, Berlin, 1902; Ephraim Eliyahu Lifshits, *Sefer Higayon Lev Ivri*, Piotrków Trybunalski, 1902; Avraham Barukh Steinberg, *Da'at Ha-Rabanim*, Warsaw, 1902; Idem., *Kol Kore: Hu Kontres Aharon*, Vilnius 1903 (all in Hebrew); Mordehai Kravinski, *Der Futerner Oyven*, Piotrków Trybunalski, 1904 (in Yiddish). On the response of the Zionist rabbis to such anti-Zionist attacks, see: Dalia Levi, "'Or Le-Yesharim'—manifest anti-tsioni—u-teguvot ahadot," *Ha-Tsi'yonut*, 19 (1995), 31–65.

20 Menachem Keren-Kratz, "*Ha-Peles*: An Orthodox Newspaper and Its Struggle with the Challenges of Modern Spirits of the Early Twentieth Century," *Kesher: Journal of Media and Communications History in Israel and the Jewish World*, 54 (2020), 43–75 (Hebrew); Yosef Salmon, "Eliyahu Akiva Rabinovits: Dovra shel ha-ortodoxia ha-yehudit be-rusia ha-tsarit," in *Al Da'at Ha-Kahal: Religion and politics in Jewish thought, essays in honor of Aviezer Ravitzky*, Vol. 2, Benjamin Brown et al. (eds.), Jerusalem: Zalman Shazar Center, 2012, 721–757.

it *Ha-Mizrahi*. This organization, which was part of the Zionist movement, also attracted criticism which castigated it as too lenient and compromising.

The only major camp which had no international organization of its own was that of the non-Zionist Orthodox Jews. Eventually, in 1912 a few of its leaders established *Agudat Israel*, the first international Orthodox organization. All these social processes came to a halt in 1914 following the beginning of World War I, which turned the world in general and the Jewish world in particular upside down. The war impacted most of the European countries in which Jews lived both by establishing new borders and by having new regimes.[21]

This was all the more so in *Eretz Israel*—Palestine. After four centuries of Ottoman, namely Muslim, government, in 1917 the country was conquered by Britain. At the same time, Britain's foreign minister, Lord Arthur James Balfour, issued a declaration in support of establishing "a national home" for the Jews in Palestine. This statement, and the fact that Britain was given an international mandate to govern Palestine, prompted a massive wave of Zionist activity throughout the Jewish world. The Zionist trend received a further boost following the USA Immigration Act of 1924, which diminished the number of Jewish immigrants from Eastern Europe by ninety percent and forced many of them to settle in Eretz Israel.

This new situation found the non-Zionist Orthodox leaders unprepared. On the one hand their objection to Zionism only intensified, but on the other hand, ignoring the growing number of secular Jews who wished to settle in Eretz Israel meant the loss of influence in all the religious aspects of life there. As a result, *Agudat Israel* began supporting various projects which assisted Orthodox Jews to settle in Eretz Israel, much like the Zionist movements.[22]

Moreover, as a result of the 1929 pogrom in *Eretz Israel*, which ended with the death of over 130 Jews and over 300 injured, and the massive wave of anti-Semitism following Hitler's rise to power in 1933, *Agudat Israel* was forced to expand its cooperation with the Zionist movement. Thus, despite

---

21 Marsha L. Rozenblit and Jonathan Karp (eds.), *World War I and the Jews: Conflict and Transformations in Europe, the Middle East, and America*, New York: Berghahn Books, 2017.
22 Gershon C. Bacon, "Imitation, rejection, cooperation: Agudat Yisrael and the Zionist movement in interwar Poland.," in: Zvi Gitelman (ed.), *The Emergence of Modern Jewish Politics: Bundism and Zionism in Eastern Europe*, Pittsburgh, PA: University of Pittsburgh Press, 2003, 85–94.

its theoretical objection to Zionism, *Agudat Israel* only strengthened its relationship with this movement. This trend resulted in *Agudat Israel* and *Ha-Mizrahi* establishing a joint party which participated in Israel's first government established in 1948.[23]

Although *Agudat Israel* represented the majority of the non-Zionist Orthodox Jews, a smaller Orthodox camp took a much harder line against Zionism and against *Agudat Israel*, which it condemned as too lenient and compromising. This group, titled Extreme Orthodoxy, was established in Hungary in the last third of the nineteenth century.

Extreme Orthodoxy and its anti-Zionist stance

In 1867 Hungarian Jews were awarded equal civil rights. Shortly thereafter the Minister of Religious Affairs summoned a general conference in order to formulate the regulations that would govern the now autonomous Jewish communities and to elect a single representative Jewish body. However, ideological conflicts between the representatives of the Orthodox and the Neolog (the Hungarian Reform movement) precluded the establishment of a single Jewish organization, and Hungarian Jewry was divided into three major camps. Consequently, the Orthodox, the Neolog, and the Status-Quo (namely the communities that joined neither the Orthodox nor the Neolog organizations) were granted the right to establish their own separate communities and to be represented by their own organization.[24]

A decade or two after the Orthodox—Neolog schism, another split began to appear, this time within the Orthodox camp itself, between two distinct factions. The larger group comprised non-Hasidic Orthodox Jews, most of whom originated from the German speaking countries to the west of Hungary and were thus known as Ashkenazim (or Germans). Although strictly observing the *halakha*, they were receptive to modernity and contemporary culture, acquired a broad education, embraced a more contemporary appearance, and by and large belonged to the higher socio-economic

---

[23] Menachem Friedman, *Society and Religion: The non-Zionist Orthodox in Eretz-Israel, 1918–1936*, Jerusalem: Yad Ben–Zvi, 1978 (Hebrew).

[24] Jacob Katz, *A House Divided: Orthodoxy and Schism in Nineteenth-Century Central European Jewry*, Hanover, NH: Brandeis University Press, 1998.

strata. They resided in Hungary's western counties in an area the Jews called Oberland. The smaller camp was located in the eastern counties, known as Unterland. Most of its members hailed from nearby Galicia, shunned modernity, were poorly educated, belonged to a lower socio-economic stratum, and many of them adhered to Hasidism.[25]

It was within this latter group that a new pattern of Orthodoxy evolved, which imparted to Hungarian Orthodoxy its unique flavor. Its leaders took a hard line not only against the non-Orthodox but also against Oberland's mainstream Orthodoxy, which they condemned for being excessively lenient and prone to compromise. While they participated in the Hungarian Orthodox Bureau, the Extreme Orthodox leaders mounted an aggressive political opposition to the ruling Ashkenazi majority.[26]

Prior to World War I the adherents of Extreme Orthodoxy constituted only a small group among Hungarian Orthodoxy, which was dominated by its mainstream leaders, who promoted a more tolerant and modern form of observant lifestyle. This, however, was not the case in Karpathorus and Transylvania, two former Hungarian regions which after the war were annexed to Czechoslovakia and Romania. In these two territories the Extreme Orthodox accounted for a far larger portion of the Jewish population. In a bid to implement their separatist agenda, Extreme Orthodox leaders sought to distinguish themselves and their followers from the more lenient mainstream Orthodoxy, thereby creating a social framework that formed an enclave within an enclave.

At first, the distinction between the mainstream and Extreme Orthodox factions was based on evaluating how strictly members of each group observed the *Halakha* and how it regarded modern trends such as general education and Western culture. This somewhat blurred border became much clearer after the establishment of the Zionist movement. Since then, every individual, community, or organization which refrained from totally banning Zionism was castigated by the Extreme Orthodox leadership as overly lenient and compromising.

---

25 Menachem Keren-Kratz, *Máramaros-Sziget: Extreme Orthodoxy and Secular Jewish Culture at the Foothills of the Carpathian Mountains*, Jerusalem: The Dov Sadan Publishing Project and Leyvik House, 2013 (in Hebrew), 39–40.
26 Menachem Keren-Kratz, "Maramaros, Hungary—The cradle of Extreme Orthodoxy," *Modern Judaism*, 35: 2 (2015), 147–174.

Consequently, while most East European and even many Hungarian rabbis joined the international Orthodox organization *Agudat Israel*, the Extreme Orthodox rabbis boycotted the movement and accused its leaders of being excessively lenient and modern and of flagrantly cooperating with the Zionist movement.[27] Given their ultra-conservative worldview, only a small number of Extreme Orthodox adherents migrated to other countries before the Holocaust. Consequently, only a handful of Extreme Orthodox Jews survived, and following the Holocaust the very concept of Extreme Orthodoxy was on the brink of extinction. The individual who almost singlehandedly preserved that tradition was Rabbi Yoel Teitelbaum—The Satmar Rebbe.

Extreme Orthodoxy after the Holocaust

Rabbi Yoel Teitelbaum descended from a well-established Hassidic dynasty.[28] Yet, being the youngest son, he was not destined to succeed his father, who was the Chief Rabbi of Sighet, Hungary, a prominent Hasidic leader and head of a yeshiva, for that right was reserved for his elder brother. Following the older brother's untimely death in 1926, Rabbi Yoel expected to replace him and thereby to secure his place in the family dynasty after all. To his disappointment, his own hometown's leaders bypassed him and chose his 14-year-old nephew instead. From that time onward he resolved to do everything in his power to gain all the public positions of which he believed he had been deprived. Employing various political tactics, he waged a six-year-long campaign to be appointed Satmar's Chief Rabbi. It took him a further three years of cunning diplomacy to get himself elected to the governing body of the Orthodox Jews in the province of Transylvania.[29]

Shortly after he had achieved these political aims, the Holocaust descended. Much to his Hasidim's consternation, he made several attempts to escape. Eventually he fled Satmar in the middle of the night, was caught

---

27 Menachem Keren-Kratz, ""Inclusion Versus Exclusion in Intra-Orthodox Politics: Between Agudat Israel and Hungarian Orthodoxy," *Modern Judaism*, 40:2 (2020), 195–226.
28 On Rabbi Yoel see: Menachem Keren-Kratz, *The Zealot: The Satmar Rebbe—Rabbi Yoel Teitelbaum*, Jerusalem: Zalman Shazar center, 2020 (in Hebrew).
29 Menachem Keren-Kratz, "The politics of a religious enclave: Orthodox Jews in interwar Transylvania, Romania," *Modern Judaism*, 37, 3 (2017), 363–391.

and sent to another ghetto. There Rabbi Yoel boarded the rescue train which was organized by the Zionist activist Israel Kasztner. After a few months' incarceration in Bergen-Belsen he was released to Switzerland.[30] Soon thereafter Rabbi Yoel settled in Jerusalem and established his own Hasidic community. After the institutes he established accumulated tremendous debts, Rabbi Yoel, persecuted by his creditors, was forced to travel to America, a country he detested, hoping to raise money to pay his debts.[31]

Upon his arrival in the United States in September 1946, Rabbi Yoel found out that his anti-Zionist views were not well received, especially among the more established American Orthodox Jews, who, by and large, were pro-Zionist. Consequently, although he raised funds in various Orthodox congregations for almost two years, he failed to gather enough money to allow him to return to Palestine and to save his crumbling institutions.[32] During that period he also discovered that the very same anti-Zionist views he expressed in his sermons struck a chord with some of the Holocaust survivors. His ultra-conservative concepts and anti-Zionist tirades reminded them of those they had heard in their former homes in Eastern Europe, the ones which no longer existed. These survivors assembled around him, encouraging him to establish his own congregation in America. This prompted Rabbi Yoel to decide against returning to Palestine, and in 1948 he settled in Williamsburg, New York.[33]

During the 1940s some dozen Hasidic rabbis who had either fled before the Holocaust or had survived it established their own courts in New York. Most of them were invited to serve as rabbis in existing congregations of Jews originating from the same European town. However, since Rabbi Yoel forbade his Hasidim to immigrate to America, and since many of them had perished in the Holocaust, no existing congregation awaited him. This meant that had he wished to establish a Hasidic court of his own, not only would he have to compete with other rabbis but he would also have to establish a congregation from scratch. In order to succeed in this mission Rabbi Yoel had

---

30 Menachem Keren-Kratz, "Hast Thou Escaped and Also Taken Possession? The Responses of the Satmar Rebbe—Rabbi Yoel Teitelbaum—and his Followers to Criticism of his Conduct During and After the Holocaust," *Dapim: Studies on the Holocaust*, 28:2 (2014), 97–120.
31 Keren-Kratz, *The Zealot*, 200–209.
32 Shlomo Ya'akov Gelbman, *Sefer Moshian Shel Israel*, Vol. 5, Monroe, NY, 1995, 146.
33 Alexander Sender Deutch, *Butsina Kadisha*, Vol. 2, Brooklyn, 2000, 61.

to offer his potential followers a unique spiritual identity that was not based primarily on mutual geographical origins.

To this end Rabbi Yoel presented himself as the only Orthodox leader after the Holocaust that was still fully committed to the most separatist, conservative, anti-Zionist, and anti-modern tradition of Extreme Orthodoxy. These unique views attracted an ever growing number of Hasidim.[34] They, presumably, found comfort in an Orthodox authority of Rabbi Yoel's magnitude who offered them a religious ideology to which they were accustomed in their East-European communities, those which were annihilated during the Holocaust.[35]

A few years after its establishment, his congregation was already considered one of the largest and most prosperous Hasidic courts in post-Holocaust America.[36] Noticing Rabbi Yoel's success, other rabbis decided to adopt the same anti-modernistic and anti-Zionist outlook. In 1955 Rabbi Yoel convened these rabbis and established the Central Rabbinical Congress. Under his guidance the CRC promoted various anti-modern and anti-Zionist activities.[37]

Writing Extreme Orthodoxy's Canonical Text

In 1958, the State of Israel celebrated its first decade of independence. During that period it became a prosperous, modern and democratic state. It won the 1956 Sinai campaign and opened its doors to almost one million immigrants, many of whom were Holocaust survivors.[38] This demonstrated that Israel succeeded in overcoming the many challenges it faced and that it was not going to disappear, as some Orthodox leaders anticipated. Although prior to its establishment Haredi leaders had feared that the Zionist regime

---

34 Menachem Keren-Kratz, "Rabbi Yoel Teitelbaum—the Satmar Rebbe—and the Rise of Anti-Zionism in American Orthodoxy," *Contemporary Jewry*, 37: 3 (2017), 457–479.
35 Gershon Greenberg, "Wartime American Orthodoxy and the Holocaust: Mizrahi and Agudat Israel religious responses," *Michael*, 15 (2000), 59–94.
36 Israel Rubin, *Satmar: An Island in the City*, Chicago: Quadrangle Books, 1972, 3–8.
37 The CRC is better known by his Hebrew/Yiddish title Hitahaduth Ha-Rabanim. On its activities see: *Sefer Milhamot Ha-Shem*, Brooklyn: Shomrei Mishmaras Ha-Kodesh, 1983 (Hebrew/Yiddish).
38 For example: S. Ilan Troen and Noah Lucas (eds.), *Israel: the first decade of independence*, Albany: State University of New York Press, 1995.

would suppress religious life, time proved them wrong. During that decade many Haredi neighborhoods and institutions were built with the support of the Israeli government. At the same time, generous social benefits allowed the Haredi population to bear more children and to send a growing number of men to spend many years in the yeshiva. The majority of the Haredim shared the patriotic spirit of the new state, and most Haredi men served in the Israeli army.[39]

These impressive achievements, which were highlighted during the official celebrations of Israel's first decade, prompted Rabbi Yoel to act. On top of his usual anti-Zionist sermons, he now began to openly accuse Zionism of having been the major cause of the Holocaust. He furthermore declared that whereas the Nazis had sought to physically exterminate Jews, the Zionists' undisclosed mission was to annihilate the very spirit of Judaism. While Nazi Germany lost the war and their extermination process was over, the Zionists had merely grown stronger and continued their efforts to annihilate Jewish tradition.[40]

This anti-Zionist campaign included a series of mass demonstrations in New York that attracted the attention of both the Israeli and international press.[41] During these protests, yeshiva students even painted swastikas on the walls of "Zionist" synagogues and on the Israeli consulate in New York. The CRC's most impressive demonstration took place in 1958 in front of the White House in Washington. It attracted the attention of the international press as Extreme Orthodox protestors waved posters comparing the newly established State of Israel to Nazi Germany.[42]

The Jewish press, as well as many spokespersons from all Jewish camps, condemned this appalling comparison and called to take action against the provocateurs. The Israeli government's and public's fury against Rabbi Yoel was such that the very future of his plans to build two Hasidic neighbor-

---

39   Menachem Friedman, *The Haredi (Ultra-Orthodox) Society: Sources, Trends and Processes*, Jerusalem: Jerusalem Institute for Israel Studies series, Vol. 41, 1991 (in Hebrew); Yair Ha-Levi, *The 'New Haredism' Revolution in Israel in the 1970s*, Ph.D. dissertation, Bar-Ilan University, 2019.
40   *Mishmeret Homatenu*, Av 5, 5718 (1958), 289–293; Deitch, *Butsina Kadisha*, Vol. 1, 310–312.
41   *Der Yid*, March 21, 1958, 1, 4; *Der Tog / Morgen Journal*, March 24, 1958, 1; *Mishmeret Homatenu*, Iyar 4, 5718 (1958), 177, 180; *New York Times*, March 24, 1958.
42   *Davar*, June 18, 1958, 2; *Der Tog / Morgen Journal*, June 20, 1958, 1; *New York Times*, June 20, 1958; *Forverts*, June 20, 1958, 1; *Ma'ariv*, June 22, 1958, 3.

hoods, one in Bnei Brak and one in Jerusalem, were in jeopardy.[43] Moreover, ten years after establishing his community and making it a leading force within America's Hasidism, Rabbi Yoel decided the time had come to transform it from a radical and reactionary movement and set it on a more conservative and relaxed trajectory. After all, by that time he was 72 years old with no son to succeed him and the only bond that united his community was an ideology that was only passed orally.

Va-Yoel Moshe

Rabbi Yoel realized that in order for his community to exist after his death and for it to perpetuate the separatist, anti-Zionist, and anti-modern Extreme Orthodox ideology he salvaged from ruins, he needed to formulate his ideology in writing. He then dedicated several hours a day to this end and asked the senior students of his yeshiva to proofread the book, while the printers were asked to verify the references to the many sources the book mentioned.[44]

In 1960, Rabbi Yoel published the first part of the book, which dealt with "the Three Oaths Midrash."[45] After completing the writing of the second section and editing an already existing responsum which became the book's third section, the book, which was titled *Va-Yoel Moshe*, appeared in its familiar form at the end of 1961. The ideology expressed in this book can be reduced to two fundamental principles. First, that Zionism in general and the State of Israel in particular are the worst sin imaginable. This sin was so grave that God's only possible response to it was the Holocaust. Second, that only those Jews who realize the severity of this sin and consequently totally ban Zionism are "true Jews," while all others who call themselves Jews are imposters who are either false or flawed. This group of "fake Jews" contains not merely secular, assimilated, Reform and Conservative Jews, but even religious and Haredi Jews. Since these are merely "fake Jews," the book sug-

---

43 *Davar*, April 28, 1958, 1; *Ma'ariv*, May 18, 1958, 3; Ibid., June 30, 1958, 6; *Forverts*, June 23, 1958, 1, 7; Ibid., June 24, 1958, 1.
44 Yakobowits, *Zekhor Yemot*, Vol. 4, 79; *Pitgamin Kadishin*, 26 Av 5,768, 32; *Mivtsar Torah Ve-Yira'h*, Vol. 1, 313–314; Deitch, *Butsina Kadisha*, Vol. 1, 369–371, 385.
45 Yoel Teitalbaum, *Sefer Va-Yoel Moshe: Le-Va'er Dinei Ha-Shalosh Shevu'ot*, Brooklyn, 5,760 (1960).

gests that there is no real need to consider their rabbis' ideological stands or *halakhic* rulings.

Rabbi Yoel lived for many years after the book's publication and continued to hammer away at the same ideas over and over. This left a permanent impression on the minds of his Hassidim for several generations, who could now not only listen to their spiritual leader but also quote and interpret his words.[46] Even after his passing, the book, and its ideas, still connected the Hasidim with his memory and became the community's ideological backbone. During the ensuing years, the book has reappeared in more than a dozen full editions and been translated into several languages. At least thirty further volumes have offered interpretations, adaptations for children, compiled digests, or reviewed its relevance to various ideological issues or *halakhic* (Jewish laws) rulings.

For more than a hundred thousand Satmar Hasidim and even a greater number of members of other Extreme Orthodox groups which are associated with organizations such as the *Edah Haredit* and *Neturei Karta* in Israel and the Central Rabbinical Congress of America (CRC, also known as *Hita'hadut Ha-Rabanim*), *Va-Yoel Moshe* became a canonical text. It is taught in special classes, both in the Yeshivas and by independent study groups, and hundreds of rabbis around the world cite the book regularly during their sermons at public events. Rabbi Yoel's successor, and even his own successors, realized the book's importance to the court's core identity, so despite each of them adopting his own leadership style and ideological nuances, each insisted that he was just interpreting Rabbi Yoel's ideas as were expressed in his books.

Neturei Karta—Extreme Orthodoxy's Most Fervent Group

Led by a Hungarian rabbi, Rabbi Yosef Haim Sonnenfeld, the non-Zionist Orthodox Jews living in Mandatory Palestine sought to establish themselves as a separate Jewish group not related to the other Jews which identified as

---

46 The fundamental role specific texts play in creating specific religious and particularly Hasidic identities deserve a separate research. Such canonic texts include for example: *Shivhei Ha-Besht* (for Hasidism in general), *Sefer Ha-Tania* (for Habad-Lubavitz), and *Likutei Moharan* (for Braslav).

Zionists. They established their own religious institutions, led an independent policy towards the Arab Question, and succeeded to convince the British authorities to grant them partial autonomy. To that end they also connected with *Agudat Israel*, which supported them both politically and financially.[47]

In time, *Agudat Israel* realized that the connection to this separatist group acted against their broader interests. Because of its Palestine branch's independent pro-Arab policy, the whole movement, which had many branches worldwide, was portrayed as overly zealous and was accused of supporting stands which contradicted the interests of the general Jewish public. This thwarted both the movement fundraising campaign and the much-needed cooperation between *Agudat Israel* and the Zionist organizations.

Although at first the movement was not worried about such cooperation, this changed following the 1929 pogroms in Palestine, the rising anti-Semitism in Europe in the early 1930s, and after realizing the consequences of the Immigration Act of 1924 which reduced the immigration of Eastern European Jews to the United States by ninety percent. Consequently, in the mid-1930s and following Rabbi Sonnenfeld's death, *Agudat Israel* sent a delegation to Eretz Israel seeking to distance itself from Jerusalem's more radical and separatist group.

While continuing to lead and support the Jerusalem organization, which became known as the *Edah Haredit*, *Agudat Israel* also appointed a separate leadership for the movement's other branches. These branches, the largest of which were in Tel Aviv and Petah Tikva, comprised members which on top of fully observing the religious laws, led a modern and productive lifestyle. While many of Jerusalem's ultra-Orthodox Jews kept to themselves, dressed in a different manner than the rest of the Jews, and led a pious lifestyle dedicating many hours to praying and Torah studies, those living in other places lived among other types of Jews, dressed the same as them, and shared the same work places.

In the late 1930s, as the gap between *Agudat Israel* and the *Edah Haredit* widened, a group of Jerusalemites established an anti-*Agudat Israel* opposition group. At first it was called the *Haim Group*, after rabbi Sonnenfeld, but later it became known as *Neturei Karta*. Initially, the group sought to influ-

---

47 Menachem Keren-Kratz, ""The rise of the Hungarian leadership of the Old Yishuv in Jerusalem during the Mandate Period," *Moreshet Israel*, 17 (2019), 107–156 (Hebrew).

ence *Agudat Israel's* policy from within, but as it failed, it established itself in opposition.

The clash between *Neturei Karta* and *Agudat Israel* reached its peak during the election to the *Edah Haredit's* leadership in 1945. While previously this organization was led by members of *Agudat Israel*, *Neturei Karta* managed to win the election and to take control over its leadership institutions. They subsequently issued new regulations which resulted in most members of *Agudat Israel* walking away from the *Edah Haredit*, making it an Extreme Orthodox, separatist, and anti-Zionist organization.[48]

The gap between the *Edah Haredit* and *Neturei Karta* on the one hand, and *Agudat Israel* on the other, expanded in the following years. It culminated following the establishment of the State of Israel and *Agudat Israel's* decision to join its first government. This resulted in establishing the two groups' separate ideologies toward the Zionist state. While *Agudat Israel* adopted a clear non-Zionist policy, it fully cooperated with the new state. In contrast, both the *Edah Haredit* and *Neturei Karta* adopted a strict anti-Zionist stand and condemned and shunned *Agudat Israel* for its lenient and compromising policy.

Extreme Orthodoxy after the Establishment of Israel

During the Mandate Period, when members of *Neturei Karta* and the *Edah Haredit* expressed anti-Zionist stands, that had very little effect on their daily life. The British Mandate authorities treated both the Zionist and the anti-Zionist in the same manner and awarded them the same rights. At that time, both *Neturei Karta* and the *Edah Haredit* had no problem in receiving state funds, being assisted by all the formal institutions, and obeying the law.[49] This, however, was not the case after the establishment of Israel. Then, the Extreme Orthodox factions refused to recognize the sovereignty of the Israeli government and its affiliated institutions, such as local municipalities and the national organizations.

---

48 Menachem Keren-Kratz, "Ha-Edah Ha-Haredit of Jerusalem in the first 25 years after the Establishment of the State of Israel," *Cathedra*, 161 (2016), 139–174.
49 Menachem Friedman, *Society and Religion: The Non-Zionist Orthodox in Eretz-Israel, 1918–1936*, Jerusalem: Yad Ben-Zvi, 1078 (Hebrew).

This unprecedented situation caused major problems for the Extreme Orthodox society. The annihilation of Europe's Orthodox communities during the Holocaust caused a total cessation of the donations which were a significant element of the economy of Jerusalem's Old Yishuv's society and its institutions. Considering accepting funds a violation of the ban on Zionism, the Extreme Orthodox leadership refused to receive either state or municipal financing. Consequently, the *Edah Haredit* suffered a major economic crisis, and its religious and educational institutions could no longer pay their workers' salaries. Seeking to provide for their families, some of them began looking for work either for institutions belonging to *Agudat Israel* or even in state sponsored ones. This threatened the continuation of the stringent separation between the Extreme Orthodox and the rest of Jewish society.[50]

Second, because *Agudat Israel* joined Israel's first governments, it was awarded significant budgets for its religious and educational institutions. The Extreme Orthodox, which refused to accept government funding and relied on self-finance and donations, were unable to compete with both the level of the teachers and the quality of religious education in *Agudat Israel's* institutions for boys and for girls. Consequently, many parents, despite theoretically supporting the Extreme Orthodox ideology, chose to send their children to the better education system. This too posed a threat for Extreme Orthodox's survival in the coming generations.[51]

Third, although *Neturei Karta*, which numbered one to two hundred families, won many seats in the *Edah Haredit's* leadership, they were not the only group of this organization, which catered to a few thousand families. In time, the *Edah's* leadership adopted a somewhat independent policy. Because so many people were dependent upon them for so many aspects of life's necessities, such as the supply of water, electricity, sewerage, gas, post, telephone, and public transportation, they were forced to cooperate with either the national or the municipal authorities.

Such cooperation and state issued authorizations were required even to maintain the *Edah's* separate identity. It, for example, required a permit to run its separate slaughtering house, rabbinical court, or burial services. They

---

50 Michal Shaul, *Beauty for Ashes: Holocaust Memory and the Rehabilitation of Ashkenazi Haredi Society in Israel, 1945–1961*, Jerusalem: Yad Ben-Zvi, 2014 (Hebrew).
51 Keren-Kratz, "Haredi (ultra-Orthodox) society and the State of Israel in its first decade as reflected in the Haredi press," *Kesher*, 52 (2019), 74–91 (Hebrew).

required permits for building their institutions, needed to formally register their real estate properties to protect their rights, or to establish new education institutions. This created a rift between *Neturei Karta*, which objected to even a minimal level of cooperation with the State or the city's authorities, and the *Edah's* leaders, who believed that a lack of cooperation with these bodies would result in a growing number of people abandoning the Extreme Orthodox camp and joining *Agudat Israel*.

The clash between these two extreme Orthodox ideologies was reflected in the fact that both the *Edah* and *Neturei Karta* published their own journals, each promoting its own values.[52] The gap was further demonstrated by *Neturei Karta's* decision to become the foremost organizer of demonstrations and public protests. This activity, which began shortly before the establishment of Israel, became the most significant characteristic of *Neturei Karta*, and particularly of its leader—Amram Blau.[53]

While initially protesting the violation of the Sabbath in their neighborhoods, in time *Neturei Karta* protested in response to other religious violations.[54] These included the opening of a mixed kindergarten for boys and girls of working mothers; the opening of a public pool where men and women could swim together; the demand made to religious girls who wanted to be exempted from military service to face a special committee; infrastructure works in areas which were suspected as former Jewish burial sites; or the performance of autopsies in hospitals.[55]

Neturei Karta justified these demonstrations, which on many occasions deteriorated into physical violence, explaining that they changed the existing status quo of the religious public lifestyle. The reasoning also bore a geographic element. They protested against driving during the Sabbath only when such incident occurred next to the Haredi neighborhoods. Other protests occurred in response to violation of other religious commands, such as mix swimming, the establishment of a sculpture garden, or the opening of a sex shop, because they desecrated the holy status of Jerusalem.

---

52 Menachem Keren-Kratz, "Walls of Separation: Neturei Karta's Magazines 1944–1958," *Kesher: Journal of Media and Communications History in Israel and the Jewish World*, 50 (2018), 71–88 (Hebrew).
53 Kimmy Caplan, *Amram Blau: The World of Neturei Karta's Leader*, Jerusalem: Yad Ben-Zvi, 2017 (Hebrew).
54 Naomi Levenkron, "The role of the Israel police in the establishment of Haredi citizenship: the protest against Sabbath desecration in Jerusalem (1948–1956)," *Police and History*, 2 (2020), 115–156 (Hebrew).
55 Motti Inbari, "The modesty campaigns of Rabbi Amram Blau and the Neturei Karta movement, 1938–1974," *Israel Studies*, 17, 1 (2012) 105–129.

During the 1950s the economic challenges of the Extreme Orthodox as well as other hardships kept the controversy between *Neturei Karta* and the *Edah Haredit* under control. This, however, changed during the 1960s as a result of what the heads of the *Edah* considered irresponsible behavior of *Neturei Karta*. This was first manifested in the kidnapping of the boy Yossale Schumacher. His parents, who just immigrated from the Soviet Union, faced financial difficulties and asked the boy's grandfather, a Haredi Jew, to raise him. A few years later, as they sought to reclaim the boy, the grandfather, who realized that the boy would not continue his Haredi upbringing, refused to return him to his parents. Soon thereafter the boy disappeared, and the police was unable to find him. It took two years and the intervention of the Mossad to discover the boy hiding under false identity in New York and to return him to his parents.[56]

In the mid-1960s the *Edah* leaders expressed their disapproval of this reckless act and forbade Amram Blau, the undisputed leader of *Neturei Karta*, to marry Ruth Ben-David, a pretty French convert some twenty years younger than Blau, who was responsible for smuggling Yossale out of Israel. When Blau disregarded the *Edah Haredit's* rabbinical court's decree, the gap between these two bodies widened even further.[57]

Israel's astonishing victory in the 1967 Six-Day War, and the liberation of holy places including the Temple Mount and the Western Wall, led many Haredi Jews to regard the state in a much more positive manner.[58] These trends even affected the Extreme Orthodox to the degree that the Satmar Rebbe, their top spiritual leader, rushed to publish a book titled *Al Ha-Geula Ve-Al Ha-Temurah* (on redemption and on transformation), in which he continued to develop the ideas expressed in his first book.[59] The book asserted that the victory was not a heavenly miracle, as many believed at the time, but one created by the devil. He consequently forbade his fol-

---

56 Motti Inbari, "The Yossele Schumacher Affair: A Case Study of Israel's Response to Ultra-Orthodox Ideological Crime," *The Journal of State and Church*, 61, 1 (2019), 20–40.

57 Kimmi Caplan, "'Hutspedike Shmotsedike Gioret': Ha-Parasha Shel Nisuei Amram Blau Ve-Ruth Ben-David," *Iunim Be-Tekumat Israel*, 20 (2010), 300–335.

58 Yair Ha-Levi, *Teguvot Ha-Zerem Ha-Haredi Ha-Merkazi Le-Milhemet Sheshet Ha-Yamim*, MA thesis, The Hebrew University of Jerusalem, 2011; Menachem Keren-Kratz, "'Al ken ein zot milhemet reshut' milhemet sheshet ha-yamim be-eiynaim harediot," *Et-Mol*, 250 (2017), 9–12 (in Hebrew).

59 Yoel Teitealbaum, *Al Ha-Geula Ve-Al Ha-Temurah*, New York: Jerusalem, 1967. Rabbi Yoel wrote the book's introduction and reviewed and edited the book chapters that were written by his students.

lowers to enjoy the fruits of this false victory and banned them from visiting the holy sites which were liberated during the war. This further expanded the gap between *Neturei Karta*, who generally obeyed Rabbi Yoel's ban on visiting the Western Wall, and the *Edah Haredit*, whose leaders disregarded it.[60]

As the result of a stroke he suffered in 1968, from which he didn't fully recover, the Satmar Rebbe's health deteriorated, as well as his influence on some of the Extreme Orthodox groups. At the same time, Amram Blau also lost much of his authority as a result of his quarrel with the *Edah Haredit's* leadership, which objected to his marriage to Ruth Ben-David. Consequently, other people, both in Israel and abroad, sought to lead *Neturei Karta* in an even stricter manner. To that end they no longer settled for protesting against the public violation of the religious status quo but publicly challenged the mere existence of Israel as a Jewish state.

For example, in May 1968, only a year after the Six-Day War, they openly burned Israeli flags in mid-Jerusalem and were immediately beaten by soldiers who passed by them.[61] A few months later, in January 1969, a few American *Neturei Karta* members protested against Israel in front of the UN building.[62] A year later, *Neturei Karta* cooperated with the PLO, the Palestine Liberation Organization which was established in 1964, and launched a mutual anti-Zionist demonstration in the UN building.[63] Since then, *Neturei Karta*, which by that time had members both in the US and in Britain, no longer settled for protesting against the violation of religious rules but also protested against Israel and claimed it should be abolished.

The Shift in Neturei Karta's Policy in the Late-Twentieth Century

In 1967 the PLO nominated Yasser Arafat as its leader, and since then the organization increased the number and scope of its terrorist attacks. In 1972, for example, Palestinian terrorists murdered eleven Israeli athletes and staff

---

60 Menachem Keren-Kratz, "Is the Jewish State the Ultimate Evil or a Golden Opportunity? Ideology vs. Politics in the Teachings and Actions of Rabbi Yoel Teitelbaum—the Satmar Rebbe," *Jewish Political Studies Review*, 29:1–2 (2018), 5–26.
61 *Maariv*, May 16, 1968, 1.
62 *Ha-Tzofe*, January 22, 1969, 2.
63 *Ma'ariv*, January 30, 1970, 1; ibid., March 13, 1970, 20.

who attended the Olympic games in Munich. The 1973 Yom Kippur War caught Israel completely unprepared. Despite eventually winning the war, this was a bitter victory, and the leaders of Israel were accused of acting in an arrogant and condescending manner toward the Arab leaders. From an Orthodox perspective, unlike the Six-Day War victory which gave the impression that God protects Israel and helps it to defeat its enemies, now the feeling was that God was no longer content with Israel and had even jeopardized its existence.

Following the Arabs' defeat in 1973 in the Yom Kippur War, the PLO decided to expand its operation in the diplomatic area. Soon thereafter, the UN recognized it as the sole representative of the Palestinian People and granted it observer status. Israel, however, considered the PLO a terrorist organization and forbade its citizens from establishing any contact with its representatives.

The war's result, and the fact that Israel almost lost it, prompted *Neturei Karta* to step up their anti-Israel campaign. This trend escalated following the death of Amram Blau in 1974, and the battle for who would succeed him caused potential candidates to present more radical stands. This was demonstrated, for example, by *Neturei Karta*'s support of Hilarion Capucci, a Syrian Catholic bishop, who was sentenced to 12 years imprisonment after using his diplomatic status to smuggle arms for the PLO into the West Bank.[64]

A year later, the leader of one Israeli *Neturei Karta* group sent a letter to Yasser Arafat expressing his support for the PLO's goals. A second letter was sent to Israel's prime minister Yitzhak Rabin demanding that he give up all the territories conquered during the Six-Day War. Both letters were condemned by the leader of the other *Neturei Karta* group.[65] By 1976 *Neturei Karta* also sent a delegate to an anti-Zionist conference held in Libya,[66] and by 1980 they freely corresponded with PLO leaders and approached the UN seeking to have it officially recognize them as representatives of all anti-Zionist Jews.[67]

---

64   *Ma'ariv*, September 1, 1974, 8; ibid., September 11, 1974, 4.
65   *Ma'ariv*, June 3, 1973, 12. Ibid., July 14, 1975, 4; ibid., July 17, 1975, 4.
66   *Ma'ariv*, August 20, 1976, 3.
67   *Ma'ariv*, March 27, 1980, 3; ibid., July 13, 1980, 3.

Although regarded as a strict anti-Zionist leader, the Satmar Rebbe, who had to consider the well-being of all the Extreme Orthodox groups, was reluctant to support *Neturei Karta's* radical stands. He made a clear distinction between "true" and "false" zealotry, and while supporting protests and demonstrations in response to Israel's violation of the religious status quo, he disapproved of anti-Israel demonstrations as such. He particularly forbade his followers from joining forces with Arab demonstrators, or using swastikas as a form of anti-Israeli protest. The Satmar Rebbe's moderating influence came to an end following his passing in 1979.

Since then, independent *Neturei Karta* groups began operating in New York and in London, while the group in Israel separated into two camps. In 1980 they demanded to participate as speakers in the UN's General Assembly when it discussed the Palestinian issue.[68] In 1984 *Neturei Karta's* leaders expressed their will that once a Palestinian Authority was established, they wanted to become its citizens. A public letter they published, in which they denounced Zionism and expressed support for the Palestinian national demands, was translated and published in several Arabic newspapers.[69]

These and many other public actions taken by various *Neturei Karta* groups tightened their relations with the PLO, and in 1985 Yasser Arafat sent them a public letter thanking them for the support for the Palestinian cause.[70] In 1988 *Neturei Karta* began hanging Palestinian flags in their neighborhood in Jerusalem. They also increased their cooperation with the PLO and their people attended many of their anti-Israeli demonstrations. As a result, Yasser Arafat announced he would appoint a *Neturei Karta* member as a minister in the government he was about to establish.[71] He fulfilled his promise in 1992 and appointed several *Neturei Karta* members as observers in the official Palestinian delegation for the peace talks in Washington. Two years later one of them was invited to take part in the official ceremony finalizing the talks between Israel and the PLO.[72]

---

68 *Davar,* July 13, 1980, 3.
69 *Davar,* February 13, 1984, 4; ibid., July 4, 1984, 3; Ibid., July 31, 1984, 3.
70 *Davar,* December 7, 1985, 3.
71 *Davar,* March 8, 1988, 3; ibid., March 14, 1988, 3; ibid., March 18, 1988, 2; ibid., December 9, 1988, 3.
72 *Davar,* April 23, 1992, 2; ibid., August 3, 1992, 4; ibid., May 1, 1994, 2; ibid., May 4, 1994, 3.

Neturei Karta in the Early Twenty-First Century

Palestinians have launched terrorist attacks against Jews and Israeli citizens since the 1920s, and since its foundation in the late 1960s, the PLO has been responsible for a large number of violent actions. But the scope and ferocity of the attacks during the second Intifada period, which began in September 2000 and lasted some five years, was nothing compared to the past. The 20,000 attacks which were launched in that period cost the lives of almost 1,200 Israelis, many of them killed by some 150 suicide terrorists. Since then, and particularly since many of the deceased were Haredi, cooperating with or supporting the PLO bore far greater consequences and was criticized even by the *Edah Haredit* and by the Satmar Rebbe, the late Rabbi Yoel Teitelbaum's nephew.

This enticed *Neturei Karta* to support both the PLO and other anti-Israeli leaders outside of Israel. In 2001 they participated in the UN conference against racism which took place in Durban, South Africa. During the conference they supported the Arab countries' claim that Israel was a racist, apartheid state which committed genocide and other war crimes.[73] In order to promote their ideas, in 2003 a group of American *Neturei Karta* established their own website (www.nkusa.org). A few years later it was followed by another *Neturei Karta* group website (www.truetorahjews.org). A few Extreme Orthodox individuals even opened their own internet forum at the Hebrew/Yiddish forums platform titled Hydepark.co.il, which was later renamed Be-Hadrei Haredim and became a major Haredi website.[74] Interestingly, as most rabbis condemned the use of modern technology, and particularly the internet and social media networks, *Neturei Karta* took full advantage of its potential.

In 2004 *Neturei Karta* participated in a public prayer held outside the Paris hospital in which Yasser Arafat lay on his death bed.[75] In 2005 they openly protested Israel's public attacks on Iranian president Mahmoud Ahmadinejad who had previously called for the annihilation of Israel. A year later a few *Neturei Karta* members visited Iran and met with Ahmadinejad

---

73 Ynet, August 29, 2001, www.ynet.co.il/articles/0,7340,L-1066629,00.html; *Ha'aretz*, September 6, 2001, https://www.haaretz.co.il/misc/1.731736.
74 Lee Cahaner, Nicola Nikola Yozgof-Orbac, and Arnon Sofer, *Ha-Haredim Be-Israel: Merhav, Hevra, Kehila*, Haifa: Haifa University, 2012, 140–141.
75 *New York Times*, November 11, 2004, www.nytimes.com/2004/11/11/world/europe/arafats-followers-kept-solemn-vigil-outside-hospital-in-france.html.

and other officials.⁷⁶ Later that year they participated in a Holocaust conference held in Iran in which many of the speakers were Holocaust deniers.⁷⁷ These radical acts could not be ignored and some of the men who participated in them were attacked, both verbally and physically, even by members of other Extreme Orthodox groups. They were even condemned by the contemporary Satmar Rebbe, who claimed they contradicted the anti-Zionist stance of his uncle—Rabbi Yoel Teitelbaum.⁷⁸

Seeking to disseminate their ideas, by 2007 several *Neturei Karta* groups began issuing several weekly and bi-weekly newsletters which they distributed via mailing lists, and a few years later they also launched their own Facebook pages. Seeking to confront these deviant tactics, former *Neturei Karta* Israeli members established an even more radical group, which was titled Sicarii (named after a radical group in the late Second Temple period, from the Latin word for 'dagger'), which acted violently both against non-Haredi Jews, particularly women, but also against those they considered too lenient Extreme Orthodox.⁷⁹

In 2011, for example, a few of them openly shouted and spit on religious women whose appearance they considered not sufficiently modest, while others physically attacked Israeli soldiers who passed near their neighborhood.⁸⁰ Such acts occurred in the following years as well. A year later a *Neturei Karta* member painted graffiti in Yad Va-Shem, Israel's central Holocaust memorial museum. The text hailed Nazi Germany for the Holocaust, which, as the text claimed, enabled the establishment of Israel.⁸¹ In 2013 another *Neturei Karta* member was accused of espionage as he collaborated with Iranian agents, for which he was convicted and imprisoned for several months.⁸²

---

76 *Nkusa.org*, October 28, 2005, www.nkusa.org/activities/Statements/2005Oct28Iran.cfm.
77 *Ynet*, December 14, 2006, www.ynet.co.il/articles/0,7340,L-3340043,00.html; *Globes*, June 13, 2008, www.globes.co.il/news/article.aspx?did=1000351025.
78 *Ynet*, December 15, 2006, www.ynet.co.il/articles/0,7340,L-3340422,00.html; ibid., February 7, 2007, www.ynet.co.il/articles/0,7340,L-3362227,00.html.
79 *Walla*, September 9, 2010, news.walla.co.il/item/1731242; *Ynet*, December 25, 2011, www.ynet.co.il/articles/0,7340,L-4166342,00.html; *Ha'aretz*, September, 7, 2011, www.haaretz.co.il/news/education/1.1448035.
80 *Ynet*, November 24, 2011, www.ynet.co.il/articles/0,7340,L-4152648,00.html; *Walla*, December 26, 2011, news.walla.co.il/item/1888315.
81 *Ynet*, June 11, 2012, www.ynet.co.il/articles/0,7340,L-4240879,00.html; Walla, June 26, 2012, news.walla.co.il/item/2544811.
82 *Ha'aretz*, August 1, 2013, www.haaretz.co.il/news/politics/1.2086896 Ibid., March 30, 2017, www.haaretz.co.il/news/politics/1.2228779.

During the twenty-first century Israel's Extreme Orthodox, namely members of the *Edah Haredit* and *Neturei Karta*, were no longer a leading force in demonstrations and protests against violation of religious norms. Instead, other Haredi groups, not usually considered part of the Extreme Orthodox camp, took their place and protested against the government's proposal to enlist more Haredi soldiers; the demand that Haredi children be taught a minimal level of general studies; or for not stopping traffic in Jerusalem's main streets near Haredi neighborhoods during the Sabbath. *Neturei Karta*, on the other hand, sought to distinguish themselves by both protesting against the very existence of the Jewish state and by collaborating with its worst enemies.

Conclusion

Throughout history, many Jewish laymen and rabbis have objected to the collective return of the Jews to *Eretz Israel*, particularly if it was motivated by nationalistic rather than religious reasons. Those who objected to the return of the Jews to Zion did so for many reasons, but the most persistent ones were those which justified their stands by religious reasonings. Anti-Zionist stands were voiced by both ends of the religious spectrum, the radical Reform on the one hand, and the ultra-Orthodox, and particularly the Extreme Orthodox, on the other.

In the last half century, and particularly since the twenty-first century, expressing anti-Zionist and anti-Israeli stands became a routine practice both among the Reform Jews and among the Extreme Orthodox ones. However, *Neturei Karta's* position that Israel should be annihilated and their open support of Israel's worst enemies has almost no equivalent on the Reform side, at least not in such a public manner.

Going back to the question which opened this article, one should wonder if there is a line which separates legitimate harsh criticism of the State of Israel from other anti-Israeli stands which according to the IHRA's working definition are simply anti-Semitic. The processes and analysis made in this article suggest that as long as expressing anti-Zionist and anti-Israeli stances remains either in the Jewish sphere, or even in the not-obviously anti-Semitic one, such views might be considered legitimate, regardless of their severity.

Iran and the terrorist organizations of Hezbollah or Hamas openly call for the abolishment of the Jewish state, claiming that Jews have no right to a state of their own, or that they have no legitimate right to protect themselves. They further deny the Jewish People's connection to *Eretz Israel*, claiming that the Palestinians are the only native people in this region. They, moreover, deny the severity of the Holocaust and claim that Jews either initiated it or at lease utilized it to get a hold in Palestine. Under the IHRA's working definition, such allegations are anti-Semitic.

Jews are not immune from expressing racist stands or from supporting anti-Semitic ones. This is true not only for individuals but also for Jewish groups and organizations. Consequently, when a Jewish group teams up and identifies with an organization which expresses anti-Semitic stands, it too should be accounted anti-Semitic. The fact that it proclaims itself to be Jewish, or justifies its acts by asserting that they derive from the Jewish tradition or the Jewish religion, does not change the obvious fact. If an individual, a group, or an organization openly identifies with an anti-Semitic body, it too can be considered anti-Semitic.

While nowadays this definition of anti-Semitic Jewish groups applies only to *Neturei Karta*, it might well be that in the future we shall see additional anti-Semitic Jewish groups from the left. While at the moment they "only" call to boycott, divest, and sanction Israel (BDS), in the future they may utterly identify with the anti-Semitic demand to abolish Israel as a Jewish state and either to expel its Jewish inhabitants, to kill them, or to make them second-class residents.

The Jewish Press in Hungary
A Brief Overview of the Hungarian Jewish Press in the 20th Century

László Bernát Veszprémy

Ever since the emancipation of Hungarian Jewry—and in fact, to some extent before that—Hungarian Jews or Hungarians of Jewish ancestry have played a vital part in Hungarian journalism. Anti-Semites have often charged that journalism as such was a "Jewish profession" in Hungary. The dry statistics have never proved this accusation, but Jews have, in fact, played a large role in Hungarian journalism for a small minority largely shunned by many even after the proclamation of equality before the law. While we cannot go into detail about Jewish journalism before the 20th century here, some of the largest or culturally most important liberal newspapers had been founded by Jews (such as *Az Est, Pesti Hirlap,* or the smaller but significant *Nyugat*), and Jews have contributed to several other important newspapers, even on the conservative side (*Budapesti Hirlap*). These newspapers, while they employed many Jews who often included some Jewish perspective in their writings, were not *Jewish* journals as such. At the same time, Hungary had a lively Jewish newspaper scene ranging from Orthodox to Neológ (Conservative) and Zionist newspapers.

Hungarian Jewry was mostly Orthodox before the Holocaust, but the Orthodox press was not as significant either in its quantity, readership or cultural impact as the smaller Neológ or Zionist press. In fact, their cultural impact, as much as it can be judged by the historian, looked like an inverted pyramid: the Zionist press was well-quoted even in non-Jewish papers, Neológ articles were sometimes debated, while the Orthodox press largely went unnoticed. The Orthodox-Neológ division, however, seems a little ambiguous here. The Zionist *Zsidó Szemle* was for a few years edited by one of the most renowned Neológ rabbis, Mózes Richtmann, even though the newspaper remained critical of Neológ declarations of Hungarian patriotism.[1] Most Zionist journalists, however, were from Kárpátalja (today: Zakarpattia Oblast, Ukraine) or Erdély (today part of Romania), peripheric areas of contemporary Hungary. The weekly *Egyenlőség* was loosely connected to the Neológ congregation of Budapest, but at times claimed that it was not a Neológ newspaper per se, and had great respect for orthodoxy.

Albeit not so significant, the culturally Zionist journal *Múlt és Jövő* has been active since the turn of the century. The Jewish press was forced to form one newspaper during the Holocaust years, the *Magyar Zsidók Lapja* (later: *Magyarországi Zsidók Lapja*). After the end of the Second World War, several smaller Jewish newspapers sprung up, only to be mostly banned or withered, this time, by the Communists. The newspaper of Budapest neology, *Új Élet*, was founded in place of *Magyar Zsidók Lapja,* at first edited by the latter's ex-editor-in-chief, Rezső Roóz. The newspaper played a dark role in supporting the emerging Communist one-party system in the 1950s. Several Hungarian-language Jewish newspapers have existed in other countries as well, some of the most important of which were *Új Kelet* (first in Romania, then in Israel), *Menóra* in Toronto, *Newyorki Figyelő* or *Hatikva* in Buenos Aires.[2] These newspapers have kept the spirit of Zionism alive among Hungarian Jews abroad.

The Jewish press from 1989 to 2010

While support for Israel had largely been buried during the Communist period—just like the Neolog-Orthodox division—, the change of system has breathed new air into Hungarian Jewish media, while also igniting healthy internal discussions and occasionally debates. Perhaps the first new Hungarian-Jewish newspaper was *Magyar Zsidó* (Hungarian Jew) in 1987, a small journal that only lived to see three numbers. The newspaper was founded and edited by György Gadó, a journalist and later parliamen-

---

1 For Zsidó Szemle see https://neokohn.hu/2019/12/04/a-zsido-aki-neokohnt-csinalt-a-horthy-korban/
2 Some issues of Új *Kelet* can be read online at https://www.nli.org.il/en/discover/newspapers/jpress while *Newyorki Figyelő* is available at https://hungaricana.hu/hu/

tarian, who in a 1995 interview said that "until 1955 I had no problems with Communism". He quit the party in 1968.[3] On the masthead of the newspaper were five aliases, all of which belonged to György Gadó. György Gadó later went on to become the editor-in-chief of *Szombat* (Shabbath), a Jewish cultural monthly which was founded in 1989 and still exists today. György Gadó held the position for a short time before writer Gábor Szántó T. took his place, fulfilling the role to this day. *Szombat* is published by the Magyar-Zsidó Kulturális Egyesület (Hungarian-Jewish Cultural Association), an organization close to the Neológ MAZSIHISZ and headed by Péter Kirschner.

The newspaper appears online and in print. The editor of *Szombat* is György Gadó's son, sociologist János Gadó. Szántó T. rarely publishes in his own journal (he wrote one article in 2020 and three in 2019), most editorials are published by János Gadó, who also writes under the pseudonym "*jég*" (meaning "ice", but also Gadó's initials read backwards). While a markedly Jewish newspaper, *Szombat* is not afraid to comment on Hungarian domestic politics, in fact, the motto of the newspaper is "Jewish political and cultural journal". *Szombat* is supportive of Israel and has close ties to MAZSIHISZ. The newspaper is mildly neoconservative in terms of foreign policy, but also has a markedly left-wing tone in domestic politics, not only supporting social progressivism in Hungary but also harshly criticizing the right wing.

Perhaps the starkest manifestation of this complicated viewpoint came in November 2006, one month after the leaked voice recording of Socialist Prime Minister Ferenc Gyurcsány had been published. On the voice recording, Gyurcsány admitted that they had been "lying morning, night and evening". Mass protests followed the leak of his words, which led to brutal police attacks on protesters, an event still ingrained into the thinking and identity of the Hungarian right today. At this point János Gadó wrote that Gyurcsány's leaked words could have been "cathartic", as he also said that "I don't want to keep doing this". But the protests organized by Fidesz were a "blow to democracy". One cannot criticize a prime minister who is "constantly the target of slander". "The opposition [Fidesz] does not see the prime minister as a partner and does not respect him as a human being. When he rises to speak, they leave the assembly. [...] This policy is familiar from the

---

3   https://www.szombat.org/archivum/a-gado and https://kanadaihirlap.com/2020/08/13/isten-eltessen-gado-gyorgy/

XXth century... This is hatred and instigation, revenge, fundamental humiliation of someone who dared defeat the Leader [Orbán]." Gadó also wrote that in reality, Gyurcsány's "message" was that "we must confront our own weakness and who we are".[4]

While not a newspaper, the Jewish cultural quarterly *Múlt és Jövő* has been revived by Jewish writer János Kőbányai.[5] It is probably the highest quality Jewish publication in Hungary now, presenting poems, essays, reviews, and annotated articles. *Múlt és Jövő* has recently launched an online edition as well. Múlt és Jövő is also a publishing house, where the books of acclaimed authors such as Ágnes Heller, Randolph L. Braham, Götzy Aly and Aleida Assman have appeared. The Jewish community channel *Heti TV* (Weekly TV), founded in 2016 and edited by Jewish journalist Péter Breuer, is also worth mentioning,[6] although its viewership is rather small.[7]

With the appearance of Chabad Lubavitch in Hungary (EMIH), new, smaller newspapers have been founded—*Egység* (Unity) in 1990, today edited by Zsófia Steiner, and *Gut Sábesz* in 1996—but these have mostly been distributed in EMIH synagogues and have not dealt with domestic politics. *Új Élet* has remained active during the change of system and the following years, now focusing almost exclusively on MAZSIHISZ's religious life. Since 1991 Holocaust survivor and Neológ rabbi Péter Kardos has been serving as the editor-in-chief of *Új Élet*. The websites of MAZSIHISZ (mazsihisz.hu) and EMIH (zsido.com) also occasionally publish news, the former is edited by Andrea Deák while the latter was for a long time edited by Tamás Ónody (who also publishes under the name Tamás Ónody-Gomperz).

While not an openly Jewish newspaper, *Hirszerzo.hu* (Secret Agent) was a strongly pro-Israel news portal edited by one-time *Szombat* editor and journalist László Seres. The news portal was also critical of the Hungarian right but had an even more blatant neoconservative drive. The editorial board was made up mostly of Hungarian Jewish journalists and Christian Zionists. *Hirszerzo.hu* was active between 2007 and 2012 and its website is now, unfortunately, offline.

---

4   https://www.szombat.org/archivum/a-kossuth-teri-forradalomrol-1354962428
5   https://multesjovo.hu
6   https://heti.tv
7   In 2018 it was not included in the list of 71 most popular channels in Hungary. https://hu.crt-tv.com/2019/02/11/magyar-csatornanezettseg-2018/

The Jewish press after 2010

With the advent of Viktor Orbán's right-wing Nemzeti Együttműködés Rendszere (System of National Cooperation, NER) Jewish journalism in Hungary has not only not dwindled, but in fact, gained ground. *Szombat* and *Új Élet*[8] are still active, and a number of other Jewish newspapers and news portals have emerged. In 2012 the Reform-aligned Kibic Zsidó Szervezetek és Közösségek Szövetsége (Kibic Alliance of Jewish Organizations and Communities) has started to publish *Kibic*, a left-leaning cultural news portal. For a long time *Kibic* was not officially functioning as a newspaper. Later it was renewed by non-Jewish journalist Attila Seres and is today edited by Judit Hidas.[9]

At the same time, EMIH has gained a sizeable chunk of the Hungarian non-Jewish left-wing press. In 2015 Brit Média (a wordplay on the Hebrew word for "alliance") has acquired the left-wing *Klub Rádió* and the left-wing weekly *168 óra* (168 Hours). The director of Brit Média at the time was András Ádám Megyeri, a former director for business development at Viasat and TV2, but later that year he was banned from running businesses by a Hungarian court because he was also the head of a venture (Agora) that was forcibly closed and had left behind some debt.[10] Megyeri is also a rabbi of EMIH and has started referring to himself online as Jonatán A. Megyeri. Brit Média has since then acquired the free tabloid *Pesti Hirlap* and the Hungarian version of the women's magazine *Elle*, while in turn, Brit Média itself was officially acquired by Jewish businessman Pál Milkovics in 2020.[11] EMIH, however, still enjoys very friendly treatment in both *168 óra* and *Pesti Hirlap*.

In 2019 Brit Média also launched the Jewish news portal *Neokohn*. The news portal's motto is "freedom, Jewry and foreign policy". The editor-in-chief of *Neokohn* was László Seres, who was later followed by Megyeri.

---

8 https://MAZSIHISZ.hu/kozossegeink/zsido-sajto/uj-elet-a-magyarorszagi-zsido-hitkozsegek-szovetsegenek-lapja
9 See the founding document of Kibic Organization here: https://akibic.hu/files/2013/10/Akibic_alapszabaly.pdf
10 http://www.szombat.org/hirek-lapszemle/eltiltas-miatt-valtozas-a-168-oranal-a-brit-medianal-es-a-klubradional
11 https://media1.hu/2020/07/10/breking-atalakul-a-168-ora-es-a-neokohn-tulajdonosi-szerkezete-a-pesti-hirlap-eddigi-tulajdonosa-a-ceg-vezetoje-lesz/

Neokohn has the largest readership of any Jewish newspaper in Hungary and has a regularly updated English version.[12] (*Szombat* also supposedly has an English version, but the last English language article was published there in 2008[13]). Some of *Neokohn*'s articles have even been picked up by the international press, a rare achievement among Hungarian newspapers.[14] With time the Jewish nature of *Neokohn*'s editorial board has somewhat dwindled, as most Jews eventually quit the newspaper. Today most of the editorial board is made up of Christian Zionists, with one Orthodox Jew, Megyeri, at the newspaper's helm. *Neokohn* has in the past published articles that have referred to Jesus as the Messiah.[15]

Smaller Jewish newspapers and blogs also exist in Hungary. *Sófár* is published by the Jewish community of Nyíregyháza, *Pesti Sólet* is the newspaper of the Dohány Street synagogue and *Sabbaton* is the newspaper of the Debrecen community. *Forrás* is the journal of the Lativ Kolel community. Recently a number of dissenting Neológ news portals and blogs have sprung up, critical of MAZSIHISZ's current leadership. *Smúzoló* was a blog of bitter language and bombastic leaks that even made it into the international press.[16] Recently, the blog has been shut down. *Azesz.com* (from the Yiddish *Der azes ponem*) still exists, with no official editorial board (the topics of the news portal, however, indicate connections to the Neológ communities in eastern Hungary). In late 2018 the *Magyar-Izraeli Média Center Egyesület* (Hungarian-Israeli Media Center Organization, MIMC) launched its website, *Huilmediacenter.com,* regularly covering Jewish subjects in the Hungarian media in English, German and Spanish.[17] The 2017 CEU research regarding Hungarian Jews found that 25% of Hungarian Jews read *Szombat* and 19% *Új Élet*. (*Kibic* was not mentioned in the research and *Neokohn* was yet to be founded back then).[18]

---

12 https://neokohn.hu/category/english/
13 https://www.szombat.org/category/english
14 https://www.jta.org/2019/06/14/global/germany-is-accused-of-downplaying-anti-semitic-attacks-by-muslims
15 https://neokohn.hu/2020/01/12/a-netflix-messiasa-ki-menti-meg-vegul-az-emberiseget/
16 https://www.ynetnews.com/article/SkzaLkxgO
17 https://huilmediacenter.com
18 https://www.szombat.org/files/2019/05/Zsidok-es-zsidasag-Magyarorszagon-2017-ben.pdf 205.

Main topics of discussion in the Hungarian Jewish press since 2010

Historically speaking the only periods in which debate was absent from the Hungarian Jewish press were periods of great strife. Today the Hungarian Jewish community enjoys relative safety compared to other parts of Europe. The discussions about security, terrorism, emigration, and negative demographic tendencies, strongly present in the Jewish press of other, mostly Western European countries, are mostly absent. Hungarian Jewish news is mostly about book launches, synagogue events, openings of kosher restaurants—and internal Jewish debates.

Jobbik's anti-Semitism

Discussions on Hungarian anti-Semitism also appeared in the Jewish press between 2010 and 2016, before the redirecting of Jobbik towards the mainstream right. Now most debates revolve around said redirection. This redirection has been regularly criticized in the Hungarian press because of the neo-Nazis and anti-Semites still present in Jobbik. To cite a few examples: Jobbik's president, Péter Jakab has a history of making anti-Semitic and anti-Roma statements, while its deputy president, Márton Gyöngyösi, is a self-described anti-Zionist who called for making a list of Jewish MPs and who called Gaza a "concentration camp" run by Israel in 2018. The party's chairman, György Szilágyi, has called for the banning of the Simon Wiesenthal Institute in Hungary, and its other chairman, Dániel Z. Kárpát, has spoken of a secret Israeli plan to conquer Hungary.[19]

Neokohn has remained strongly critical of Jobbik's masquerade and published articles such as "Deputy mayor of Ózd resigned due to Nazi photos", "Jobbik politician is convinced their anti-Semitic and homophobic candidate 'has changed'", "The Anti-Semites are coming: A chronicle of the unification of Hungary's Left and the far-right Jobbik party".[20] *Szombat*, on

---

[19] https://huilmediacenter.com/2021/06/14/long-gone-is-the-far-right-worldview-kafkadesk-whitewashes-far-right-jobbik/
[20] https://neokohn.hu/2021/10/12/deputy-mayor-of-ozd-resigned-due-to-nazi-photos/, https://neokohn.hu/2021/08/09/jobbik-politician-is-convinced-their-anti-Semitic-and-homophobic-candidate-has-changed/, https://neokohn.hu/2021/08/02/the-Anti-Semitess-are-coming-a-chronicle-of-the-unification-of-hungarys-left-and-the-far-right-jobbik-party/

the other hand, has emphasized the necessity of removing Orbán from power and has cautiously made steps towards accepting Jobbik. Editor-in-chief Szántó T. published an article in 2017 detailing under what conditions he would accept the left-wing parties' cooperation with Jobbik. Szántó T. wrote that "in order for Jobbik to become a force of civilized, democratic politics," it would have to "make clear its position on Holocaust memory", "openly condemn anti-Semitic and racist groups and forums" and "make clear their position regarding Israel".[21] Szántó T. has not demanded that any anti-Semitic or racist politicians leave Jobbik or be removed from the party. At this point the party was still headed by well-known anti-Semite Gábor Vona, and among its members was a politician with a skinhead past, Tamás Sneider. One must compare this with the opinion of EMIH-aligned anti-Semitism expert Kálmán Szalai, voiced in a *Neokohn* article: "Jobbik can only become authentic if it dissolves itself".[22]

These different opinions have naturally led to a heated debate. In May 2021 *Neokohn* editor-in-chief Megyeri wrote a bitter, Jewish *J'Accuse* directed at *Szombat*, titled: "The ten greatest lies of *Szombat*".[23] Many of Megyeri's charges involved the treatment of Jobbik at *Szombat* in recent years. In summer 2019, Megyeri related, Szombat translated a piece by *JTA*, titled "In Hungary, some left-wing Jews ready to work with party led by former neo-Nazi". *Szombat* had omitted a line from the report regarding MAZSIHISZ rabbi Zoltán Radnóti calling Hungarian Chabad leaders "Jobbik bashers." *Szombat* also changed the title of the article to "EMIH rabbi: the Orbán-government is close to ideal from a Jewish point of view". Megyeri also cited *Szombat's* failure to report the anti-Semitic scandals of ex-Jobbik spokesman Ádám Mirkóczki.

Mirkóczki, who is now independent mayor of the city of Eger, had previously made national news when an e-mail from him emerged in which he wrote the following: "I quote from the M1 TV's news tonight: 'in the short three years of the operation of the Auschwitz death camp, almost 2 million people were killed...' This of course means that for three years every single day they killed and burned 2000 people! If they missed one day, the next

---

[21] https://www.szombat.org/politika/mitol-valhatna-a-jobbik-a-civilizalt-demokratikus-kozelet-reszeve
[22] https://neokohn.hu/2020/10/22/a-jobbik-csak-akkor-lehet-hiteles-ha-feloszlatja-magat/
[23] https://neokohn.hu/2021/04/30/a-szombat-tiz-legnagyobb-torzitasa/

day they had to kill 4000. This is not very likely." Mirkóczki failed to apologize for his remarks. When right-wing channel *Hír TV* asked him about his comments, he said: "Sue me, I don't know what to say". Earlier this year it was also found that Mirkóczki's one time assistant, Kristóf Hajnády, had previously pictured himself in Auschwitz, showing the sign "V" with his hand, a sign of victory. As Megyeri pointed out, *Szombat* reported none of these scandals.

On the one hand, Megyeri's charge seems to be justifiable: a report published by the Hungarian-Israeli Media Center Organization has found that *Szombat* consistently failed to report on the anti-Semitic scandals of a Jobbik politician who ran for parliament in the Borsod county by-election in 2020.[24] On the other hand, the entire exchange of articles lacked finesse and probably didn't serve the best interests of Hungarian Jewry. *Szombat,* in an unsigned editorial, decided not to properly react to the charges, merely saying that Megyeri's "soul had been bought" and that "naturally" they were not going to reply to an attack like that. This incident highlights that inter-Jewish debates in contemporary Hungary revolve more around the question of what the proper Jewish conduct toward the state and the Hungarian right is, and less about the issue of anti-Semitism *per se*. Megyeri clearly picked the subject because he wanted to show that the left-wing alliance with Jobbik was a morally undefendable one—but no reference can be found in his article about right-wing anti-Semitism *not* connected to the opposition. *Szombat,* on the other hand, has signaled that defeating Orbán was a cause superior to all other causes—probably even to the Jewish one. Orbán had to go—or so went *Szombat*'s reasoning—and therefore whitewashing Jobbik's anti-Semitism was justified.

The Jewish relation to NER and the opposition

This paper has already, to some extent, presented the left-wing Jewish attitude to the right-wing NER and the right-wing Jewish criticism of the opposition. However, few if any articles can be found in the left-wing Jewish press condemning anti-Semitism coming from the left, and a similar blind-

---

24 https://huilmediacenter.com/wp-content/uploads/2020/10/2020-October-Biro-report-pdf-2-bw.pdf

ness seems to have taken over the conservative Jewish press regarding anti-Semitism coming from the non-opposition right. *Szombat* editor János Gadó commented on his public Facebook page in August 2021 on an article from the strongly anti-Israel left-wing news portal *Mérce*. The *Mérce* article's title read: "Pro-Israel Jair Bolsonaro hosted the grandson of Hitler's minister, now an AfD politician". Gadó wrote that "this is how you put Israel and Netanyahu [sic! Netanyahu was not in the title—L. B. V.] and Hitler into the same title. A great achievement by *Mérce*".[25] He was, however, careful *not* to write an article about this. Public Facebook posts are, in fact, a loophole for Jewish pundits to comment on things but not leave a trace. A left-wing Jewish commentator might want to occasionally condemn anti-Semitism on the left but might feel that an opinion piece would be too strong: therefore, he writes a Facebook post, knowing well that most people do not save the links or the screenshots of such posts. (Alas, the historian does.) Perhaps as a sole exception, *Neokohn* once defended the left-wing Jewish organization Auróra when it was attacked by neo-Nazis who were not related to Jobbik.[26]

The conservative Jewish argument for Orbán has basically been summarized by Tamir Wertzberger, the foreign affairs director of Likud. In his article, published in *Neokohn*, Wertzberger saw Orbán as a protector of Europe from a left-wing onslaught that would, in the end, harm Israel: "Left-wing parties are not traditionally anti-Semitic, but belong to political groups in the EU such as the Swedish Social Democrats, who are known to be anti-Israel, or the British Labor Party, which was recently led by Jeremy Corbyn, the same Corbyn who considers Hezbollah and Hamas his 'friends'… The battle for Hungary will be decisive: an ideological and values-based battle between the conservative right and the progressive left. If the left defeats Victor Orbán, there will be no one who can stop the radical revolution of progressives and the creation of a new world order—and there will be no one who can stop anti-Israel sentiment in the EU, along with growing anti-Semi-

---

[25] https://www.facebook.com/janos.gado.1/posts/10223136550753845. In general, left-wing news portals and newspapers in Hungary tend to be critical of Israel; right-wing newspapers tend to be pro-Israel. On this phenomenon see: https://huilmediacenter.com/wp-content/uploads/2021/06/MIMC-2021-May-Final-Pdf.pdf

[26] See my own article: https://neokohn.hu/2019/10/27/nazis-see-no-difference-between-zionist-and-pro-palestine-jews/

tism. If, on the other hand, the progressives lose in Hungary, the trend could be reversed, and this could re-ignite conservatives from other countries to return to power and prevent the risk posed by the progressive Left to the traditional values of Western civilization and democracy."[27]

The Hungarian-Jewish connection to Israel

Another source of division seems to be the Hungarian Jewish attitude toward Israel and Zionism. While Zionism is a colorful palette of different political views and Israel has many political parties ranging from the post-Zionist left to the religious-nationalist right, it would perhaps not be an overstatement to say that Zionism is generally seen as a form a nationalism among scholars and Israel is generally labelled a right-wing country. The Hungarian Jewish divide over Israel is therefore also to some extent a debate about the "proper" Jewish attitude to nationalism and the right.

No other case has highlighted this debate more than the 2020 scandal of MAZSIHISZ rabbi Gábor Fináli. Fináli, the young rabbi of the Ohel Avraham synagogue of Budapest, had in 2020 written public Facebook comments (in English) regarding Israel and the Holocaust. Fináli wrote: "Israel took all the benefits and most of the compensation from Germany for the death and suffering of our relatives. The chaos that Israel has been causing since 1948 is the reason for most, if not all, attacks on Jews in the Diaspora. The money spent on security until recently (2018) was because we suffer the consequences, we're the soft targets... Herzl's mission failed because it didn't stop the Holocaust, but soon it will lead to a new one."[28]

In response, the Rabbinical Board of MAZSIHISZ distanced itself from Fináli and wrote a message of apology to the Israeli ambassador to Hungary. (Fináli has since then quit the Rabbinical Board for reasons of different internal conflicts.[29]) The Fináli case shows a number of things. Hungarian Jews still strongly support Israel. The 2017 CEU research regarding Hungarian

---

27   https://neokohn.hu/2021/06/22/battle-for-hungary/
28   https://www.timesofisrael.com/hungarian-jewish-group-expels-rabbi-who-said-zionism-will-cause-2nd-holocaust/
29   See his letter of resignation here: https://MAZSIHISZ.hu/vakbarat/hirek-a-zsido-vilagbol/MAZSIHISZ-hirek/a-MAZSIHISZ-tobb-rabbija-kilep-a-rona-tamas-altal-vezetett-rabbitestuletbol

Jews found that a majority of Hungarian Jews have felt "some" or "strong connection" to Israel in every age group.[30] Yet most respondents who said that they had "mostly negative feelings" towards Israel (7%) were among the youngest, 18-24-year-old group. Perhaps it is not surprising that Fináli speaks to this rebellious youth who dare question the Zionist convictions of their parents and grandparents. On a different note, *Neokohn* was eager to cover the case, probably in order to gain good points among pro-Israel Hungarian Jews and Christian Zionists.[31]

During the Socialist period Hungary was opposed to Israel, but this apparently hasn't had an effect even on the older generation, at least regarding their relationship with the Jewish state. Hungarian Jews are still generally left-wing, but this is an older kind of left, one that doesn't demonize Israel. Because of that, MAZSIHISZ had difficulty dealing with a strong internal voice that was saying something very different from the official line. There were consequences, but not too strong consequences.

Most responses were messages of condemnation. Few have tried to understand what Fináli was saying.[32] In a sense, MAZSIHISZ is struggling with its own anti-Zionist tradition. *Neológism* used to be strongly against Zionism because they thought that the idea that Jews are a distinct nation with a "real" homeland somewhere else played into the hands of anti-Semites. This was a quite common point of view back then: for example, the 5th September 1925 headline of the Neológ *Egyenlőség* read: "We must not be Zionists!" The author of the article was Simon Hevesi, then chief rabbi of the Dohány Street synagogue.[33] When one combines this tradition with a "flock" that is pro-Israel, it clearly creates problems. Fináli might have rediscovered something that was very much within the Neológ tradition but has been buried for a long time. The debate certainly didn't revolve around Fináli's authenticity—which nobody questioned—but rather around his choice of words.

---

30 https://www.szombat.org/files/2019/05/Zsidok-es-zsidasag-Magyarorszagon-2017-ben.pdf 127.
31 See their articles of Fináli: https://neokohn.hu/tag/finali-gabor/
32 See my own attempt at analyzing Fináli's worldview: https://neokohn.hu/2020/02/21/miert-sodrodik-az-anticionizmus-fele-a-neologia/
33 For the article scanned see: ibid.

Summary

A quick analysis of the contemporary Jewish press in Hungary shows surprising colorfulness and vividity. The are many news organs—both online and in print—that represent a variety of Jewish traditions, ranging from reform to conservative to orthodox, from Zionist-right-wing to progressive. There are Jewish newspapers even in the countryside, a rare feat for a European country where most Jewish communities were eradicated during the Holocaust. I have presented the most important actors in the Hungarian Jewish media scene, namely *Szombat, Kibic* and *Neokohn*. I have also presented some important topics of discussion, namely on Jobbik's anti-Semitism, the "proper" Jewish response to Orbán's NER and the opposition, and the Hungarian-Jewish divide over Israel. In conclusion, the strong divisions inside Hungarian Jewry are well reflected in the Hungarian Jewish press, whereas most newspapers are busier attacking each other than presenting a united Jewish front against outside dangers—however small these might be. This also reflects the security of the community, as the topics unfortunately so "popular" in foreign Jewish newspapers—terrorism, immigration, anti-Semitic attacks—are mostly missing from the Hungarian Jewish press. In a historical sense, the Jewish press has always been acting within certain limits set out by the majority of the society (i.e. the non-Jews)—this is a fact more or less ingrained within diaspora-existence. The Hungarian Jewish press today is perhaps also a sad example of that.

Disclaimer: the author of this article was a journalist at Szombat *for 2016-2018 and the deputy editor-in-chief of* Neokohn *for 2019-2021, and is currently a member of the MIMC Organization.*

When the Cultic Milieu Goes Mainstream: Anti-Semitism and Violence in the Digital Age

Jeffrey Kaplan

The Cultic Milieu

The cultic milieu is the metaphorical domain that throughout recorded history has given sanctuary and solace to the seekers, rebels and misfits for whom the dross of everyday life in mainstream society is unbearable. The cultic milieu is a marketplace for the hidden, suppressed and sometimes utterly chimerical beliefs that exist on the fringes of every society. Most of these ideas are banished to the realm of the cultic milieu permanently. Others, suitably refined and cleverly marketed, may enter the mainstream for a time, sometimes to the benefit of society and at other times to its great detriment. Women's suffrage, and indeed the early strains of modern feminism, emerged from the worlds of left wing thought, communalism and new religious movements to become a fixture of mainstream Western society. Belief in an age-old Jewish conspiracy, blood libels and the bricolage of anti-Semitic beliefs too have entered the mainstream at times, often with tragic results.

What happens when cultic beliefs become mainstream is a fascinating study, but one that has become increasingly vital in the internet age. Currently, the availability of communications technology, the increasing dominance of social media, and the pervasive sense of social crisis powered by the pandemic has served to erase the borders that once separated the cultic milieu from the social mainstream, making conspiratorialism increasingly plausible to many and powering the rise of the far right from the fringes to the mainstream—a process much accelerated by the more than tacit government approval manifested by the Trump Administration.

Entering the Cultic Milieu

In the late 1980s I was in search of a dissertation topic related to millenarian and messianic violence. In the course of this quest, I came across a book that would have a profound impact on the way I looked at the world, Norman Cohn's *Pursuit of the Millennium*.[1] In these pages were dazed medieval millenarians in the throes of crisis who rejected the corrupt leadership of the church in a time when the medieval world was in its death throes. Cohn's discussion of German National Socialism as a modern variant of the medieval apocalyptic malady was not yet included, although the propensity of such movements for anti-Semitic violence was very much to the fore. It was a topic that Cohn would cover in his *Warrant for Genocide*, which compliments the much earlier work by Joshua Trachtenberg, *The Devil and the Jews: The Medieval Conception of the Jew and Its Relation to Modern Antisemitism*.[2]

What gave Cohn's work so much influence over my thinking was that it accorded with my own experience. I had just returned to the US after two years as a Fulbright lecturer at the University Graduates Union in Hebron in the West Bank. These were the years of the first Intifada, and as I became more and more acquainted with the Islamist activists in the area, occasionally being allowed to accompany them on their *da'wa*[3] calls on various families in the region, I also had an opportunity to observe at close proximity the Gush Emunim settler movement, both in the occupation of the Hebron Casbah and in their recreation of a Texas suburb around Kiryat Arba. The religious and often apocalyptic currents that swirled through the discourse and actions of both indeed harked back to the pages of *Pursuit of the Millennium*.

The Intifada, which involved many of my Palestinian students in Hebron and which was later lionized in Nizar Qabbani's poem "The Trilogy of the

---

[1] Norman Cohn, *The Pursuit of the Millennium: Revolutionary Millenarians and Mystical Anarchists of the Middle Ages*, Revised and expanded ed. (London,: Maurice Temple Smith Ltd., 1970).

[2] *Warrant for Genocide; the Myth of the Jewish World-Conspiracy and the Protocols of the Elders of Zion* (London: Eyre & Spottiswoode, 1967). Joshua Trachtenberg and Yale University, *The Devil and the Jews, the Medieval Conception of the Jew and Its Relation to Modern Antisemitism* (New Haven: Yale University Press, 1943).

[3] *Da'wa* is not an easy term to translate from the Arabic. Literally 'the call', it refers to calling people to the truth of Islam. In Islamist circles is more akin to gentle proselytization and is not to be confused with *takfir*, which is the violent expulsion of Muslims from the faith.

Children of the Stones,"⁴ reinforced the many lessons I learned from being by happenstance in Iran in the early stages of the Iranian Revolution. From Iran, I got a job in Dammam, Saudi Arabia, in the immediate aftermath of the takeover of the Mecca Mosque by the would-be messiah Juhayman al-Otaybi and more immediately, the violent suppression of the Shi'ite uprising in Qatif.

It was an interesting decade, but for me America seemed, to quote Talking Heads' depiction of life in heaven, a place where nothing ever happens. In this quest for a topic, I happened on a nearly forgotten article published long ago in an annual of British sociology by Colin Campbell, "The Cult, the Cultic Milieu and Socialization."⁵ Starting with the near impenetrable prose of Ernst Troeltsch whose conceptual trilogy of 'cult, sect, church' as the evolutionary path of global religions still remained a staple of Divinity School classes, Campbell offers the first sketches of a map of a religious world far outside the mainstream. It is a world I had come to know, love, and sometimes fear in the Middle East.

The Cultic Milieu Defined

A Cliff Notes version of Troeltsch's theory might in an undergraduate class go something like this. A church is an institutional religious entity with multiple interests and ideas, a bureaucratic structure that invests religious charisma as Max Weber defined it in the institution rather than in a particular leader. It does not depend on religious virtuosi, and its teachings limit mysticism in the interests of institutional stability.

Cults by contrast are ephemeral in nature, highly unstable in composition, imbued with mysticism and led by charismatic individuals whose charisma is rarely passed down to a successor.⁶ A cult's beliefs are heterodox when compared to those of a church, its demands on its followers are

---

4   Translated in Tariq Ali, *The Clash of Fundamentalisms: Crusades, Jihads and Modernity* (London: Verso, 2003), 141–2.
5   Colin Campbell, "The Cult, the Cultic Milieu and Secularization," *A Sociological Yearbook of Religion in Britain* 5 (1972): 119–36.
6   Timothy Miller, *When Prophets Die: The Postcharismatic Fate of New Religious Movements* (Albany, NY: SUNY Press, 1991).

high, and it significantly lacks structure beyond the charisma of its founder. Few survive the passing of the founder to enter an intermediate stage, which Troeltsch defines as sects.[7]

Later scholars added the important caveat that cults are oppositional in nature.[8] According to Campbell:

> Given that cultic groups have a tendency to be ephemeral and highly unstable, it is a fact that new ones are being born just as fast as the old ones die. There is a continual process of cult formation and collapse which parallels the high turnover of membership at the individual level. Clearly, therefore, cults must exist within a milieu which, if not conducive to the maintenance of individual cults, is clearly highly conducive to the spawning of cults in general... Thus, whereas cults are by definition a largely transitory phenomenon, the cultic milieu is... a constant feature of society.[9]

Campbell adds two more elements that will be key to what follows. First, he notes that the cultic milieu is marked by a remarkable tolerance for the beliefs of other denizens of the milieu, even if those beliefs are antithetical to one's own. Second, the milieu is composed of a small but shifting number of true seekers whose quest for ultimate truth is never ending.

Years later, in a conference in Stockholm Sweden, I and my co-author Heléne Lööw would expand this definition of the cultic milieu:

> The cultic milieu is oppositional by nature. The cultic milieu is a zone in which proscribed and/or forbidden knowledge is the coin of the realm, a place in which ideas, theories and speculations are to be found, exchanged, modified and, eventually, adopted or rejected by adherents of countless, primarily ephemeral groups whose leaders come and go and whose membership constitute a permanent class of seekers whose adherence to any particular leader or organization tends to be fleeting at best. The ideas generated within the cultic milieu may eventually become

---

7   Ernst Troeltsch, *The Social Teachings of the Christian Churches* (New York: Macmillan, 1931, 1992).
8   Campbell, "The Cult, the Cultic Milieu and Secularization," 13.
9   Ibid., 14.

mainstream, but long before they come to the attention of the dominant culture, they will have been thoroughly vetted, debated, reformulated, and ultimately, adopted or rejected within the cultic milieu itself. The sole thread that unites the denizens of the cultic milieu—true seekers all—is a shared rejection of the paradigms, the orthodoxies, of their societies. Beyond this element of seekership, the cultic milieu is a strikingly diverse and remarkably tolerant ethos. Ideas unacceptable to the social, cultural and political mainstream flourish.[10]

The cultic milieu is vast and it is timeless. It is not a mere product of modernity, for every society of which we have historical record has spawned its own cultic milieu. It is ever present and open to all who would dare to follow its myriad byways. Entry into the cultic milieu has a single prerequisite—a simple act of negation, that is, to reject the religious, social and political status quo of the day. The seeker must be secure in the belief that there must be something else, something better, something more true. One must become in other words, a seeker after ultimate truth. As the "X-Files" would have it, the truth is out there. It is real and accessible, and we have but to transcend the dross of everyday life to find it. The cultic milieu is the realm where hidden and suppressed knowledge beckon.

The cultic milieu is an antinomian world where the mores of one's own society no longer hold sway. It is a place freed from the injustices of society, although it is often a path fraught with peril, for the powers of this world, no less than the ties of family and faith, enact penalties upon those who would reject its ways. It is more than the Bible's "House of many rooms" (John 14:2). It is a vast world of concentric neighborhoods with depth and breadth which can be measured by its conceptual distance from the mainstream.

Every epoch had its cultic milieu. Whether the Mystery Cults of ancient Greece, the heresies of the Middle Ages, the messianic excitement of Sabatai Zevi, the occultism of the Illuminati or the Golden Dawn and Aleister Crowley in the 19th century, or the cults of the 1960s whose emergence moved Campbell to write his treatise on the cultic milieu, this oppositional realm has always been with us.

---

10 Jeffrey Kaplan and Heléne Lööw, *The Cultic Milieu: Oppositional Subcultures in an Age of Globalization* (Walnut Creek, CA: AltaMira Press, 2002), 3–4.

For my dissertation research I was determined to plunge fully into the American and later European cultic milieu in search of an exotic and extremely poorly studied subculture; the radical right and the world of racism and extreme anti-Semitism. It was a world that was poorly documented in the academic literature. There were some works, most notably *The Politics of Unreason*, which was funded by the Anti-Defamation League, although the ADL's material on the American radical right only occasionally had a nodding acquaintance with the truth.[11] There was really little else that was not based on the work of the ADL or other watchdog groups. The radical right was therefore an ideal topic for a dissertation, although my dissertation supervisors were rather appalled at the idea of making personal contact with people who were in those years cultural and political pariahs.

The quest began when by sheer chance I happened upon a cassette tape by Christian Identity minister Dan Gayman, whose Church of Israel was then a leading Identity ministry. Christian Identity in the 1980s was much feared, particularly after Robert Mathews' revolutionary group popularly known as The Order had murdered radio shock jock Alan Berg in my native Denver, robbed several armored trucks to finance their activities, and allegedly committed several other murders as well before the FBI eventually smashed the group and jailed many of its members, including David Lane, whose 14 words, "We must secure the existence of our people and a future for white children," remain ubiquitous in the movement to this day. Mathews himself was killed in a shootout with the FBI in 1984. The Order was composed of a mix of Identity and Odinist adherents, Odinism being a racist recreation of the Norse/Germanic pantheon. Anti-Semitism and the belief in a *Protocols*-driven immemorial Jewish conspiracy were their central tenants of faith.[12]

Despite the fact that Kaplan is a suspiciously Jewish sounding name, Pastor Gayman granted multiple interviews and thus was born my first published article, which centered on Identity and the wider American radical

---

11 Seymour Martin Lipset and Earl Raab, *The Politics of Unreason: Right-Wing Extremism in America, 1790–1977*, 2d ed. (Chicago: University of Chicago Press, 1978). Cf. Jeffrey Kaplan, "The Anti-Cult Movement in America: An History of Culture Perspective," *Syzygy: A Journal of Alternative Religion and Culture* 2, no. 3–4 (1993): 267–96.

12 On the Order, Kevin Flynn and Gary Gerhardt, *The Silent Brotherhood: Inside America's Racist Underground* (New York: Free Press, 1989). On all of these, Jeffrey Kaplan, *Encyclopedia of White Power: A Sourcebook on the Radical Racist Right* (Walnut Creek: AltaMira Press, 2000).

right.[13] I kept a post office box in these years, which was soon flooded with *samizdat* from a plethora of groups and movements. This began a years' long sojourn in the cultic milieu of the Euro-American radical right, as well as such esoteric byways as Satanism, radical environmentalism, new religious movements, the violent faction of the pro-life groups (rescue movement), and many, many more. In these pre-Windows 95 days interviews were in person, often in the homes or the headquarters of those that I interviewed.

Those interviews were many and quite diverse. Members of Nazi and skinhead groups, Identity adherents, followers of the Church of the Creator, Holocaust deniers, militia members, Odinists and bikers, numerous prison interviews—all of which yielded a remarkable trove of cassette tapes and many volumes of movement literature, activists' personal letters and diaries and much more. But what all with whom I spoke had in common was that each had an almost encyclopedic knowledge of the milieu. No matter how distant or arcane the belief system, whether they regarded its source as friend or foe, they were aware of many of the neighborhoods of the cultic milieu.

In the cultic milieu, ideas are fungible but people are not. For example, Sevetri Devi, was a first generation Nazi, a true Hitler worshipper, who herself would be anathema to the leftist and sometimes painfully politically correct activists in the radical environmental subculture. But she also wrote one of the first books on animal rights, and her belief in ecological purity travelled well, although she herself would never be embraced in the world of 'deep green'.[14]

There are groups in the cultic milieu whose passion in life is fighting each other. In Europe, the skinhead groups and ANTIFA specialized in street fights, while football ultras find fulfillment in fighting supporters of other clubs, for example. Yet for most, despite their hostility to the mainstream, and for the radical right, their hatred of Jews, Muslims and other races, there was a marked tolerance for the disparate ideas and groups within the milieu. All are united by their rejection of the mainstream. Individuals in the milieu have exquisitely sensitive antennae for bits of information, gleaned from

---

13   This article and many more on the far right are gathered in my 'greatest hits' volume, *Millennial Violence: Past, Present, and Future* (London Frank Cass & Co., 2002).

14   Nicholas Goodrick-Clarke, *Hitler's Priestess: Savitri Devi, the Hindu-Aryan Myth, and Neo-Nazism* (Albany, NY: NYU Press, 2000). Jeffrey Kaplan, "Savitri Devi and the National Socialist Religion of Nature," *The Pomegranate* 13, no. 7 (1999): 4–12.

mimeographed newsletters and from word of mouth by the constant drift of seekers who sample first one group then another. They gather a bricolage of ideas and concept, and pass them on to others. In many ways, they serve as a kind of canary in the coal mine for ideas and trends that seek to enter the mainstream.

And Now

And now we see a world transformed. Cohn's millenarians were wrenched by the changes wrought by the Black Death, which for the first time created a market value for labor, by the decay of the feudal system, by the rise of the urban centers, by the increasingly visible corruption of the institutional church, and much more. The printing press accelerated these changes, turning out religious broadsides in vernacular languages until at last the revolutionary Taborites under the command of Jan Žižka demonstrated that popular insurgencies could humble the might of both church and state.[15]

Our own time offers considerable parallels. Where the printing press could reach a literate audience who could read the tracts to others, the internet and the power of social media brings ideas that once floated primarily on the fringes of the cultic milieu into every home that wishes to partake of its wares. Once again, the decline of authority, be it governmental or religious, the established press or the wisdom of the educated elites, is ubiquitous. In a world where every man or woman can make his or her own truth, where the world of alternate news gives what Kelly Anne Conway presciently deemed 'alternative facts', established truths break down. If there are no truths, there are no lies, and the anomy of the cultic milieu becomes the reality of the mainstream. Elections can be contested and recounted by those most invested in changing their outcomes, and in such a world, systems crumble. The violence of 6 January 2021 in Washington will surely be a harbinger of things to come.

The anti-Semitic and Islamophobic words and beliefs that I documented in the cultic milieu have become the realities of Christchurch and

---

15 *Apocalypse, Revolution and Terrorism: From the Sicari to the American Revolt against the Modern World* (New York: Routledge, 2018), chapter 1.

Pittsburgh, and each new atrocity is streamed online to a receptive audience of true believers via social media channels from Facebook to Telegram and beyond. The conspiratorial fantasies that feed these events are broadcast most powerfully by Q-Anon and its many imitators, creating a cultic following in the mainstream as many displaced from work by the pandemic have endless hours to devote to searching their online worlds for answers. As these ideas enter the mainstream, their converts are untouched by the tolerance for ideas that marked the seekers of the cultic milieu. In the contemporary mainstream, divisiveness and rage have become the order of the day.

As Cohn demonstrates however, these disruptions, however violent, may change their societies but are never permanent. In political terms, Arthur Schlesinger's generational theory is instructive. American politics, he suggests, follow a cyclical pattern which begins with a generation who reject the status quo in favor of social activism. After a time however, they tire of the excitement and give way to another generation who return to the private acquisitiveness that marks American culture.[16]

Those of us who lived the 1960s know this pattern well. The anti-war movement decayed and turned in on itself long before the 1973 withdrawal from Vietnam. The broad coalition of the Civil Rights Movement radicalized and fragmented even before the 1968 assassination of Martin Luther King. On a far greater scale, Mao's putative permanent revolution convulsed China in the massive destruction of the Cultural Revolution until it reached its Thermidor and gave way to Deng Xiaoping's reforms.

Similarly, the anti-Semitic wave of the 1920s, driven by the Depression era demagogues and the Red Scare of the 1950s burned hot for a time in the 1950s, but faded long before the fall of the Berlin Wall in 1989.

This too shall pass. But not soon.

---

16 Arthur Meier Schlesinger, *The Cycles of American History* (Boston: Houghton Mifflin, 1986).

Contributors

TRISTAN AZBEJ is State Secretary for the Aid of Persecuted Christians and for the Hungary Helps Program at the Hungarian Prime Minister's Office. Prior to this assignment, he served as a diplomat in Israel for four years. He received his Ph.D. degree in Geosciences at Virginia Tech. After returning to Hungary, he has become actively involved in politics as a member of the Hungarian Christian Democratic People's Party. At present, he is serving as vice president in the party.

RABBI ANDREW BAKER is the Director of International Jewish Affairs of the American Jewish Committee and Personal Representative on Combating Anti-Semitism of the Chairperson-in-Office of the Organization for Security and Cooperation in Europe (OSCE). In recognition of his work in Europe he was decorated by the presidents of Germany, Lithuania, Latvia and Romania. He is a past president of the Interfaith Conference of Washington, a former commissioner of the District of Columbia Human Rights Commission, and a past president of the Washington Board of Rabbis.

BÉLA BODÓ was born in Hungary and completed his undergraduate education at the University Debrecen and the University of Toronto in 1990. He received his M.A in 1991 and his Ph. D. in 1998 from York University in Toronto, Canada. He is a professor of East European History at the University of Bonn, Germany. His latest book, *The White Terror: Antisemitic and Paramilitary in Hungary*, was published by Rutledge, London, in 2019.

RABBI RÓBERT FRÖLICH is currently the Chief Rabbi of Hungary. He was the Neolog Chief Rabbi of the Dohány Street Synagogue since 1993. From 2015 until his resignation in 2018 he was the National Chief Rabbi. He graduated from Anna Frank High School (today: Scheiber Sándor high school) in 1984 and then went on to study at the Jewish Theological Seminary, University of Jewish Studies (OR-ZSE) in Budapest, where he completed his studies in 1990 and was ordained as a rabbi. He also completed two rabbinical training courses in Jerusalem in 1990 and 1991. Between 1986 and 1988, he worked as a religion teacher at the Bethlen Square Synagogue. He was the Deputy Rabbi at the Dózsa György út Synagogue in 1989. Then, in 1990 he became the rabbi of Újpest Synagogue and in 1991 he was the rabbi of the Páva Street Synagogue. In 1991, he joined the Ministry of Defense, where he first was a religious expert in the Office of Church Experts and then in 1993 he became an inferior pastor of the Military Pastoral Office. Since 1993 he has been Chief Rabbi of the Dohány Street Synagogue. In 1995 he was appointed as a Brigadier General. On January 26, 2020, he received an honorary doctorate from the American sister institution of OR-ZSE, the Jewish Theological Seminary of America (JTS) in New York.

VIRÁG GULYÁS is a former diplomat to the EU, communications consultant and journalist, who just earned her 2nd Master's degree in Jewish Studies at Touro College, Manhattan. As a woman who admits growing up around anti-Semitic jokes and vibes, today she writes and speaks about her journey and is well-known for her raw, honest blog, *The Almost Jewish*, in the U.S., Europe and Israel. As a loud pro-Israel voice, a Hungarian, and a non-Jewish Zionist, she has created an ideology that aims to change the stereotypes about Israel and the Jewish people one day at a time. She has been working on several high-profile educational and PR campaigns that helped to burst the bubble of false narratives around Israel by pointing a finger at the falsification of history led by Palestinian Arab propaganda work (backed up by such organizations as the U.N.). She is the NYC Coordinator for the grassroots movement called End Jew Hatred.

H.E. AMBASSADOR YACOV HADAS-HANDELSMAN is the Israeli Ambassador to Hungary. Earlier he was Special Envoy for Sustainability and Climate Change in the Ministry of Foreign Affairs. He represented Israel as Ambassador to Germany for five and half years, and prior to that he was Ambassador to the European Union and NATO in Brussels. As a Middle East expert he was in charge of Israel's relations with the Arab world and a member of the negotiating team with the Palestinians as Deputy Director General, Head of the Middle East and Peace Process Division. He also was a policy advisor to the Deputy Foreign Minister. He spent three years as ambassador to Jordan and was the head of the Israeli Trade Representation Office in Doha, Qatar. He joined the Ministry of Foreign Affairs in 1986 and had been Deputy Chief of Mission in Austria and Turkey. Mr. Hadas-Handelsman holds a B.A. degree from the University of Tel Aviv, International Relations and Near East Studies and an M.A. in Near East Studies from Hebrew University Jerusalem.

JEHUDA HARTMAN specializes in the history of Hungarian Jews in modern times. He holds a Ph.D. in Jewish History from Bar-Ilan University and a Ph.D. in mathematics from the University of California in Los Angeles. He was associated with several universities and research institutions in Israel, the US and Canada. Professor Hartman developed computerized mathematical systems, which were implemented in Europe, Japan and the US. He founded an Israeli company for developing industrial optimization systems and was its chief scientist. Hartman is a recipient of the Israel National Defense Prize. His book *Patriots without Homeland: Hungarian Jewish Orthodoxy from Emancipation to Holocaust* appeared in 2020.

ANDRÁS HEISLER was born in 1955. Mr. Heisler is married and has two sons. He has degrees as an engineer and as an economist, and he runs his own company. He was recently re-elected as president of the Federation of Jewish Communities in Hungary (MAZSIHISZ). He speaks English and French. He has been a member for decades of the Dohány Street synagogue where his father served as chairman. Mr. Heisler is the founder of the Jewish Community Forum and the charity organization Limmud Hungary. He is tirelessly working for the sake of the Hungarian Jewish community and for future Jewish generations. He is dedicated to preserving the memory of the Shoah as an integral part of history and to furthering the commemoration policy in Hungary.

JEFFREY KAPLAN has published some twenty-three books and anthologies and over 100 journal articles and anthology chapters since his graduation from the University of Chicago in 1993. His most recent books include *The 21st Century Cold War: A New World Order?*, *Apocalypse, Revolution and*

Terrorism: From the Sicari to the American Revolt against the Modern World, and the first volume in the Routledge Distinguished Author series, *Radical Religion and Violence: Theory and Case Studies*. He has researched and taught in many countries, most recently in China, Saudi Arabia, Pakistan and Hungary. He is currently a Senior Distinguished Fellow at the Danube Institute in Budapest, as well as a member of the Scientific Advisory Board of Trends in Abu Dhabi, United Arab Emirates.

MENACHEM KEREN-KRATZ is an independent scholar. In 2009 he completed a Ph.D. in Yiddish literature (summa cum laude, Bar-Ilan University, Israel), and in 2013 he received an additional Ph.D. in Jewish History (Tel-Aviv University, Israel). His first book was *Maramaros-Sziget: Extreme Orthodoxy and Secular Jewish Culture at the Foothills of the Carpathian Mountains* (Jerusalem: The Dov Sadan Publishing Project of the Hebrew University, 2013, in Hebrew). His most recent book is *The Zealot: The Satmar Rebbe—Rabbi Yoel Teitelbaum* (Jerusalem: Zalman Shazar Center, 2020, in Hebrew). His upcoming book is *Zealotry and Piety: Jewish Hungarian Orthodoxy*. Over sixty of his articles, both in Hebrew and in English, were accepted for publication in academic and semi-academic publications. These included several peer-reviewed article collections as well as in many academic journals such as: *Dapim: Studies on the Holocaust, Modern Judaism, Contemporary Jewry, Israel Studies Review, Journal of Modern Jewish Studies, Jewish Political Studies Review, Association of Jewish Studies Review, Jewish Studies Quarterly, Jewish Quarterly Review*, and *Tradition* (in English), and *Identities, Cathedra, Kesher, Da'at, Moreshet Israel, Dor Le-Dor* and *Yalkut Moreshet* (in Hebrew). He also lectured in many local and international conferences.

TAMÁS KOVÁCS is the director of Holocaust Memorial Center and an associate professor at the National University of Public Service. His publications include "On the Margin of a Historic Friendship: Polish Jewish Refugees in Hungary during the Second World War" and " Polish Jewish Refugees in Hungary during the Second World War."

RABBI SLOMÓ KÖVES is a leading Orthodox rabbi and Chief Rabbi of EMIH (Egységes Magyarországi Izraelita Hitközség), which is an affiliate of

Chabad-Lubavitch in Hungary, which is led by Rabbi Baruch Oberlander. He received his Ph.D. in Hungarian Jewish History in 2007 from the University of Debrecen. His activities are almost too numerous to list, but he is the founder of the Hungarian Action and Protection League and is heading the House of Fates Holocaust Museum project.

MAREK KUCIA is a professor of Social Sciences at the Institute of Sociology of the Jagiellonian University in Kraków, Poland. His major research interests are Holocaust Memory and the memory of Auschwitz in Poland. His publications include articles in English, German, Hebrew and Polish, and he authored the book (in Polish) *Auschwitz as a Social Fact: The History, Present and Social Consciousness of KL Auschwitz in Poland* (2005).

LÁSZLÓ KÜRTI is a cultural anthropologist (Ph.D. University of Massachusetts) with extensive fieldwork experience in Hungary, Romania, and the USA. He taught at American University in Washington, DC and Eötvös Loránd University in Budapest. He is presently a professor at the Institute of Applied Social Sciences, University of Miskolc, Hungary. His English-language books include: *The Remote Borderland* (2001), *Youth and the State in Hungary* (2002), and he served as co-editor for *Beyond Borders* (1996), *Working Images* (2004), *Post-Socialist Europe* (2009), and *Every Day's a Festival: Diversity on Show* (2011). From 2001 to 2006 he was secretary of the European Association of Social Anthropologists. Currently he serves on the international editorial board of *Visual Studies, Urbanities, Ethnological Debates* and *Region: Regional Studies of Russia, Eastern Europe, and Central Asia*.

SHAUL MAGID is a Senior Fellow of the Kogod Research Center at the Shalom Hartman Institute of North America. He is a professor of Jewish Studies at Dartmouth College, where he teaches Jewish Studies and Religion. He is the rabbi of the Fire Island Synagogue in Sea View, NY. He is a contributing editor of *Tablet Magazine* and Editor of Jewish Thought and Culture at *Tikkun Magazine*. He is also a member of the American Academy for Jewish Research. Professor Magid received his rabbinical ordination in Jerusalem and his Ph.D. from Brandeis University. He is the author of many books on Jewish thought and culture. His latest book is

Meir Kahane: The Public Life and Political Thought of an American Jewish Radical (Princeton University Press, 2021).

DÁVID NAGY is a researcher at the Danube Institute. He studied International Security and Defence Policy at the National University of Public Service and at the University of Haifa. His main research fields include terrorism and radicalism in the Middle East.

RABBI BÁRUCH OBERLANDER is an Orthodox Hasidic Jewish religious leader, founder and chief leader of the Chábád-Lubavitz Hungary and the head of the Budapest Orthodox Rabbinate. He studied in Israeli and American yeshivas and was inaugurated as a rabbi in 1998 at Tmimim Lubavitz in Central Yeshiva Tomche in Brooklyn, NY. In 1989 he moved to Budapest with his wife and founded the Chábád Lubavitz Jewish Education Association and Foundation. He has been teaching Hebrew law at the Faculty of Law of Eötvös Loránd University since 1990–1991 and Jewish medical ethics at Semmelweis University academic year since 2008–2009. In 2004 Rabbi Oberlander together with Rabbi Slomo Köves, the newly inaugurated rabbi, founded the United Hungarian Jewish Community (EMIH). Since 2005 he has been the president of the Central and Eastern European Rabbinical Council (KERT). On August 20, 2012, on behalf of the Hungarian president of the Republic, Zoltán Balog, the Minister of Human Resources, he was awarded the Officer's Cross of the Order of Merit of Hungary.

TAMÁS ORBÁN was born in Transylvania and studied Contemporary History and International Relations in Kolozsvár (Cluj Napoca). He works as a research fellow of the Danube Institute and is a columnist for the *Hungarian Conservative*.

LIDIA PAPP is a researcher at the Danube Institute. Mrs. Papp is an international relations expert. Her primary research interests are the Middle East, humanitarian assistance, and the protection of religious freedom.

TIBOR PÉCSI is an historian and theologian. His research interests include the history of the Holocaust and Zionism, with special regard to moral issues and the dilemmas of the protagonists. He has been a teacher at Bornemisza Péter High School since 1997. Between 2004 and 2015 he was an educational expert at the Holocaust Memorial Center in Budapest. Since 2011 he has been an historian and pedagogical expert for the March of the Living Hungary. He is married and is the father of two children.

SEBASTIAN REJAK is the acting director of the American Jewish Committee of Central Europe, which has a demonstrated history of working in the governmental relations industry. He is skilled in international relations, non-profit organizations, foreign affairs, diplomacy and community relations. He is a strong program and project management professional who graduated from National School of Public Administration (KSAP) in Warsaw.

SÁRON SUGÁR is a researcher at the Danube Institute and is a columnist for the *Hungarian Conservative*. She studied international relations at Eötvös Loránd University. Her main research fields include events in the Middle East, especially the changes in the Israeli-Palestinian conflict, and the worldwide persecution of Christians.

GYÖRGY SZABÓ is the president of the Hungarian Jewish Heritage of Public Endowment (MAZSÖK), which serves Holocaust survivors and other members of the Hungarian Jewish community. It is also responsible for Jewish trusts. He was awarded the Knight's Cross of the Hungarian Order of Merit (civic section) for his service.

KÁLMÁN SZALAI is the executive director of the Action and Protection League.

ZSÓFIA TÓTH-BÍRÓ is a researcher at the Danube Institute. She is the online editor of *Hungarian Conservative* and the deputy editor of a Hungarian journal, *Reaktor*. She is currently studying law at Pázmány Péter Catholic University.

TAMIR WERTZBERGER is the Action and Protection League Director of Foreign Affairs at the European Parliament. He is an expert on Israel advocacy, public diplomacy, and international relations. Since September

2016 he has held a position in the Likud Party as International Relations Coordinator. He was an intelligence officer (captain) and he studied for a B.A. in political science and the Middle East. He founded the advocacy page "whole truth about the Israeli-Palestinian conflict" in 2010. Between 2011–2014 he worked with Jewish communities abroad to strengthen the communities and their connection to Israel for the Jewish Agency. He is fighting against Anti-Semitism.

Articles Glossary

Aliya. The Hebrew term for Jews migrating to Israel.

Antinomian. Literally, the rejection of religious laws or morality. It signifies a pattern of behavior that is amoral and pays no heed to the rights of others.

Anti-Soros campaign. A government financed media campaign, the most visible of which were giant posters throughout the country that blamed George Soros for the 2015 migration crisis. Many claimed that the campaign had anti-Semitic connotations.

Arrow Cross Party (Nyilaskeresztes Párt). The Arrow Cross Party was a Hungarian fascist group which was founded as the Party of National Will by Ferenc Szálasi in 1935. It came to power under the German occupation from October 1944 to April 1945. It was responsible to a considerable degree for the Hungarian participation in the Holocaust.

István Bethlen. Hungary's Prime Minister between 1921–1931, when the Numerus Clausus laws (see relevant glossary entry) were passed in Parliament.

Black Zionism. Black Zionism is a seldom used term for Jews who support Zionism from places like Ethiopia, where a community of Jews immigrated to Israel from the 1970s–1990s. It is a controversial term because of its widespread use in black nationalist movements from the Marcus Garvey era and more recently with sectarian Back to Africa groups who have no connection with the state of Israel.

Blood libels. Blood libels refers to the charge that Jews kill Christian children in order to use their blood to make matzoh (unleavened bread) for Passover. The earliest were in the 12th century but have been a regular feature of anti-Semitism leading to violent pogroms well into the 20th century.

Christian Zionists. Christian Zionists are the small groups of Protestant Christians who, for eschatological reasons, support the Zionist enterprise in Israel. Some Christian Zionists belive that it will hasten the Second Coming of Jesus, while other Christian Zionists support Israel because of the covenental relationship of the Jews to God. The movement is particularly strong in the United States but has a significant community of adherents in Hungary.

Folk anti-Semitism. Folk anti-Semitism refers to popular anti-Semitic tropes which are heavily colored by Christian beliefs. In this view, the Jews are either themselves satanic or willing servants of Satan. In Hungary, this form of anti-Semitism was prevalent in the villages.

Győzike show. A popular Hungarian reality show that ran on Hungary's largest commercial TV channel which featured a Roma celebrity and his family.

Gyurcsány, Ferenc. A socialist politician who was Prime Minister of Hungary between 2002–2008. He is currently the president of Hungary's largest opposition party Democratic Coalition (DK).

Horthy, Admiral Miklós. Admiral Horthy is a controversial figure in Hungarian Jewish history. Appointed Regent of Hungary in 1920 by the National Assembly, Horthy's regime saw the passage of the anti-Jewish Numerus Clausus laws and other anti-Semitic legislation. Horthy described himself as an anti-Semite and was cautiously allied with the Nazi government in Germany in its war with Russia. Yet he is credited with trying, with mixed success, to prevent the deportation of the Jews of Budapest to Nazi concentration camps.

Hungarian Guard. The Hungarian Guard was a violent racist movement targeting Jews and Roma throughout Hungary. From 2008–2010 it allied with Jobbik (Movement for a Better Hungary) and took part in mass rallies and parliamentary elections. It was banned by the Hungarian government in 2009.

Hungary Helps Program. Hungary Helps is a program set up by the Hungarian government in 2017 to assist with issues of international development but it concentrates particularly on religious oppression with a special emphasis on persecuted Christians. It is currently led by Tristan Azbej, State Secretary for the Aid of Persecuted Christians and for the Hungary Helps Program.

Hungarian Jewish Heritage of Public and Endowment. It was founded in 1997 as a product of negotiations between, the Federation of Hungarian Jewish Communities (WJRO) and the government of Hungary. The Foundation's mission is to assist Hungarian Holocaust survivors and enhance the Jewish cultural heritage and traditions in Hungary. MAZSÖK currently provides modest monthly pension supplements to over 6,700 Holocaust survivors.

Institute of National Remembrance. The Institute of National Remembrance is a Polish research organization, founded in 1990, to investigate crimes against Polish citizens from World War II through the end of the communist era in 1990.

Jobbik (Movement for Hungary). Jobbik is a far-right party, which was founded in 2003 by Gábor Vona. It was widely criticized for its anti-Jewish and anti-Roma rhetoric. It claimed to have changed its stance on anti-Semitism in 2017.

Komárom Fortress. After the Arrow Cross takeover in October 1944, the Komárom Fortress became an internment camp from which thousands of Jews and Gypsies were sent to extermination camps.

Kunmadaras events. In May 1946, a pogrom took place in the village of Kunmadaras which targeted Jews returning from Holocaust deportation camps. The causes of the violence were complex, with anti-Semitism the most obvious but the theft of the property of Jewish deportees by their neighbors also had much to do with the violence.

Magyar Demokrata Fórum [Hungarian Democratic Forum/MDF]. The ruling party between 1990–1994. It was an opposition party until it was dissolved in 2011. The MDF proposed to reinstate the position of a military rabbinate.

Numerus Clausus. The Numerus Clausus were a series of laws passed in September, 1920, that, among other things, severely limited the access of Jews and women to higher education. It was part of a series of the so-called 'Jewish Laws' which were passed between 1938–1941.

Szálasi, Ferenc. The founder of Hungary's National Socialist Party, the Arrow Cross (see the relevant entry). He orchestrated the coup against Admiral Horthy after Hungary's occupation by Nazi Germany. He was executed in 1946.

Teleki, Count Pál. A Hungarian politician and government minister between 1920–1921. He was one of the main opponents of the so-called Jewish laws.

Three Oath Midrash. The Three Oaths (*Shalosh Shavuot*) are associated with the Satmar Rebbe, Rav Yoel Teitelbaum. Strongly anti-Zionist in intent, they bound the Jews to not "break through the wall," and enter the Land of Israel; to not rebel against the nations (gentile states); and that the nations should not oppress the Jews too heavily.

Index

"1945" (Hungarian Movie, 127
"Borat" (movie), 127
"Music Box" (movie), 127
"Son of Saul" (movie), 127
"Sunshine" (movie), 127
"Sweet Transylvania" (song), 124
14 words, 232
168 óra (168 hours), 217

A

Abramson, Henry, 156
Action and Protection, 8, 13, 26, 27, 54, 111, 113, 117, 118, 241, 243
AFD (Alternative für Deutschland/Alternative for Germany), 222
Africa, 128, 152
Agudat Israel, 191, 192, 194, 200–3
Ahmadinejad, Mahmoud, 89, 208
Al Assad, Bashar, 109
Al Ha-Geula Ve-Al Ha-Temurah (On redemption and on transformation), 204
Aliya, 186, 245
al-Otaybi, Juhayman, 229
Aly, Götzy, 216
American Jewish Committee, 59, 237, 243
Anti-Defamation League [ADL], 39, 113, 138, 159, 232
ANTIFA (anti-Fascist Action), 233
anti-Israelism, 27, 30, 40, 57, 92, 119, 129, 138, 140, 145, 153, 154, 185, 206–8, 210, 222
anti-Roma, 11, 12, 123, 124, 219, 247
anti-Soros campaign, 18, 19, 127, 245
anti-Zionism, 16, 30, 50, 60, 86, 89, 119, 133, 145, 154
apartheid, 86, 208
Apponyi, Albert, 70–72
Arafat, Yasser, 205–8
Arendt, Hannah, 149
Armageddon, 153
Ashkenazi Jews, 10, 12, 186, 192, 193
assimilation, 12, 78, 198

Assman, Aleida, 216
Auschwitz, 11, 29, 31, 43, 49, 105, 120, 123, 124, 126, 128, 160, 161, 164, 220, 221, 241
Avarffy, Elek, 74, 75
Az Est, 213

B

Baker, Rabbi Andrew, 177, 237
Baldwin, James, 147, 153
Balfour, Arthur James, 191
Bandholtz, General Harry Hill, 72
Bar Mitzvah, 11, 137
Baumhom, Lipót, 105
BDS Movement, 86, 90, 136, 137, 139, 141, 154, 211
Be-Hadrei Haredim, 208
Ben-David, Ruth, 204, 205
Bennett, Naftali, 154
Beregi, Ármin, 76
Berg, Alan, 232
Bergen, D.L., 149
Berlin Wall, 235
Bethlen, István, 70, 71, 245
Biden, Joe President, 139, 148
Billing, Michael, 122
Black Anti-Semitism and Jewish Racism, 149
Black National Caucus, 152
Blau, Amram, 203–6
Blinken, Anthony, 148
blood libel, 142, 227, 245
Blood Libel (skinhead band), 124
Bnei Brak, 198
Boas, Franz, 121
Bodó, Béla, 69, 104, 237
Bolsheviks, 123
Book of Revelation, 153
Braham, Randolph L., 216
Breuer, Péter, 216
Brit Média, 217
brit milah, 61
British Labor Party, 60, 222
Brussels, 108, 114, 139, 140, 238

Budapest, 4, 6, 10, 14, 22, 26, 33, 39, 43, 47, 48, 72–74, 76, 77, 94, 95, 104, 126, 179, 182, 214, 223, 238, 240, 241, 242, 243, 246
Budapesti Hirlap, 213
Buenos Aires, 214

C

Campbell, Colin, 229–31
Capucci, Hilarion, 206
Carter, Jimmie, 151
Catholic Church, 70, 83, 160, 164
Central Rabbinical Congress
Central Rabbinical Congress of America (CRC, also known as *Hita'hadut Ha-Rabanim*
Chabad [Lubavitcher Movement], 6–8, 50n6, 216, 220, 241, 242
Christchurch Mosque attack, 234
Christian dispensationalism, 153
Christian Identity, 232
Christian Zionists, 153, 155, 216, 218, 224, 245
Church of the Creator, 233
Churchill, Winston, 45
Civil Rights Movement, 235
Clemenceau, Georges, 83
Cohen, Sacha Baron, 127
Cohn, Norman, 228, 234, 235
Cold War, 17, 151, 180
communism, 73–75, 86, 135, 151, 179, 215
Conway, Kelly Anne, 234
Corbyn, Jeremy, 60, 222
Coughlin, Father Charles, 151
Critical Race Theory, 152, 155, 156
Crowley, Aleister, 231
Csernoch, Prelate János, 70
cultic milieu, 227–35
cultural Judaism, 5
Cultural Revolution, 235

D

Dammam, 229
Deák, Andrea, 216
Democratic Socialism, 151
Depression era, 235
Devi, Sevetri, 233
Diaspora, 90, 93, 223, 225
Division ADA (skinhead band), 121
Dohány Street Synagogue, 4, 6, 26, 31, 77, 81, 126, 218, 224, 237, 238, 239

Dombováry, Géza, 72
Durban, 59, 208

E

Edah Haredit, 199–205, 208, 210
Eger, 220
Egyenlőség, 74–76, 98, 99, 214, 224
Egység, 216
Elle, 217
EMIH, 6–10, 14, 18, 19, 26, 33, 50n6, 111, 216, 217, 220, 240, 242
Eötvös Loránd Research Network, 105
Epstein, Jeffrey, 151
Erdély, 22, 124, 193, 194, 214, 242
Eretz Israel, 185–88, 190, 191, 200, 210, 211
EU Agency for Fundamental Rights, 13, 53, 62, 161
European Commission, 8, 51, 118
European Monitoring Center, 62
European Parliament, 12, 117, 119, 120, 138, 178, 243
Evangelical Christians, 153, 155
Extreme Orthodoxy, 89–92, 192–94, 196, 201, 240

F

Facebook, 48n3, 133–35, 209, 222, 223, 235
Faludy, György, 82
Fear, 85
Federal Bureau of Investigation (FBI), 232
Fidesz, 14, 18, 48n3, 215
Final Solution (skinhead band), 124
Fináli, Rabbi Gábor, 223, 224
First World War, 76, 91, 99, 191, 193
Forrás, 218
France, 54, 57, 108, 139, 153
Fredrickson, George, 146
Freedom Riders, 152
Freedom Summer, 152
Friedrich, István, 76
Fürj, Lajos, 83

G

Gadó, János, 215, 216, 222
Gadó, György, 214, 215
Galicia, 193
Gavras, Costa, 127
Gayman, Dan, 232

Index

Germany, 11, 86, 123, 146, 149, 150, 171, 197, 209, 223, 237, 238, 246, 247
Golden Dawn, 231
Goldhagen, Jonah, 149
Goldwater, Barry, 147
Goodman, Andrew, 152
Gore, Al, 151
Greece, 118, 119, 231
Gross, Jan T., 85
Gulyás, Virág, 27, 120, 238
Gush Emunim, 228
Gut Sábesz, 216
Gyöngyösi, Márton, 11, 29, 219
Győzike show, 122, 246
Gypsies *see* Roma
Gyurcsány, Ferenc, 215, 246

H

Hagee, John, 153
halakha, 4, 5, 95, 188, 192, 193
Halakhic Jews, 5, 9
Halimi, Sarah, 87, 107, 108, 139
Hamas, 90, 130, 133, 137, 211, 222
Ha-Mizrahi, 191, 192
Hassidic (Hassidism), 7, 194, 199
Hatam Sofer, 188
Hatikva, 214
Healthy Skinhead (skinhead band), 124
Hebron, 228
Heisler, András, 7–10, 18, 26, 45, 55, 239
Heller, Ágnes, 216
Hertzberg, Arthur, 146, 148, 155
Heti TV, 216
Hevesi, Ferenc, 81
Hevesi, Simon, 224
Hezbollah, 211, 222
Hibat Tzion (the love of Zion), 186
Hidas, Judit, 217
Hír TV, 221
Hit Gyülekezete (Faith Church), 29
Hitler, Adolf, 48, 123, 131, 132, 135, 136, 191, 222, 233
Hitler's Willing Executioners, 149
Hohler, Thomas, 72
Holocaust denial, 50, 55, 64, 90, 111, 131, 132, 135
Holocaust Documentation Center, 103, 104
Holocaust identity, 32
Holocaust Memorial Center, 103, 240, 243

Holocaust Memorial Museum, 151, 209
Holocaust Museum, 8, 12, 55, 132, 241
Holocaust Remembrance Year, 64, 65
Holocaust survivors, 17, 180, 195, 196, 243, 247
Holy Temple (Second Temple), 43
Horowitz, Nathan, 72, 73
Horthy, Miklós, 31, 49, 69–73, 76, 77, 82, 125, 246, 247
House of Fates, 8, 241
Hungarian 1848–49 revolution, 81
Hungarian Army, 81, 127
Hungarian Christian Democrats, 63
Hungarian Conservative, 242, 243
Hungarian Democratic Forum [MDF], 82, 247
Hungarian Guard, 10, 86, 246
Hungarian military chaplains, 81, 83
Hungarian Parliament, 3, 11, 29, 74, 125, 178, 179
Hungary Helps Program, 65, 66, 237, 246
Hypercacher store attack, 108

I

Ignác Goldziher Jewish Historical and Cultural Research Institute, 49
IHRA (The International Holocaust Remembrance Alliance), 62, 132, 141, 145, 150, 154, 185, 210, 211
Illuminati, 231
Immigration Act of 1924, 191, 200
Institute of National Remembrance, 163, 246
International Memorial Day, 104
intifada, 110, 133, 134, 208, 228
intolerance, 62, 63
Iran, 89, 208, 209, 211, 229
Iranian Revolution, 229
Iraq, 66
Islamophobia, 148, 153
Israel, 5, 8, 12, 14, 17, 22, 23, 29, 31, 40, 50, 57, 59, 63, 86, 87, 89, 90, 92, 93, 104, 108–10, 117, 119, 120, 122, 125, 130, 132, 133, 135, 138, 145, 148, 150–56, 177–80, 185–87, 189, 196–99, 201, 203–11, 214, 215, 219, 220, 222, 223–25, 237, 238, 239, 240, 243, 244, 245, 247
Israeli Defense Forces, 57

J

Jakab, Péter, 12, 219
Jenkins, Jerry, 153

Jerusalem, 9, 31, 43, 87, 90, 135, 136, 153, 195, 198, 200, 202, 203, 205, 207, 210, 238, 239, 241
Jerusalem Document, 145, 154
Jewish cemeteries, 122, 169, 172
Jewish Community Relations Council, 148
Jobbik, 10–12, 29, 30, 48n5, 111, 113, 179, 219–22, 225, 246, 247

K

Kahane, Rabbi Meir, 151
Kamenets-Podolsky mass murders, 105
Karácsony, Gergely, 48n3
Kardos, Rabbi Péter, 216
Kárpát, Dániel Z., 219
Kárpátalja, 214
Karpathorus, 193
Kazakhs, 127
Kertész, Imre, 126, 128
Key Concepts in the Study of Anti-Semitism, 149
Kibic Zsidó Szervezetek és Közösségek Szövetsége, 217
Kibic, 217, 218, 225
Kibbutz movement, 86
Kielce pogrom in Poland, 85
King, Martin Luther, 152, 235
Kirschner, Péter, 215
Kiryat Arba, 228
Klub Rádió, 217
Kőbányai, János, 216
Kohn, Sámuel, 94, 95
Komárom Fortress, 105, 247
Kosher food, 108, 219
Kossuth, Lajos, 81
Kosztolányi, Dezső, 75
Köves, Rabbi Slomó, 6–10, 12, 18, 19, 26, 45, 111, 112, 240, 242

L

Ladocsi, Gáspár, 83
LaHaye, Tim, 153
Lane, David, 232
Lativ Kolel, 218
Left Behind series, 153
Legal Aid Office of the Pest Community, 72
Liberal Party (Germany), 149
Lieberman, Joe, 151
Likud, 222, 244
Lipstadt, Deborah, 148
Lööw, Heléne, 230
Löw, Emmanuel, 81
Löw, Immanuel, 71, 72
Löw, Leopold, 81
Lubavitcher Rebbe, 6, 7
Lubavitchers, 7, 51

M

Madoff, Bernie, 151
Magyar Demokrata Fórum (MDF), *see* Hungarian Democratic Forum
Magyar Zsidók Lapja, 214
Magyar-Izraeli Média Center Egyesület, 218
Magyar-Zsidó Kulturális Egyesület, 215
Makkabea, 76, 77
March of the Living, 31, 243
Marom, 14, 15n24
Marshall, Louis, 146, 150, 155
Mathews, Robert, 232
MAZSIHISZ, 4–9, 19, 26, 49, 83, 84, 178, 215, 216, 218, 220, 223, 224, 239
Mazsök [Hungarian Jewish Heritage of Public Endowment], 57, 58, 243, 246
Mecca Mosque, 229
Megyeri, András Ádám (Megyeri, Jonatán A.), 217, 218, 220, 221
Memorial Collection Public Foundation, 103
Menóra, 214
Mérce, 222
Messianism, 7
Mikes, Count János, 70
Milkovics, Pál, 217
Millenarian, 228, 234
Milton Friedman University, 8
Ministry of Foreign Affairs (Hungary), 238, 239
Mirkóczki, Ádám, 220, 221
mitzvoth (religious commands), 187
Muslims, 22, 60–62, 66, 87, 148, 191, 228n3, 233
Múlt és Jövő, 214, 216
Muzsikás (folk music band), 126
My Happy Days From Hell, 82
Mystery Cults, 231

N

National Association of Jewish University Students, 76, 77
National Socialism, 228

NATO, 82, 238
Natural Born Killers (skinhead band), 124
Nemzeti Együttműködés Rendszere, 217–25
Neokohn, 8, 217
Neolog, 5, 6, 22, 74, 77, 79, 94, 97, 98, 192, 213–16, 218, 224, 237
Netanyahu, Benjamin, 8, 17, 18, 157, 180, 222
Neturei Karta, 199–210
New Left's New Politics Conference, 152
New *Yishuv*, 187, 188
Newyorki Figyelő, 214
Notes of a Native Son, 147
Numerus Clausus, 70, 71, 74, 78, 97, 99, 245, 246, 247
Nyíregyháza, 217
Nyírő, József, 125
Nyugat, 213

O

Oberlander, Rabbi Baruch, 6, 7, 9, 241, 242
Oblath family, 78
Odinism, 232
Ohel Avraham synagogue, 223
Old *Yishuv*, 187, 188, 202
Omar, Ilhan, 148
Ónody, Tamás (Ónody-Gomperz, Tamás), 216
Orbán government, 9, 19, 103
Orbán, Viktor, 8, 17–19, 47, 50, 64, 180, 216, 217, 220–22, 225
Organization for Security and Cooperation in Europe, 59, 237
Orthodox Jews, 4, 90, 91, 99, 187, 190–92, 194, 195, 199, 200
Ózd, 219

P

Palestine, 16, 30, 40, 91, 109, 136, 137, 186, 189, 190, 191, 195, 199, 200, 205, 211
Palestinians, 108, 153, 156, 208, 211, 239
Paris, 72, 108, 208
Páva Street synagogue, 105, 106, 238
Pelle, János, 85
Pesti Hírlap, 213, 217
Pesti Sólet, 218
Petah Tikva, 200
Petrás, Mária, 126
Pittsburgh synagogue attack, 145, 147, 152, 235

PLO (Palestine Liberation Organization), 205–8
pogroms, 69–71, 76, 85, 134, 187, 200, 245
Pogromshchiki, 77
Poland, 12, 31, 85, 124, 150, 159–64, 168, 172
Post-Holocaust trauma, 47, 48
Prohászka, Ottokár, 70
Prónay, Pál, 70, 72, 73
Pursuit of the Millennium, 228

Q

Q-Anon, 235
Qatif, 229

R

Raab, Earl, 148, 149, 151
Rabin, Yitzak, 206
racism, 30, 59, 62, 121, 128, 147, 151–54, 156, 208, 232
Radnóti, Rabbi Zoltán, 220
Raffay, Ernő, 83
Recsk, 82
Red scare, 235
Reform Movement, 189, 192
Reform Jews, 6, 210
Richtmann, Mózes, 214
Rohingyas, 66
Roma 29, 122, 123, 127, 171, 246, 247
Roma Holocaust Memorial Day, 104
Roman Catholic Church, 160
Romania, 13, 90, 126, 131, 193, 214, 237, 241
Roóz, Rezső, 214
Rosenberg trial, 151
Rumbach Street Synagogue, 47

S

Sabbaton, 218
Said, Edward, 156
Sanders, Bernie, 151
Satmar Hasidim, 194–96, 199
Satmar Rebbe, 89, 90, 194, 204, 205, 207–9, 240, 247
Saudi Arabia, 229, 240
Schlesinger, Arthur, 235
Schneerson, Rabbi Menachem Mendel, 6, 7
Schumacher, Yossale, 204
Schwimmer, Michael, 152
second coming of Christ, 153, 155, 245

Second World War, 30, 81, 86, 108, 123, 159, 162–64, 170, 171, 181, 214, 240, 246
Self-Defense League (Önvédelmi Liga), 76
Sephardic Jews, 66
Seres, Attila, 217
Seres, László, 216
Settlers (Palestine), 136, 188
Shabbat, 137, 140, 215
Shechita, 61
Shoah, 30–32, 64, 85, 132, 133, 138, 239
Simmel, George, 123
Simon Wiesenthal Institute, 219
Six-Day War, 152, 204–6
skinhead movement, 233
Smith, Anthony, 125
Smithsonian Institute, 152
Smúzoló, 218
Sneider, Tamás, 220
Sofer, Rabbi Moshe, 95, 96
Sonnenfeld, Rabbi Yosef Haim, 199, 200
Soros, György (George), 112, 123, 245
South Africa, 59, 128, 208
Soviet Union, 86, 204
SS officers, 171
Steiner, Zsófia, 216
Students for a Democratic Society, 152
Stuyvesant, Peter, 150
swastika, 112, 122, 123, 197, 207
Sweden, 230
Szabó, György, 14, 45, 243
Szabolcsi, Lajos, 74, 76
Szalai, Kálmán, 26, 111, 220, 243
Szálasi, Ferenc, 45, 48, 123, 125, 245, 247
Szántó T., Gábor, 215, 220
Szegedi, Csanád, 11, 12
Szilágyi, György, 219
Szombat, 215–22, 225

T

Tabódy, István, 82
Taborites, 234
Takaró, Károly, 83
Talking Heads, 229
Talmud, 43, 53, 187
Talmudic teachings, 95, 188
Tamir, Aharon
Teitelbaum, Rabbi Mózes
Tel Aviv, 200
Teleki, Count Pál, 71, 72, 77, 247

Temple Mount, 87, 204
The Black Revolution and the Jewish Question, 149
The Devil and the Jews: The Medieval Conception of the Jew and Its Relation to Modern Antisemitism, 228
The International Jew, 151
The Jewish Stake in Vietnam, 151
The Order, 232
The Politics of Unreason, 232
The Question of Palestine, 156
The Trilogy of the Children of the Stones, 228–29
Three Oath Midrash, 188, 198, 247
Times of Israel, 8, 18, 50
Tiszaeszlár blood libel, 95, 124
Torah, 7, 21, 187, 188, 200
Tormay, Cécile, 45
Toronto, 214
Trachtenberg, Joshua, 228
Transylvania *see* Erdély
Tree of Life synagogue *see* Pittsburgh synagogue attack
Troeltsch, Ernst, 229, 230
Trump, Donald, 19, 139, 148, 181, 227
Turanic Nations, 127
TV2, 217

U

Új Élet, 214, 216–18
Új Nemzedék, 71
United Jewish Community of Hungary *see* EMIH
UN General Assembly, 109, 207
UN Human Rights Council, 109, 132
UN Security Council, 109
United Nations (UN), 40, 109, 132, 137, 205, 208
University Graduates Union, 228
Unterland, 193

V

Va-Yoel Moshe, 198, 199
Viasat, 217
Vietnam, 151, 235
Volkgeist, 146
Volksstaat, 146
von Bismarck, Otto, 149
von der Leyen, Ursula, 8, 51
von Habsburg, Archduke Ágost József, 70

Vona, Gábor, 11, 220, 247

W

Warrant for Genocide, 228
Warsaw Pact, 83
Washington, George, 150
Washington Holocaust Museum, 151, 152
Wass, Albert, 45, 125
Weinstein, Harvey, 151
Weiss, Bari, 145
Wertzberger, Tamir, 27, 139, 222, 243
West Bank, 109, 206, 228
Western Wall, 204, 205
Wiesel, Elie, 29

Y

Yad Vashem, 104, 105
Yarmulke, 148
Yazidis, 66
Yeshiva, 6, 12, 194, 197–99, 242
Yishuv Eretz Israel, 186, 188, 190
Yom Kippur, 206

Z

Zadravecz, István, 70–72
Zakarpattia Oblast (Ukraine), 214
Závada, Pál, 85
Zero tolerance, 24, 34, 39, 47, 50, 64, 132, 139, 141
Zevi, Sabatai, 231
Zionism, 12, 40, 86, 90, 91, 133, 154, 155, 168, 185, 186, 189–93, 197, 198, 202, 207, 214, 224, 224, 242, 245
Žižka, Jan, 234

H.E. Mr. Yacov Hadas-Handelsman, Israeli Ambassador to Hungary.

Tristan Azbej - State Secretary for the Aid of Persecuted Christians and the Hungary Helps Program.

Sámuel Glitzenstein, the rabbi of Zsilip, the modern Jewish synagogue and cultural center of the Hungarian Orthodox Jewish Community proudly showing the recently built Jewish centrum's huge playground to researchers from the Danube Institute.

Interior of the Dohány Street Synagogue, the largest synagogue in Europe, a center of Neolog Judaism.

Memorial in the courtyard of the Dohány Street Synagogue. The caption in Hungarian reads "Children of one Mother".

The Dohány Street Synagogue, also known as the Great Synagogue or *Tabakgasse* Synagogue, is a historical building in Erzsébetváros, the 7th district of Budapest, Hungary.

Róbert Fröhlich chief rabbi of the Dohány Street Synagogue, Budapest.

András Heisler, president of MAZSIHISZ.

The inside of Kazinczy Street Orthodox Synagogue which was ...built in 1911–13 and restored after 1945. The synagogue has the only Mikvah in Budapest. Kazinczy Street Synagogue is in Budapest Jewish Quarter and in its courtyard, there is an Orthodox Glatt Kosher restaurant called Hanna and nearby there is a kosher delicatessen and butcher.

Thousands commemorate with torches at the annual Hungarian March of the Living in Budapest, on Hungary's Holocaust Memorial Day on April 15, 2019. At the end of the March the holocaust survivor Chief Rabbi Péter Kardos said a Jewish mourning prayer.

Thousands attend the annual Hungarian March of the Living in Budapest, on Hungary's Holocaust Memorial Day on April 15, 2019. That year's march was led by Scottish secretary David Mundell and commemorated the life and work of Scottish missionary Jane Haining, who sacrificed her life to protect her Hungarian Jewish pupils during WWII. Haining was caught and killed in Auschwitz by the Nazis.

The inside of the Óbudai's Orthodox synagogue, which is the oldest functioning synagogue in Budapest. The building was inaugurated in 1821 and fully renovated in 2016 by EMIH (Egységes Magyarországi Izraelita Hitközség – Unified Hungarian Jewish Community).

Edith Bán Kiss's stone relief shows a moment of Deportation: a Hungarian policeman directs Jews to cattle trucks for deportation.

Edith Bán Kiss's stone relief shows a moment of Forced Labor: an Arrow Cross Party guard oversees men in a labor battalion.

Edith Bán Kiss's stone relief shows the last moment before death: a Nazi guard herds Jews into the gas chambers.

Edith Bán Kiss's stone relief shows the moment of Liberation: Red Army soldiers welcome Jews in Budapest.

Shoes on the Danube Bank is a memorial of the victims shot and pushed into the Danube by Arrow Cross militiamen in 1944–45. It gives remembrance to the 3,500 people, 800 of them Jews, who were killed on the river bank.

Slomó Köves, a leading Orthodox rabbi and chief rabbi of EMIH, an affiliate of Chabad-Lubavitch in Hungary.

The controversial monument of the memorial for victims of the German Occupation at Budapest, Szabadság Square. The memorial has sparked controversy and angered the Jewish community, with critics alleging that the monument absolves the Hungarian state and Hungarians of their collaboration with Nazi Germany and complicity in the Holocaust.

György Szabó, the president of the Hungarian Jewish Heritage Public Foundation.

Kálmán Szalai, executive director of the Action and Protection Foundation, and Tamir Weitzberger, foreign affairs director of the Action and Protection League.

A Hungarian orthodox Jewish man gives a Hebrew lesson to a young child in the recently built Zsilip, which is a modern Jewish synagogue and cultural center of the Hungarian Orthodox Jewish Community.

Organizers of the conference titled Anti-Semitism in Hungary: Appearance and Reality. From the left to the right: Lídia Papp, Dorina Dósa, Dávid Nagy, Tamás Orbán, Jeffrey Kaplan, Zsófia Tóth-Bíró, Sáron Sugár.

10,000 Hungarian people protest against anti-Semtism and against far-right politician Marton Gyongyosi's anti-Semitic remarks in Budapest on November 27, 2012. The protester holds up a sign in which the following can be read in Hungarian: We say **no** to listings. We say **no** to another Holocaust. We say **no** to the legacy of Ferenc Szálasi. **We will no longer tolerate the neo-Názi Jobbik party in the Parliament.**

10,000 Hungarian people protest against anti-Semtism and far-right politician Marton Gyongyosi's anti-Semitic remarks in front of the Parliament in Budapest, November 27, 2012. The rally was held after a Hungarian far-right opposition politician had urged the government to draw up lists of Jews who pose a national security risk. The government released a terse condemnation of the remarks.

Virág Gulyás, New York City coordinator for End Jew Hatred.

Elie Wiesel spoke in 2009 in Faith Church (*Hit Gyülekezete*), which is a Hungarian nondenominational megachurch. Many important Hungarian politicians, Jewish representatives, ambassadors attended the event.

Playground at Zsilip, which is a recently built modern Jewish synagogue and cultural center of the Hungarian Orthodox Jewish Community. Researchers from the Danube Institute visit the modern Jewish center. One of its aims is to attract young Jewish people to the community.

www.ingramcontent.com/pod-product-compliance
Lightning Source LLC
Chambersburg PA
CBHW070507240426
43673CB00024B/470/J